The City of Women

The City of
W·O·M·E·N

Ruth Landes

INTRODUCTION BY SALLY COLE

University of New Mexico Press
Albuquerque

First published by the Macmillan Company, 1947
© 1947 Institute for the Study of Man, New York
Introduction © 1994 Institute for the Study of Man
All rights reserved.

FIRST UNIVERSITY OF NEW MEXICO PRESS EDITION

All illustrations are reproduced by courtesy of the
Smithsonian Institution, Washington, D. C.

Library of Congress Cataloging-in-Publication Data
Landes, Ruth, 1908–1991.
The city of women / Ruth Landes; Introduction by Sally Cole.—
1st University of New Mexico Press ed.
p.   cm.
Originally published: New York: Macmillan, 1947.
Includes bibliographical references.
ISBN 0–8263–1555–0. —ISBN 0–8263–1556–9 (pbk.)
1. Candomblé (Cult) — Brazil —Salvador — Case Studies.
2. Salvador (Brazil) — Religious life and customs — Case studies.
3. Brazil — Religious life and customs — Case studies. I. Title.
BL2592.C35L36   1994
299'.67—dc20   94–18707
CIP

Contents

Ruth Landes in Brazil

WRITING, RACE, AND GENDER IN 1930S
AMERICAN ANTHROPOLOGY

Sally Cole

In the 1980s anthropologists challenged the scientific authority and objectification of their subjects in ethnographic writing (Clifford and Marcus 1986). More recently, scholars and writers have situated the debate in the context of postcolonial and feminist critiques of anthropology, condemning the discipline's effective erasure of critical theoretical writing about race and gender (Abu-Lughod 1991; Harrison 1991, 1992; hooks 1990; Lutz 1990; Mohanty 1991; Morgen 1989; Trinh 1989; Wolf 1992). Professional ethnography has typically been characterized by a style of writing that Jonathan Spencer calls "ethnographic naturalism," "the creation of a taken-for-granted representation of reality through the use of certain standard devices such as free indirect speech and the absence of any tangible point of view" (1989: 152).[1] Increasingly, historians are recognizing that the emergence of scientific ethnography was not inevitable or natural but was the product of the hegemonic processes of canon making by influential individuals and powerful institutions. Scientific ethnography came to dominate the field by marginalizing other types of writing, theorizing, and anthropology. Rethinking ethnography has encouraged a fresh reading of the history of anthropology and especially of the development of the professional scientific monograph.

Ruth Landes' *The City of Women*, marginalized during the making of the disciplinary canon, warrants contemporary rereading as an early ethnography of race and gender. The book is a study of the women-led Afro-Brazilian spirit possession religion, *candomblé*, in the ancient seaport city of Bahia in northeastern Brazil. Landes conducted field work in Brazil during 1938 and 1939 and published her study through the New York publisher, Macmillan, eight years later in 1947. Written in descriptive prose and dialogue, *The City of Women* is based on Landes' experiences with female and male ritual specialists and on her observation of cult rites and ceremonies. Landes' remarkable study is a testament to the vitality and dignity of the candomblé practitioners, who helped give meaning to the lives of Afro-Brazilians living in the poverty and under the military repression of Brazil in the 1930s. Landes also wrote *The City of Women* as a personal memoir of her year in Brazil, making herself one of the main characters in the book. Favorably reviewed as a "very intelligent travel work" (Honigman 1948) and a "tourist account" (Mishnun 1948) on the one hand, *The City of Women* was rejected as unscientific by the anthropological profession (Herskovits 1948) on the other. When the book appeared in 1947, the field of anthropology was working to expand its institutional base in universities, professionalize its ranks of practitioners, and cultivate its respectability as the "science of culture" (Gordon 1990; Yans-McLaughlin 1986). In the three decades between 1930 and 1960, 'culture' replaced 'race' as the discipline's central paradigm. Within this new framework, anthropologists catalogued cultural traits and represented cultures in scientific monographs. In this professional context, *The City of Women* was problematic, for Ruth Landes' theoretical interests lay in questions of race, gender, and sexuality. She inserted her own experience and relationships into the text. She refused to produce an ethnographic portrait of candomblé (and Afro-Brazilian culture) as homogeneous, integrated, and static, the then-standard approach among her professional peers. Instead, she described internal conflicts, dialogues, and contestations of meaning in a context of change and fluidity, and she situated Afro-Brazilian culture in the past—the history of colonial and nineteenth-century slavery and of the urbanization and proletarianization of Brazil. These characteristics, which located the book on the margins of anthropology in its day, are the very reasons we have for turning to it again at the end of the twentieth century.

Beginning in 1538 and over the next three centuries an estimated three and a half million slaves were brought from Angola, the Congo, and West Africa to labor for the Portuguese colonization of Brazil. From their African homelands, they brought a rich ceremonial life centred on beliefs in powerful spirit beings *(orixás)* who visit the human world through specially designated human priest-mediums. Perfunctorily baptised in Roman Catholicism upon their arrival and left to their own devices in their plantation quarters, slaves freely interpreted Iberian Catholic imagery in the context of their African beliefs. The result was the birth of Afro-Brazilian religions that were neither African nor Iberian but a blending of the two that took diverse regional forms. In Bahia, the Afro-Brazilian religion is known as candomblé.

Following the abolition of slavery in 1888, freed slaves migrated to cities in search of wage employment. The period following slavery was a time of uncertain social and economic status for African Brazilians. Some scholars have suggested that the re-emergence and fluorescence of candomblé cults in Bahia by the turn of the century represented the efforts of former slaves, who were now the urban poor, to establish a new cultural identity through an assertion of cultural continuity with their slave history (Eco 1983: 106). By the 1930s there were an estimated 100 to 150 candomblé cult centers, or *terreiros*, in Bahia, each sanctified by one of a pantheon of orixás, each led by its own high priestess or priest *(mãe de santo* or *pai de santo)* and core of initiates, the spirit mediums *(filhas de santo)*, and each observing its own ceremonial festival days, rituals, and practices. Ruth Landes concentrated her studies on two of these terreiros, Engenho Velho and Gantois.

The social and political turmoil of the 1930s was reflected in the emergence of new cults. Combining Amerindian beliefs with African and Catholic imagery, *candomblé de caboclo* was practised at the terreiro of the priestess, Sabina, described by Landes in *The City of Women*. *Umbanda* emerged in Rio de Janeiro during the 1930s and spread rapidly throughout the country, taking on many regional manifestations (Gabriel 1980). Umbanda incorporated elements of

African religions, Catholicism, occultism, and Allan Kardec spiritualism. By the 1960s, the cult had between five and ten million followers—in Rio de Janeiro alone there were over twenty thousand cult centers—and attracted a growing middle-class following (Brown 1986).

African possession religions centered around a belief in a cosmology of spirits or culture heroes, the orixás. To the accompaniment of drumming and public ritualized dancing, orixás visit the human world by possessing or "riding" selected human spirit mediums. Most prevalent in Bahia in the 1930s were the Yoruban male spirits: Xangô, spirit of lightning and thunder; Ogún, of war; Omolu, of illness; Oxalá, of the sky and procreation; and Oxóce, of the hunt. There were also female spirits: Iemanjá, spirit of the sea and of salt water; Iansã, of wind and storm; and Oxún, of the river Oxún and of fresh water. The orixás were not conceived to be persons or gods but rather to be "natural forces . . . cosmic vibrations, water, wind, leaves, rainbow" (Eco 1983: 105). Each was associated with particular symbols, colors, clothing, food, ceremonial days or seasons, invocations, and dances. In the Afro-Brazilian cults these African spirits became loosely identified with Christian saints and symbols, a practice that simultaneously enabled the Roman Catholic Church to declare the slaves to be practising Catholics and that enabled slaves to keep alive African beliefs and ritual life. The strong attachment of Iberian Catholics to great liturgical festivals and spectacular processions as well as their devotion to the cult of the Virgin Mary and the saints resonated for the slaves, who similarly loved the ceremonies for the African orixas. This shared love of spectacle and festiveness eased the integration of Catholic and African rituals in the emergent Afro-Brazilian religions.

Each terreiro or cult house was presided over by a priestess (mãe de santo) or priest (pai de santo). When Landes reached Bahia in 1938, by far the majority of terreiros were led by women, although leaders of the caboclo and other new mixed cults were often homosexual men (Carneiro 1940; Landes 1940a; Pierson 1942). The responsibilities of the priest or priestess were to identify the manifesting spirits during trance and possession, to supervise the lengthy initiation rites of the mediums (filhas de santo), to perform sacred rituals, and to preside at public ceremonies. In addition, considered to have divining and curing powers, the priests and priestesses counselled people on all matters whether they were related to business, politics, disputes, or love. In the Yoruban candomblés of Bahia, these spiritual leaders were individuals who had inherited their title and who were highly trained in African religious knowledge and ritual. They were both dignified and charismatic, and their comportment and knowledge brought high levels of prestige to their terreiros.

Other functionaries of a terreiro were the *ogans*, the *mãe pequena*, the *ekedi*, and the *filhas de santo*. Honorary male members, ogans are financial sponsors of a terreiro or perform ritual roles such as drumming at ceremonies or the slaughtering of sacrificial animals. The mãe pequena (literally, "little mother") was the next in authority to the priestess. She was usually designated to inherit the terreiro upon the death of its leader and was responsible for ensuring that initiates carried out their ritual obligations. The mãe pequena also made the propitiatory food offering *(despacho)* to Exú, whose spirit must be appeased before any ceremony can begin. Also resident in the terreiro are the ekedi, servants who assisted and cared for the initiates, especially in the emotional aftermath of spirit possession. The mediums (filhas de santo) were almost always young women. Once they had been possessed by an orixá, they were said to have been chosen by the spirit to speak his or her will and were required to undergo a severe initiation in order to bring under control this ability to be possessed. Following a rigidly prescribed sequence of events that might last from six months to a year, initiation included food, drink, and sex taboos, hair cutting, and learning the rituals and songs of the orixá, usually in the Yoruban language. The candomblé temples were hierarchically organized with the priestess commanding authority to enforce rules and taboos regarding food and sex for initiates and, when necessary, to order severe discipline for any offenders.

Landes reported a great deal of rivalry among the candomblés of Bahia. Each tried to outdo the other by displaying the most elaborate ceremonies, costumes, and accessories, offering the most abundant food, claiming the most knowledgeable and respected leader, and so on. This competition encouraged rigid definitions of "tradition" and generated contested assertions of authenticity. As the terreiros jockeyed for supremacy, established temples publicly censured new cult houses as "unorthodox," such as those of caboclo leaders, Sabina and João, described by Landes (cf. Brown and Bick 1987). The commercialization of the candomblés for tourism was also emerging in the 1930s. In *The City of Women*, however, Landes focussed on the more conservative—what were considered to be the most "African"—sects.

Candomblé was not exclusively a religious organization; it was also a social and economic institution. As Landes describes, common-law marriage was the preferred form for cult leaders, spirit mediums, and initiates. Only women and children lived in the candomblé itself: the priestess and her biological daughters; and her female spirit medium initiates and their children. Husbands visited their wives in the terreiro, and sometimes lived or stayed in huts on the temple grounds. The women were usually engaged in the informal economy—market and street vending, sewing, and laundering, or midwifery, healing, divining, and administering death rites. Many women worked for years to save enough money to fulfill their obligations to the orixás. The ritual life of the candomblés mirrored the economic and social autonomy of the women and the female-centeredness of Afro-Brazilian households in Bahia. Removed from political and economic representation in Bahian society, Afro-Brazilian women endowed their domestic lives with meaning through creative elaborations and modifications of the possession religion.

The candomblés also operated as mutual aid societies and provided a basis for female solidarity under social and economic conditions of poverty, sickness, discrimination, and other adversities (cf. McCarthy Brown 1991; Constantinides 1982; Kendall 1985). Women could obtain loans of money, advice and counsel, cures for illnesses and other misfortunes, and shelter from abuse or homelessness. Candomblés were self-sufficient economic systems; initiates paid room and board during the months or years of their initiation and offered gifts at each stage of their indoctrination. Husbands and ogans provided economic and other support to the cult houses.

Nonmembers or clients visited the temple to consult the mãe de santo and paid her to impart knowledge, expertise, and counsel. At the public ceremonies often attended by several hundred people, participants and spectators made cash donations to the priestess. As Landes reports, some priestesses achieved wealth and high social status through their cult activities.

Early scholars predicted that the candomblés would disappear with "assimilation" (Nina Rodrigues 1932; Pierson 1942; Ramos 1935). However, not only have they persisted but new cults have emerged to express the increasing regional diversity and socioeconomic and ethnic complexity of Brazil. New generations of scholars continue to study the Afro-Brazilian and Caribbean possession religions (McCarthy Brown 1991; Brown 1986; Gabriel 1980; Galembo 1993; Thompson 1993; Wafer 1991), which have shown an apparently limitless potential for growth based on their flexibility and creativity, and the fundamentally individual relationships that people develop with the spirits and their human mediums. The continued vitality of candomblé is also due to its resonance for women. Candomblé makes visible women's experience, and offers women well-defined roles, personal access to a multiplicity of spirits who speak to women's needs, and access to extended personal networks and material resources. Innovation that simultaneously maintains continuity with history—a history now symbolized not only in the folklore of the orixas but in stories about the lives of earlier generations of cult leaders over more than a century—endows candomblé with a persistent vitality, symbolic value, and continued utility in contemporary contexts of gender, class, and ethnic struggle.

RUTH LANDES, BOASIAN ANTHROPOLOGIST, 1908–1991

Born in 1908, Ruth Landes was the daughter of Russian Jewish immigrants to the United States and was raised in Brooklyn. Her father, Joseph Schlossberg was cofounder of the American Clothing Workers of America, and her family moved in social circles that included Jewish and African American intellectuals, writers, and political activists. Through her family she met W.E.B. DuBois,

Alain Locke, James Weldon Johnson, Walter White, and Zora Neale Hurston and developed an early interest in African American cultural life. After completing a bachelor's degree at New York University, Landes began a graduate program in social work and undertook a four-year study of Harlem storefront churches in the 1920s for her master's thesis, which was later published as "Negro Jews in Harlem" (1967). During this time Landes' father's long-time friend, anthropologist Alexander Goldenweiser, introduced her to Franz Boas and Ruth Benedict, both of whom strongly encouraged her to consider graduate work in anthropology. Wanting to pursue her interest in African American culture and seeking a commitment outside the "confines of my early marriage" (1970a: 120), Ruth Landes began a Ph.D. in anthropology at Columbia University in 1932. Boas and Benedict, her professors at Columbia, became and remained the two strongest influences upon her work throughout her life.

Historians consider Franz Boas to be the father of American anthropology.[2] He had long shown a particular interest in African American culture. As early as 1906 he tried to establish an African American Museum and to introduce a course in African American studies at Columbia. Both of these projects were discouraged and eventually foundered. Boas, however, continued to encourage students to undertake research on African Americans, for this research was central to his vision of anthropology as an antiracist science. The Boasian vision was instrumental in Ruth Landes' entering the discipline and in the development of her own humanist and anti-racist anthropology.

A German Jew, Boas emigrated to the United States in 1883. Never feeling fully "American," he always saw himself as "immigrant" and "other." His central contribution to anthropology—the development of the scientific concept of culture and the analytical separation of culture and race—was a theoretical response to his personal experience of scientific racism and anti-immigration sentiment in early twentieth century America (Boas 1928; 1948). Scientific racism was rooted in nineteenth-century social Darwinism, which linked race and culture in a single hierarchical evolutionary sequence. Mendelian laws of heredity and the developing field of genetics dominated scientific views on race and fed public opinion. The early twentieth century was a period of massive immigration, especially Jewish and Italian, to the United States. Fearing the dilution of Anglo Protestant domination, conservative political forces mobilized to stem the tide of increasing cultural and social diversification. At the time, increasing immigration and ethnic diversity was largely a phenomenon of the cities of the northeastern seaboard, particularly New York, while Jim Crow laws racially segregated blacks and whites in the southern United States. Under mounting pressure to pass anti-immigration laws, the Congress commissioned in 1911 and published a forty-volume scientific report that linked the "deterioration" of the American "stock" to immigration (Barkan 1992). Only Boas' contribution to the survey argued against racial determinism and focussed instead on the role of environmental influences. At Columbia Boas engaged his students in studies of immigrant populations and of southern blacks who had migrated to the North. Their work documented how environment and history modified culture. Far from being linked to biological race, culture was the adaptive and expressive vehicle for the social and economic conditions of human populations. Boas' cultural anthropology strongly influenced Ruth Landes as a young student and professional scholar.

The second important influence in Landes' anthropological training was Ruth Benedict. In her journals, Landes has likened her dependence upon Benedict during this time to her earlier dependence upon her parents and suggests that Benedict came to replace her parents. Her choice of a Ph.D. dissertation topic—the social organization of the Ojibwa of northern Ontario, Canada—can be traced directly to Benedict's influence. Landes writes that, when she arrived at Columbia, she was "given the choice of studying Negro life anywhere or examining the life of an American-Indian tribe" (1970a: 120): "Negroes were regarded even by liberals and scholars as a sort of tribe—not the same as white men, not the same as modern men" (1947: 3). That she chose to study the Ojibwa and not African Americans reflects Benedict's research interests and her influence over Landes. Fieldwork among the Ojibwa resulted in three books, *Ojibwa Sociology* (1937), *The Ojibwa Woman* (1938), and

xv

Ojibwa Religion and the Midewiwin (1968). After receiving her Ph.D. in 1935, Landes continued research under Benedict's direction. She worked with the Santee Dakota in the summer of 1935 and among the Kansas Potawatami in the fall and winter of 1935 and 1936. Although she did not write up the results of this research for many years, Landes collected material for two future books, *The Mystic Lake Sioux* (1969) and *The Prairie Potawatami* (1970b).

The focus on religion and the collection of texts and stories in Landes' writing on Native American cultures is consistent in style and approach with Boasian ethnography of the period. Her interest in women and gender relations was mirrored in the research and writing of other women students of Boas and Benedict (cf. Parezo 1993). Landes' recording of Native American shamanistic practices and her early interest in sexuality may be traced to Benedict's book *Patterns of Culture* and to her paper "Anthropology and the Abnormal," both of which appeared in 1934. Benedict described how other cultures accommodate behaviour deemed "deviant" in America and how spirit possession, homosexuality, paranoia, and megalomania, for example, are sometimes the foundation of authority and leadership. Benedict's work carried an explicit critique of the intolerance in American society and she urged ethnographic research on these subjects. In this historical context, Landes' study of candomblé in Bahia owes much to Ruth Benedict's influence.

RUTH LANDES IN BAHIA, BRAZIL, 1938–1939

In the context of emerging United States political and economic interest in South America, Boas and Benedict initiated American anthropological research in Brazil during the late 1930s. At this time Landes again considered research on the African American experience, deciding to study race relations in Bahia. Columbia University also sent four young male anthropologists—Buell Quain, Charles Wagley, Jules Henry, and Walter Lipkind—to study the culture and conditions of Indians in the Amazon basin. Landes alone undertook fieldwork in an urban setting and among Afro-Brazilians.

White Brazilian sociologist Gilberto Freyre profoundly influenced students of race relations in the United States. His two books, *The Masters and the Slaves* ([1933] 1986a) and *The Mansions and the Shanties* ([1936] 1986b) were much discussed among academics at the time. Freyre had done graduate studies at Columbia, and his writings on the history of race relations in Brazil reflected his observations of segregation in the United States. His description of a unique Brazilian "racial democracy" drew American scholars to that country to study its race relations at first hand. Landes writes: ". . . we had heard . . . that Brazil's large Negro population lived decently among the general population; and we wanted to examine the details" (1970a: 120).

There was a great deal of scholarly interest in Afro-Brazilian studies in the 1930s. As early as 1896, physician and professor of forensic medicine, Raymundo Nina Rodrigues (1862–1906), a native of Bahia, studied spirit possession (1935; 1976). Following his death, scholars at the Institute that bears his name, the Instituto Nina Rodrigues in Bahia, continued this work. Of these, Artur Ramos became the most well-known internationally. A physician specializing in clinical psychiatry and forensic medicine, Ramos moved to Rio de Janeiro where he taught forensic medicine and where he began research on spirit-possession religions in 1926. Ramos published extensively on the subject, taking a special interest in the physical and psychological characteristics of trance and possession (1935). Held in 1933 and 1937 were two Afro-Brazilian congresses at which white Brazilian and American scholars and Afro-Brazilian ritual specialists collaborated in furthering the study of candomblé. During the same decade in the United States, Donald Pierson, a student at the University of Chicago, wrote his book *Negroes in Brazil: A Study of Race Contact in Bahia*, which was based on two years' fieldwork (1935–1937). After conducting research in Africa, Melville Herskovits, professor of Anthropology at Northwestern University, undertook comparative studies of African religions in the New World, focussing on Haiti, Cuba, and Brazil (1937; 1943; 1969; [1941] 1990). Likewise, French anthropologists Claude Levi-Strauss and Roger Bastide conducted research in Brazil in the late 1930s. While the former worked in the

Amazon (1961), the latter began a life's work on the African religions of Brazil (1978). Thus when Landes arrived in Bahia in 1938, candomblé had a relatively high profile in the local intellectual and cultural community.

Prior to going to Brazil, however, Landes spent a year (1937–1938) at Fisk, the African American University in Tennessee on the advice of Robert Park. Her charge was "to teach, to study the collection, and to 'get used to Negroes'" (1947: 2–3). She taught classes, worked with the university's extensive African American library collection, and experienced American "racial etiquette" in the segregated South (1970a: 120). Eight years later, when writing *The City of Women*, Landes reflected:

> . . . it seems unbelievable that the distance between the races in our country could have been so great as to justify my spending a year among Negroes just because I was white and therefore had to become accustomed to them. Looking back, it seems amazing that I should have been sent to another country to study the workings of its racial policy, on the simple assumption that the peaceful coexistence of two physical types of men requires special regulatory devices (1947: 3).

Within weeks of her arrival in Bahia, Landes herself recognized the inherent racism in such an approach and abandoned the study of race relations in order to focus on candomblé. Although she claims that *The City of Women* "does not discuss race problems because there were none" (1947:vi), the book tells us a lot about race in both the United States and Brazil largely through Landes' situating herself and her subjects in historical context.

In *The City of Women*, Landes clearly locates the Afro-Brazilian candomblé practitioners as the politically and economically powerless in Bahia and herself as a white woman and a Jew. With Brazil experiencing the rise of Nazism in the 1930s, Landes was conscious of her Jewish identity. More than once, she recalls "star[ing] miserably at official portraits of Hitler on the walls" when she dealt with the Brazilian bureaucracy (1947: 9). Being a woman, however, presented the greatest difficulty in initiating her research. Donald

Pierson, a white male, had apparently worked without hindrance in Bahia a few years earlier and had been taken on as an *ogan* by one of the male cult leaders. Landes, on the other hand, described her frustration in finding that she could not even get close to the candomblé temples—the cultural centre of Afro-Brazilian life in Bahia. Discouraging Landes' efforts, Brazilian officials and scholars explained that a "respectable" white woman did not enter the black neighborhoods without an escort. "[W]omen were as handicapped in their movements as political opponents," she writes (1947: 9).

Landes was frustrated by race, class, and gender codes in 1930s Brazil on many levels. Personally, she felt imprisoned. She had lived unhappily under the color bar at Fisk, and she refused to accept similar barriers in her Bahian relationships. Professionally, she was determined to immerse herself in Afro-Brazilian culture and to apply what anthropologists today call participant-observation field methods. She wanted to experience a very different kind of field research than she had in the Native American reservations, "where it is possible to hire individuals to sit in a chair for months and tell about themselves" (1947:16). In *The City of Women*, she writes: "I wanted to see them live their own lives instead of merely hearing them answer my questions. Indeed, I myself could not ask questions before I knew about their lives" (1947:18). At another point, she explains, "I should have to persuade the Bahians to take me into their life. I should have to force my way into the flow and become part of it. To study the people I should have to live with them, to like them, and I should have to try assiduously to make them like me." (1947:16).

Landes' endeavour was aided immeasurably through her meeting Edison Carneiro soon after her arrival. Carneiro was twenty-eight, a Bahian-born *homem de côr* (man of color), journalist, and folklorist. He was also part of a group of communist intellectuals in Bahia. At the time he was himself engaged in a study of the candomblés (1940; 1978; 1981). During her stay Carneiro became Landes' key informant and her constant companion. His escort enabled her to travel throughout the city and its black districts, to spend nights in the candomblés observing the stages of trance, possession and their aftermath, and to meet key figures in Bahian cult life, including Martiniano do Bonfim, Mãe Menininha, and other Brazilian intellectuals and observers of candomblé. Carneiro was also Landes' lover during her year in Bahia.[3]

Ruth Landes' first publications on her Brazilian research were two articles written in 1940: "A Cult Matriarchate and Male Homosexuality" published in the Harvard-based journal of the American Psychological Association, the *Journal of Abnormal and Social Psychology*; and "Fetish Worship in Brazil" published in the *Journal of American Folklore*. In these two pieces and in a later article entitled "Negro Slavery and Female Status" (1953), Landes adopts what was the then-standard style of ethnological description, cataloguing the pantheon of African spirits and their associations with Catholic beliefs and practices. However, her description of the candomblés as led by and for women was new as was her observation that the male leaders of the emerging mixed caboclo cults were homosexual or transvestite. According to Edison Carneiro (1964), these articles were unfavorably received by influential Brazilian and American scholars, and it was difficult afterwards for Landes to find an academic publisher for *The City of Women*. Although this was probably true, Landes was also seeking her own voice as a writer and was no longer located in an academic context. Landes herself, was proud of the book. In her diary in 1951 she wrote, ". . . again, I want to write a thing of beauty—like my City of Women!" She had written *The City of Women* some years after returning from the field. By this time she had worked as a researcher for Gunnar Myrdal on the Carnegie-funded "American Negro" project and as a director on President Roosevelt's Fair Employment Practices Commission (FEPC) in Washington, D.C., during World War II. Academic jobs were few, and she was uncertain about her future and wondered if she might be a writer.

The City of Women was published as a trade book in 1947. It is a

personal and descriptive account of Landes' encounters with candomblé leaders and of her own participation in and observation of
cult ceremonies. Landes and Carneiro are central personages in the
text. Landes' recording of her own experiences and feelings and of
her friendship with Carneiro were unconventional in her day but
resulted in a style of ethnographic writing that is reflexive, dialogi-
cal, and experiential. The writing was different in important ways
from other studies of that period. According to French anthropologist Roger Bastide, Landes' peers too often treated Afro-Brazilian
spirit religions as "museum specimens." In his opinion, only two
books about the candomblés gave "an adequate idea of their dense,
teeming vitality" (1978: 221): Henri-Georges Clouzot's *Le Cheval
des Dieux* and Ruth Landes' *The City of Women*. Roger Bastide, however, was alone among his contemporaries in lauding Landes'
ethnography. A review of the book for the discipline's flagship journal *American Anthropologist*, laid out the profession's concerns about
Landes' work in Brazil: First was her portrayal of the respective
roles of women and men in candomblé; second was her contextual-
ization of Afro-Brazilian religions as emerging out of local history
and experience rather than as representing African "survivals"; and
third were her methods and personal comportment in the field.

The reviewer, Melville Herskovits, claimed that Landes gave a
"false perspective on the role of men and women in the culture that
gives the book its misleading title" (1948: 124). He continued:

> What Miss Landes does not realize is that men have places that are
> quite as important as those of the women; that the African counter-
> parts of the Bahian cults have priestesses as well as priests. . . . The
> basic thesis is also wrong because of the misreading of an economic
> cause—that is, few men are initiates, in Bahia no less than in Africa,
> because they cannot afford the time its takes, because in Africa it is
> easier to support a woman in the culthouse than to withdraw a man
> from productive labor for months on end. Miss Landes overstresses
> the homosexuality of male priests—there are many "orthodox" as
> well as caboclo priests in Bahia who have no tendency toward inver-
> sion (Ibid.).

Herskovits maintained that Landes had misinterpreted the relations of men and women in the candomblés because she had not been adequately trained "in the Africanist field." He wrote that she had been "ill prepared" to conduct research in Bahia because "she knew so little of the African background of the material she was to study that she had no perspective" (Ibid.). His assertion was based on the limited ethnographic knowledge of gender roles in West African societies at the time; abundant subsequent research has shown these relations to be women-centered in ways consistent with Landes' early understanding of social roles in Bahia (Potash 1989). Recent research has also supported Landes' early observations about homosexuality in the cults (Wafer 1991).

Melville Herskovits was engaged in developing "Afro-American culture" as a field of study in anthropology and had conducted research in West Africa, Surinam, Haiti and the southern United States (1937; 1943; [1941] 1990). Like Pierson and Brazilian ethnologists of the Nina Rodrigues school, Herskovits argued that the "survival" of African culture was evident in music, art, language, family structure, and religion and especially in the continuing African American belief in spirit possession. According to Walter Jackson, Herskovits had come "to see himself as an interpreter of Africa to Afro-Americans" (1986: 109). Gertrude Fraser has recently noted that anthropologists who conducted research on African Americans in the 1930s and 1940s envisioned only two possible analytical frameworks: One was to measure degrees of assimilation into white American society; the other was, like Herskovits, to look to Africa for explanations of the cultural differences between African Americans and whites. Fraser writes, "In either case, African-American culture was largely examined in terms of something or somewhere else" (1991: 407).

As *The City of Women* illustrates, Ruth Landes, who observed Afro-Brazilian religion on its own terms, was working within a third and alternative framework. Landes believed that she was studying a new living Brazilian religion, and she wanted to portray candomblé as fully integrated in the way of life of the urban poor of Bahia. She was especially concerned to understand the ways that the candomblés met the needs and structured the lives of women, a perspective that developed from her field methods. Landes tells us that she decided early on not to conduct research in what was apparently the style of most scholars of Brazil at the time—conducting formal interviews in their university offices or relying on second-hand reports. Nor would she focus, as they had, on obtaining technical descriptions of the physiological characteristics of spirit possession or on dissecting the Catholic and African origins of the religions. Instead, Landes was determined to undertake participant-observation as American anthropology was beginning to define it: "entering deeply into the field culture, joining it twenty-four hours a day, each day, all the months or years of research" (1970a: 121).

As noted above, participant-observation in Brazil proved difficult for Landes. Boundaries of gender, race, and class effectively controlled social interaction, and the police spied on the candomblés, which were believed to harbor opponents of the military regime of Getulio Vargas. Indeed, fieldwork only became possible for Landes when she met Edison Carneiro. In a short time the two combined their research efforts. Ruth Landes recognized the link between her experience and her ethnographic understanding of the culture, and she sought to explore this relationship in her writing. For Landes, "Field work serves an idiosyncrasy of perception that cannot separate the sensuousness of life from its abstractions, nor the researcher's personality from his experiences. The culture a field worker reports is the one he experiences, filtered through trained observations. . . . Through field work at the pleasure of the host culture one learns one's place there and that is one's only vantage point for penetrating the culture" (1970a: 121; 138).

Landes' field methods were, however, Herskovits' major criticism. He wrote that her training on American Indian reservations had not prepared her for "what might be called the diplomatic aspects of fieldwork. . . . Students of acculturated societies must be . . . taught how to conduct themselves in the capital as well as in the bush, told how to turn the corners of calling cards, when to leave them, and how to 'sign the book.'" In *The City of Women* Landes describes how she had been given letters of introduction to elite and official people in Bahia but that she found these contacts to be distant from the people and life of the candomblés. She therefore chose not to spend her time socializing with the elite of Bahian society but instead to devote her energies to getting to know people for whom the beliefs and practices of the cult houses held profound meaning. *The City of Women* is filled with the names and stories of these people, who were descended from African slaves and who worked as stevedores, bricklayers, fishermen, seamstresses, laundresses, and street vendors. Landes wrote, "I felt it was fine just to be among them, and I wanted to be of them" (1947:15).

Herskovits' criticism of Ruth Landes' field methods was an indirect criticism of her personal comportment in the field and of her alliance with Edison Carneiro, a nonelite, nonwhite candomblé aficionado. Landes' affair with Carneiro was well-known at the time. Although she understood that the relationship had given her intimate access to life in the candomblés, her critics believed that it had compromised her anthropology.[4]

REREADING *The City of Women*

Anthropologists are beginning to acknowledge that the processes of professionalization erased much early work on race and gender during the creation of the disciplinary canon and are still at work in the profession (Harrison 1992; Lutz 1990; Morgen 1989). Rereading the ethnography of Ruth Landes and reconstructing the processes by which her work was marginalized and her career controlled offers an illustrative case study.[5] Especially compelling is the recognition that many characteristics of Landes' writing in *The City of Women* are incorporated in what anthropologists now call "new" and "experimental" ethnography: reflexive writing about one's subjective experience in the field and one's situated position as an author; acknowledgement of the role of friendship; the naming of friends as persons in ethnography rather than keeping them nameless informants (cf. Behar 1993; Trawick 1991; McCarthy Brown 1991); and attempts to reduce "othering" and objectification through the writing of multivocal ethnographies that seek to provide other people, the ethnographic subjects, textual space to represent their subjective experience in their own words and voices. Furthermore, Landes' focus on race and gender, unconventional and criticized in the 1930s and 1940s, is the critical focus of postcolonial and feminist anthropology in the late twentieth century.

In a recent paper, Lila Abu-Lughod has argued that the centrality of the concept of culture in anthropology has served to endorse a self-other distinction embodying hierarchy and denying other cultures' history (1991: 137–138, 146). She urges that anthropologists begin to adopt a variety of strategies—theoretical, substantive, and textual—that constitute "writing against culture," what she describes as "a decolonization at the level of the text" (1990: 11). These strategies, she argues, are at work in the recent writing of feminist and "halfie" ethnographers and include not only the textual practices of reflexivity and multivocality but also, through recognition that the self participates in multiple identifications and that the other is also partially the self, a blurring of the self-other dichotomy.[6] For Abu-Lughod, writing against culture involves more than experimental writing styles or "textual innovations"; it requires fundamental shifts in the theory and substance of basic research.

Exploring the history of writing in anthropology and rereading the ethnography of earlier practitioners in the discipline reveals that writing has continually been subject to critique and revision in the context of the theoretical concerns of the day. The reprinting of *The City of Women* not only makes Landes' work available to a new and contemporary audience but also serves as a reminder that theoretical debates about race and gender and debates about writing and textual authority have a long history in our discipline. Knowing that history may help us to move toward progressive debate rather than to reproduce processes of silencing and marginalization.

Rereading the ethnography of Ruth Landes, we learn that "writing against culture" has long been a subtext in anthropology. During the period of its professionalization, however, the discipline marginalized such writing because it threatened the authority of the scientific concept of culture upon which its new professionalism was based (Gordon 1990). In 1935, when Landes received her Ph.D. and began her professional career, anthropology was defining itself as a science of culture engaged in the search for general laws and in developing a scientific style of writing. The reasons it is important to know about Landes' work today are the very reasons

xxv

she did not receive recognition in her lifetime. Landes did not escape the exoticization of cultural difference of her day, but she did resist her peers' rhetorical strategies of "othering." She rejected the scientific writing style of ethnographic naturalism to assert textual authority; she resisted the cataloguing of cultural traits and the removal of culture from its social, political, and economic contexts; and she did not write out of her texts the contradictions of history and of "unruly experience" (Clifford 1988: 25) in order to construct an integrated cultural whole in her ethnography. She defined race and gender as topics for scientific research and was conscious of the politics of race and gender in her field research situations. Finally, she insisted on situating herself as a Jew and a woman in her writing—a practice that, although increasingly current in present-day anthropology (especially among feminist and halfie ethnographers), was anathema to the rhetorical assertions of ethnographic authority in her day.

Writing against culture requires more than textual innovation and, more importantly, takes place at the levels where basic research questions are defined and addressed and thus at the level where theory is generated. For Ruth Landes, questions of race and gender were fundamental to anthropological inquiry, and scientific theories were inadequate to address them. "My training in pure science had left me unprepared for such events," she wrote after a few weeks' immersion in the race and gender politics of 1930s Brazil. She thus let go of academic reference points and scientific theories of culture and endeavoured to let Brazil speak to her on its own terms, a process she writes about in *The City of Women*. In making this decision, she effectively chose a life course on the borders of a discipline that was at the time seeking to legitimate its professional status as the "science of the study of man." While it may be that "systematic, sharply new methods or epistemologies" (Clifford 1988: 23) are needed in anthropology today, we also have much to learn from historical analysis of how the discipline handled epistemological crises in the past. Recent movements in ethnographic writing and theory may not be as novel as they appear if we examine some of the historical casualties of the process of disciplinary professionalization.

In *The City of Women* Ruth Landes describes the ritual cleansing (*axêxê*) of a candomblé temple after a year of mourning following the death of one of the temple leaders:

> I attended the mass with Zézé, and that afternoon I returned to the temple. Under Hilda's direction, the axêxê was concluding in a weary spirit. It was a farewell, and a resumption of life. The temple was freed of death. Visitors had their footsteps "cleaned" at the doorway, as Hilda handed them water to throw to the right, to the left, and before the door. Mother Dada was dancing alone, and the daughters were kneeling and reverencing with uplifted hands as they sang in Yoruba:
>
> > Dada, good mother,
> > Ah, tender Mother,
> > Dada, precious Mother,
> > Who shares all with us,
> > Look upon me.

It was a sort of invocation to life (1947:231).

Ruth Landes invoked life in her ethnography. As a result her writing, censured in its day, continues to speak to us more than half a century later.

ACKNOWLEDGEMENTS

My wish to arrange for a reprinting of *The City of Women* emerged as part of my work on a biography of Ruth Landes. The arguments I make in this Introduction are developed further in this larger project. I would like to thank Jo Glorie, formerly of Paragon House, (now defunct) for her initial interest. I would like to thank Nancy Parezo for introducing me to editor Larry Ball at the University of New Mexico Press and Larry for his unfailing enthusiasm for this project. I also thank Lambros Comitas, director of the Research Institute for the Study of Man (RISM), holder of the copyright on all of Ruth Landes' published works, for facilitating the reprinting. I would also like to thank RISM for funding for my initial trip to the National Anthropological Archives to look at the Ruth Landes Papers. Subsequent research has been supported under a grant from the Social Sciences and Humanities Research Council of Canada. Finally, I thank David Howes and Leni Silverstein for their readings of an earlier version of this introduction.

NOTES

1. Spencer continues, "Ethnographic naturalism, while working with ostensibly unproblematic literary devices, in fact constructs a kind of object — a world robbed of its idiosyncracies and foibles — which is foreign to the experience of its readers" (1989: 153–4).

2. The contradictions and tensions in Boas' own writing must be separated from his oral teachings and mentoring of his students. According to George Stocking (1974), Franz Boas is the single most important force shaping American anthropology, and the debates of twentieth century American anthropology can be largely understood as the working out in time of the wide-ranging and sometimes contradictory positions that Boas developed over his career, which began in 1881 and spanned more than half a century.

3. More than eighty letters from Carneiro to Landes, written after she returned to the United States, are a testimony to their affair. This unpublished correspondence was among the papers that Ruth Landes arranged for deposition in the National Anthropological Archives at the Smithsonian Institute upon her death.

4. I have elaborated this argument elsewhere (Cole 1993; 1995 [in press]). Landes has recorded her own thoughts on the episode in her 1970 essay "A Woman Anthropologist in Brazil" (1970a).

5. Although Ruth Landes received her Ph.D. in 1935, she did not find a permanent academic appointment until thirty years later when, in 1965, she was hired at McMaster University in Hamilton, Ontario, Canada—on the strength of her research on the Ontario Ojibwa. Until this appointment, she had supported herself through a variety of short-term consulting and teaching contracts in the field of what was known as "applied anthropology." In addition to her work in Washington on President Roosevelt's Fair Employment Practices Committee (1941–45), Landes conducted research on Mexican American youth for the Los Angeles Metropolitan Welfare Council (1946–47); was a research director for the American Jewish Committee (1948–51); was a Fulbright Scholar in Britain studying Caribbean immigration (1951–52); lectured at the New School for Social Research (1953–55); and taught in the School of Social Work at the University of Southern California and at the

Claremont Graduate School in the Anthropology and Education Program and consulted for various California state and Los Angeles city agencies (1957–63). She died in Hamilton in February 1991, professor emerita at McMaster.

6. "Halfie" is a term that Abu-Lughod (1990; 1991) uses to denote anthropologists who are also by birth or ancestry part of the cultures they study but who by virtue of their or their parents' emigration to the United States and their academic training in anthropology find themselves to be both part and not part of the culture.

REFERENCES

Abu-Lughod, Lila
1990 Can There be a Feminist Ethnography? *Women and Performance* 5(1): 7–27.
1991 Writing Against Culture. In *Recapturing Anthropology: Working in the Present*. Richard Fox, ed. Pp. 137–162. Santa Fe: School of American Research.

Barkan, Elazar
1992 *The Retreat of Scientific Racism: Changing Concepts of Race in Britain and the United States Between the World Wars.* Cambridge: Cambridge University Press.

Bastide, Roger
1978 *The African Religions of Brazil.* Trans. by Helen Sebba. Baltimore: The Johns Hopkins University Press.

Behar, Ruth
1993 *Translated Woman: Crossing the Border with Esperanza's Story.* Boston: Beacon Press.

Benedict, Ruth
1934a *Patterns of Culture.* Boston: Houghton Mifflin
1934b Anthropology and the Abnormal. *Journal of General Psychology* 10(2): 59–82.

Boas, Franz
1928 *Anthropology and Modern Life.* New York: Norton.
1948 *Race, Language and Culture.* New York: Macmillan.

Brown, Diana
1986 *Umbanda: Religion and Politics in Urban Brazil.* Ann Arbor: UMI Research Press.

Brown, Diana and Mario Bick
1987 Religion, Class, and Context: Continuities and Discontinuities in Brazilian Umbanda. *American Ethnologist* 14: 73–93.

Brown, Karen McCarthy
1991 *Mama Lola: Vodou Priestess of Brooklyn.* Berkeley: University of California Press.

Carneiro, Edison
1940 The Structure of African Cults in Bahia. *Journal of American Folklore* 53: 271–278.
1964 Uma "Falseta" de Artur Ramos. In *Ladinos e Crioulos: Estudos sobre o Negro no Brasil.* E. Carneiro, ed. Rio de Janeiro: Civilização Brasileira. Pp. 223–227.
1978 *Candomblés da Bahia.* 6th ed. Rio de Janeiro: Civilização Brasileira.
1981 *Religiões Negras.* Negros Bantus. 2nd. ed. (orig. published separately in 1936 and 1937). Rio de Janeiro: Civilização Brasileira.

Clifford, James and George Marcus, eds.
1986 *Writing Culture: The Poetics and Politics of Ethnography.* Berkeley: University of California Press.

Clifford, James
1988 *The Predicament of Culture: Twentieth-Century Ethnography, Literature and Art.* Cambridge: Harvard University Press.

Cole, Sally
1993 Biography as Historical Anthropology: Ruth Landes and the Science of Culture. Paper presented at the Annual Meeting of the History of Science Society, Santa Fe, New Mexico, November 11–13, 1993.
1995 Ruth Landes and the Early Ethnography of Race and Gender. In *Women Writing Culture/Culture Writing Women.* Ruth Behar and Deborah Gordon, eds. Berkeley: University of California Press. (In Press.)

Constantinides, Pamela
1982 Women's Spirit Possession and Urban Adaptation. In *Women United, Women Divided: Comparative Studies of Ten Contemporary Cultures.* Patricia Caplan and Janet Bujra, eds. Pp. 185–205. Bloomington: Indiana University Press.

Eco, Umberto
1983 *Travels in Hyperreality.* Trans. by William Weaver. New York: Harcourt Brace Jovanovich.

Fraser, Gertrude
1991 Race, Class, and Difference in Hortense Powdermaker's *After Freedom: A Cultural Study of the Deep South. Journal of Anthropological Research. Special Issue: The Legacy of Hortense Powdermaker* 47 (4): 403–415.

Freyre, Gilberto
1986a The Masters and the Slaves: A Study in the Development of Brazilian Civilization. 1933. Reprint, Berkeley: University of California Press.
1986b *The Mansions and the Shanties: The Making of Modern Brazil.* 1936. Reprint, Berkeley: University of California Press.

Gabriel, Chester
1980 Communications of the Spirits: Umbanda, Regional Cults in Manaus and the Dynamics of Mediumistic Trance. Ph.D. diss., Department of Anthropology, McGill University, Montreal.

Galembo, Phyllis
1993 *Divine Inspiration.* Albuquerque: University of New Mexico Press.

Gordon, Deborah
1990 The Politics of Ethnographic Authority: Race and Writing in the Ethnography of Margaret Mead and Zora Neale Hurston. In *Modernist Anthropology: From Fieldwork to Text.* Marc Manganaro, ed. Pp. 146–162. Princeton: Princeton University Press.

Harrison, Faye V.
1991 Anthropology as an Agent of Transformation: Introductory Comments and Queries. In *Decolonizing Anthropology: Moving Further Toward an Anthropology for Liberation.* Faye V. Harrison, ed. Pp. 1–14. Washington, D.C.: American Anthropological Association.
1992 The DuBoisian Legacy in Anthropology. *Critique of Anthropology* 12(3): 239–260.

Herskovits, Melville
1937 African Gods and Catholic Saints in New World Negro Belief. *American Anthropologist* 39: 635–643.
1948 Review of *The City of Women. American Anthropologist* 50:123–125.
1969 The Social Organization of the Candomblé. In *The New World Negro.* Francis Herskovits, ed. Pp. 226–247. Bloomington: Indiana University Press.
1990 *The Myth of the Negro Past.* Introduction by Sidney W. Mintz. 1941. Reprint, Boston: Beacon Press.

Herskovits, Melville and Francis
1943 The Negroes of Brazil. *Yale Review* 32: 263–279.

Honigmann, John
1947 Review of *The City of Women*. Social Forces 26: 227.

hooks, bell
1990 *Yearning: Race, Gender and Cultural Politics*. Toronto: Between-the-
Lines.

Jackson, Walter
1986 Melville Herskovits and the Search for Afro-American Culture. In
*Malinowski, Rivers, Benedict and Others: Essays on Culture and Personality. History
of Anthropology*, vol. 4. George Stocking, ed. Pp. 95–126. Madison: University
of Wisconsin Press.

Kendall, Laura
1985 *Shamans, Housewives and Other Restless Spirits: Women in Korean Ritual
Life*. Honolulu: University of Hawaii Press.

Landes, Ruth Schlossberg
1937 *Ojibwa Sociology*. New York: Columbia University Press.
1938 *The Ojibwa Woman*. New York: Columbia University Press.
1940a A Cult Matriarchate and Male Homosexuality. *Journal of Abnormal
and Social Psychology* 35: 386–397.
1940b Fetish Worship in Brazil. *Journal of American Folklore* 53: 261–270.
1947 *The City of Women*. New York: Macmillan.
1953 Negro Slavery and Female Status. *Journal of African Affairs*.
1967 Negro Jews in Harlem. *Jewish Journal of Sociology* 9(2): 175–189.
1968 *Ojibwa Religion and the Midewiwin*. Madison: University of Wisconsin
Press.
1969 *The Mystic Lake Sioux*. Madison: University of Wisconsin Press.
1970a A Woman Anthropologist in Brazil. In *Women in the Field:
Anthropological Experiences*. Peggy Golde, ed. Pp. 117–139. Chicago: Aldine.
1970b *The Prairie Potawatami*. Madison: University of Wisconsin Press.

Leacock, Seth and Ruth
1975 *Spirits of the Deep: A Study of an Afro-Brazilian Cult*. New York:
Anchor Books.

Levi-Strauss, Claude
1961 *A World on the Wane*. Trans. by John Russell. London: Hutchinson.

Lutz, Catherine
1990 The Erasure of Women's Writing in Sociocultural Anthropology.
American Ethnologist 17(4): 611–627.

Mishnun, Virginia
1947 Review of *The City of Women. The Nation* 165:128.

Mohanty, Chandra
1991 Under Western Eyes: Feminist Scholarship and Colonial Discourse.
In *Third World Women and the Politics of Feminism.* Chandra Mohanty, Ann
Russo, and Lourdes Torres, eds. Pp. 51–80. Bloomington: Indiana University
Press.

Morgen, Sandra
1989 Gender and Anthropology: Introductory Essay. In *Gender and
Anthropology: Critical Reviews for Teaching.* Sandra Morgen, ed. Pp. 1–20.
Washington: American Anthropological Association.

Nina Rodrigues, Raymundo
1935 *O animismo fetichista dos negros bahianos.* Rio de Janeiro: Civilização
Brasileira.
1976 *Os africanos no Brasil.* 4th ed. 1932. Reprint, São Paulo: Companhia
Editora Nacional.

Parezo, Nancy, ed.
1993 *Hidden Scholars: Women Anthropologists and the Native American
Southwest.* Albuquerque: University of New Mexico Press.

Pierson, Donald
1942 *Negroes in Brazil: A Study of Race Contact in Bahia.* Chicago: University
of Chicago Press.

Potash, Betty
1989 Gender Relations in Sub-Saharan Africa. In *Gender and Anthropology:
Critical Reviews for Teaching.* Sandra Morgen, ed. Pp. 189–227. Washington:
American Anthropological Association.

Ramos, Artur
1935 *O folk-lore negro do Brasil.* Rio de Janeiro: Civilização Brasileira.

Scheper-Hughes, Nancy
1992 *Death without Weeping: The Violence of Everyday Life in Brazil.*
Berkeley: University of California Press.

Spencer, Jonathan
1989 Anthropology as a Kind of Writing. *Man* 24:145–164.

Stocking, George, ed.
1974 *The Shaping of American Anthropology, 1883–1911: A Franz Boas Reader*. New York.

Thompson, Robert Faris
1993 *Face of the Gods: Art and Altars of Africa and the African Americas*. New York: The Museum for African Art.

Trawick, Margaret
1991 *Notes on Love in a Tamil Family*. Berkeley: University of California Press.

Trinh, Minh-ha
1989 *Woman, Native, Other: Writing Postcoloniality and Feminism*. Bloomington: Indiana University Press.

Wafer, Jim
1991 *The Taste of Blood: Spirit Possession in Brazilian Candomblé*. Philadelphia: University of Pennsylvania Press.

Wolf, Margery
1992 *A Thrice-Told Tale: Feminism, Postmodernism and Ethnographic Responsibility*. Palo Alto: Stanford University Press.

Yans-McLaughlin, Virginia
1986 Science, Democracy, and Ethics: Mobilizing Culture and Personality for World War II. In *Malinowski, Rivers, Benedict and Others: Essays on Culture and Personality*. George Stocking, ed. Pp. 184–217. Madison: University of Wisconsin Press.

FOREWORD

THE MATERIAL for this book about Brazil was gathered during an anthropological field trip in Bahia and Rio de Janeiro in 1938 and 1939, which was generously supported by the Council for Research in the Social Sciences of Columbia University, and directed by the Anthropology department of the University. Many persons aided whole-heartedly in many ways, with indispensable advice, guidance, and criticism. In the United States, Dr. Ruth Benedict and the late Dr. Franz Boas of Columbia University gave me unfailing sympathy and support. Equally kind and instructive were Dr. Charles S. Johnson, Dr. and Mrs. Donald Pierson and the late Dr. Robert E. Park of Fisk University, Mr. Walter White of the National Association for the Advancement of Colored People, and Dr. Margaret Mead of the American Museum of Natural History. Mr. Morris Ernst, Mr. Alexander Lindey, and Mr. Drew Pearson furnished me with valuable introductions.

In Brazil, every person I met taught me much. My constant tutors, without whom I should have been lost, and whose indulgent patience I will always remember, were the ethnologists Dr. Edison Carneiro and Dr. Arthur Ramos, the noted missionaries Dr. and Mrs. Hugh C. Tucker, D. Héloisa A. Torres, director of the Museu Nacional of Rio, D. Dina Venancio Filho, who taught me Portuguese, and Miss Isabel do Prado, Mrs. Kate di Pierri and Miss Maria Julia Pourchet who were my particular friends in Rio. Besides, in Bahia, I had invaluable discussions with Dr. Nestor Duarte, who was studying the role of Negro women in Brazilian history; with Dr. Hosannah de Oliveira, a distinguished specialist in children's ailments; with Canon Manoel Barbosa, who was a leader of liberal thought; with the gifted young poet Dr. Aydano de Couto Ferraz; with the American

Consul Robert Janz and his staff, especially George Hasselman; with the missionary Peter Baker; with all the other persons whom I name in my story, and with some who prefer not to be named.

Brazil gave me an entirely unexpected realization of the ease with which different races could live together civilly and profitably. So when I left for home, I looked at my own country with fresh criticism. Afterwards, working during the war years on the staff of the President's Committee on Fair Employment Practices, and living for a time in the deep South, I became lost in the unending instances of "racial conflict" that it was my duty to handle. Finally, after six years, I returned to my memories of the harmony in Brazil. This book about Brazil does not discuss race problems there because there were none. It simply describes the life of Brazilians of the Negro race, a gracious poised people whose charm is proverbial in their own land, and undying in my memory.

RUTH LANDES

I

SHORTLY BEFORE the Second World War, Columbia University sent me to Brazil to make an anthropological study of Negro life there. We had heard that the large Negro population lived with ease and freedom among the general population, and we wanted to know the details. We wanted also to know how that interracial situation differed from our own in the United States. It was a sociological project which excited the imaginations of few people. Not until a year or so later did the crash of war make the Negro people and their problems a part of the day's news.

We knew extremely little about Brazil at that time, and the general feeling among my colleagues was that I was being sent to the margins of the tableland of the world, where only luck could keep me from falling off. Tensely, I attended to the precautions that were recommended. I was inoculated with five or six serums, like those given a few years later to combat troops in the Pacific. I bought many dresses and shoes because of a notion we had that they could not be bought there. One whole trunk was filled with soap and other toilet articles, so that later the Customs in Rio debated whether to charge me the duty regularly levied on commercial merchandise; they abandoned the idea only after I had persuaded them to verify my letter of introduction to the International Health Division of the Rockefeller Foundation. I was instructed in the conduct proper to young ladies in a Latin country.

Much that we knew about Brazil in those years was far from reassuring. The Amazon region was a "green hell," according to an English novelist; the great jungle between the tall eastern plateau and the Andes, called the Mato Grosso, was a land where untamed Indians roamed and shot white men. Only General Rondon had penetrated its wildest corners, to direct the construction of telephone communications. The coast was the safest region, with a dense population living in great cities. President Vargas had become dictator, wiping out overnight all democratic institutions: popular elections, local and federal congresses, the free press, free labor unions, free public gatherings. Some American magazines and newspapers reported how the opposition was hunted down, denounced as "communists," driven into hiding or exile, sometimes imprisoned and sometimes tortured.

About the people, the nonpolitical world, we knew practically nothing. They had none of the glamour and warmth associated with Mexico and the Caribbean. Rio de Janeiro was four thousand miles by water from New York harbor—a tremendous distance before the war, as the price of the passage indicated. In the back of our minds lurked the black-face stereotypes of South Americans that O. Henry had given us a generation ago in devastating satires. And the Portuguese language of Brazil, quite different from Spanish and spoken in only this one of the Latin countries, helped further to estrange our sympathies. Our nation's last large-scale contact with Brazil had been during the First World War, when the Navy stationed ships at Bahia and Rio; but not even memories remained of this period.

Specialists had gone to Brazil, as I now was going, and had written excellent reports in the fields of geology, engineering, and history. The books were little known and were collected in a few libraries in distant parts of the country for the benefit of a handful of students. So when I, as a research fellow of Columbia University, tried to secure information about Brazil in the superb libraries of New York City, I found practically nothing. The resources were unbelievably skimpy.

At about this time I learned that Fisk University, the Negro college in Nashville, Tennessee, had the best collection of books and other materials on the subject east of the Mississippi. In fact, some members of the faculty had spent years of research in Negro centers in Brazil. I learned this by chance at a tea party, and almost as casually I was invited down there to teach, to study the collection, and to "get used to Negroes" before I left for the gloomy green land below the equator.

Eight years have passed since then, and at the present date it seems unbelievable that the distance between the races in our country could have been so great as to justify my spending a year among Negroes just because I was white and therefore had to become accustomed to them. Looking back, it seems amazing that I should have been sent to another country to study the workings of its racial policy, on the simple assumption that the peaceful coexistence of two physical types of men requires special regulatory devices. I think the Brazilian consul was also amazed when I visited his office in New York for my visa and explained my purpose. "Negroes!" he said. "Why must you *study* them? They are no different from other citizens of my country!" And he asked to see my police record. But in the United States, Negroes were regarded even by liberals and scholars as a sort of tribe—not the same as white men, not the same as modern men. I recall how this was crystallized for me ten or twelve years ago when I was offered the opportunity to conduct anthropological research either on an American Indian reservation or among Negroes.

So I went to Fisk. That was daring, not because the school was southern but because it was Negro. There was Tennessee's tradition of Jim Crow, and of occasional lynching, with the dreadful accompaniments of anger, pity, horror, hysteria. Reared in rebellious New York City, trained in the challenging dialectic of my science which declared that all races of man are alike human and in that sense equal, I arrived in the Nashville station cocked for controversy. I was met by the head of the department in which I was to work, a Negro scholar of international reputation, suave and humorous in conversation. I know that he was wary and tense. In those days it was a flamboyant experiment for whites and Negroes to work as equals in a white-collar field, and only now as I write do I fully realize how skillfully this scholar kept the lid on a boiling caldron.

I got used to Negroes, as I was supposed to, but in a strained new way. These Negroes of the University—my faculty superiors and associates, the students in my class, most of them of very humble origins—were angry and self-conscious about their position in America, and possibly they became angrier at the sight of me and the two or three other white instructors brought down from Columbia University. We Northerners were so innocent and earnest. The Negroes taught us something of the race-ways of the South as they had learned them, with fear and mistrust; and in one manner or another they soon made it plain to me that I had better not pretend to act as an equal in a devout equation of races and classes, but as a well bred patron of the classical arrangement. That way there would be less suffering for everyone. The South taints all those who come to it, they believed.

This was not what my advisers had in mind when they urged me to prepare myself for Negroes in Brazil by living among Negroes at Fisk University. Intellectuals in New York do not know the South, and are always shocked by brief exposure to it. On the other hand, my Negro friends in the South had never experienced the absence of obsessive race-thinking that distinguishes Brazil. "You whites come here to teach us," a brilliant colored student at Fisk told me confidentially, "because you can't find employment in a respectable white school. You are exploiting us. If you were really competent in your profession, you'd be hired at a white college." This defiant statement, laden with mistrust of even white sympathizers, was peculiarly American. As I was later to realize, it had nothing to do with the attitudes of the Negro race in Brazil.

*　　*　　*

The boat trip to Rio was long—twelve brilliant calm days in April over the Atlantic. Latin Americans of different nationalities were returning to their homes, and it was an Argentinian from Buenos Aires, a producer in the new moving picture industry there, who showed me how well his group was learning a North American kind of intolerance.

"Are you going to that monkey land!" he exclaimed in scorn and disappointment when I said I planned to spend about a year and a half in Brazil. "Why, they're all blacks, as backward as in Africa!" I was astonished at his vehemence because in those days we were less familiar with the ideologies in Argentina. "You'll find them swinging by their tails from trees," he went on. "You'd better come to Argentina, where the white people are."

With my experience at Fisk University in mind, I tried to be reasonable. I said: "You would change your mind if you met a charming, well educated Negro. And some of them are as fair as I am—you might not recognize them!"

He scrutinized me then. "So you're a Negro," he said in a shocked and disconcerted tone, and I did not trouble to correct him. "I can hardly believe it," he added, "and I am sorry that I won't be able to see you in Rio." He left me a little note when we landed, addressed to "My dear *Negrita*."

Arriving in Rio, it was necessary for me to be presented to high officials of the government and of the federal police, in order to establish my identity and the political innocence of my proposed studies. The administration was fearful of spies at that time, and all persons under suspicion were tormented as "communists." One well known scholar of north Brazil, of excellent family, who belonged to the opposing political faction, was labeled "communist" with an official explanation that he had studied at Teachers College of Columbia University, and he was thrown into jail. Now here was I, from Columbia University. People cautioned me not to "talk," not to discuss Brazilian politics, not to discuss democratic principles or government, or Russia, or communism, not to discuss public figures like President Roosevelt, not to ask questions, not to take pictures, not to talk with the lower class who might be disaffected by the inflation and the general political insecurity.

Finally I was introduced to a distinguished minister of the government, of international repute, deservedly honored for his allegiance to the democratic nations and their principles. He was a big handsome man of fair coloring, who came from the prosperous, Europeanized state of Rio Grande do Sul adjoining the Argentine border. I gave him a letter from a mutual friend in Washington.

"Welcome," he said with a charming smile, and shook hands.

5

He gave me a seat beside his desk in the enormous cool room that was his office, overlooking a delightful, rose-tinted patio whose center fountain sparkled in the dazzling sunlight as the water sprayed into the air. "This letter says that you are not one of those sensational reporters. Fine. Brazil needs to be correctly reported. Especially her political situation. And since you are going to study Negroes, I must tell you that our political backwardness, which made this dictatorship necessary, is due entirely to our Negro blood. Unfortunate. So we are trying to breed the blood out, making one nation of all the people, 'whitening the Brazilian race.'" He left me somewhat confused and disturbed.

I was painfully bewildered in those days. The way life was arranged in New York City, and again in Nashville, and again in Rio de Janeiro varied like different worlds on different planets. In Rio I felt that I was on the rim of the world I had known. The climate and the people, the sounds and the smells, were strange, alien, difficult. But the principal difficulty was that I did not know the language.

I suppose only a North American can feel impatient over the necessity of learning a new tongue, the business of memorizing grammatical rules and exceptions, and of catching the idioms which really make one a citizen of that universe. I fretted with impatience, but obviously I could do nothing without acquiring the ability to use Portuguese. The impotence of being without a language, of being without human speech, defies description. One cannot give, one cannot receive, one's thinking is paralyzed, and all one's intuitions falter. The effort of learning to speak, the drive to understand, convulse one's very brain so that at times I wondered dumbly at the ingenuity of those early human ancestors who cared to invent spoken words.

Three months passed this way in Rio, clumsily acquiring the involved and idiomatic speech, and learning also the language that is not of the tongue but is expressed by fingers and hands, even by sweeping movements of the arms and shoulders, by glances of the eye and the many fine movements that travel lightly over a face and color the tones of the voice. All these make up the citizen of Rio, the special carioca personality, and they were the bridge over which I traveled towards the stranger, remoter life in the northeastern city Bahia, where I planned to concentrate my studies.

Bahia had been my goal from the start. A great seaport town, capital of the rich state of Bahia, and once the capital of the brief empire of Brazil, it has always played a critical role in the nation's domestic and foreign affairs. Because of former slavery and a rich plantation economy, it has a dense Negroid population. So have other states in the northeast, but Bahia is known for the unique quality of her Negro folk life. What the Negroes do in Bahia is "typical" of Brazil. The lyrics and melodies they compose and inspire, the manner of singing, the types of orchestration, the dances, sports, amusements, foods, drinks, dress, literature, the Carnival that lasts for months, the forms of religious worship, even the personality and physical beauty of the women are a dear part of Brazil. Out of Bahia come forms and symbols for national chauvinism to cling to. Carmen Miranda later brought these to Broadway and Hollywood. Heitor Villa-Lobos brought the melodic themes and harmonies to Carnegie Hall. Candido Portinari painted the Rio echoes of that life, and the Museum of Modern Art exhibited them after the World's Fair had closed its showing. Bahia Negroes have inspired a rich and varied literature, have attracted scientists and novelists. The newspapers cover their activities as a matter of course. Brazil's social scientists devote themselves to these Negro citizens as completely as Mexican scientists do to the Indians, and in a similar mood of gallant appreciation and of expiation for the past.

So I went to Bahia, and I was consciously uneasy for the first time in this exploration through different worlds of ideas. I was uneasy now because I had already learned enough to realize that I had no point of reference, no theory or belief to support or explode. I knew, however, that I should never be as naïve about the language of "racial equality" as when I arrived in Nashville. In Nashville, a man could be tortured and killed because of his physical color. In Brazil that could happen only because of his political color. But it could happen, and so there was no question of "safety" or "freedom" despite the difference in phrasing. In Nashville a Negro could go to college, but his soul was always sick. In Bahia every Negro could hold up his head, people said, but in Rio they laughed, or pretended to, over his African ways. In particular the Rio people—but not the scholars—warned me against the cult groups that have been inherited from the African history of these people. They are called "candomblé" in Bahia, and "macumba" in Rio, the terminology differing because of the differing African languages that were once spoken in these cities. Gossip spread spine-chilling stories of sorcery practiced by the groups, leading to madness, violence, and death. Bahia was the Mecca for all these interests, and so sometimes people called the city "The Old Mulatto."

"Must you go there?" my Brazilian teacher wailed. She screwed up her cheerful young face and shivered in mock horror. Then she laughed. " 'Let Bahia stay there!' " she quoted a song, " 'and we'll stay here!' "

"A white woman up there alone?" an American from Georgia said disapprovingly. "You know what those blacks will do."

I could not leave before I had cleared with the Department of Agriculture and secured military approval. I was an alien, actually unwelcome, but tolerated because I was identified as a "scientist" who would not be gainfully employed but would on the contrary spend money. I was supposed to report to authorities in Bahia, and when I neglected to do this—thinking that the polite letters were merely letters of introduction which I would use only in case of necessity—the secret police were notified, and I was trailed assiduously, and finally ordered deported from the area. But that was months later.

This well intentioned study of race relations could not avoid the rumblings of the times. Naturally not, since fascist ideologies were only newer versions of the widespread motivations that had crystallized out in our country as race bitterness. Rio was a dumping ground for German, and Italian, and Japanese manufactures, and Brazil was among the many South American countries that had felt the appeal of easy and favorable trade arrangements with the Axis nations. Consequently Axis ocean liners crowded Rio's huge harbor, and gave passengers much more efficient coastal service than did the fleets of other countries or of Brazil itself. I could have flown to Bahia, but it was incomparably more economical to take passage on a German boat. Walking up the gangplank of the clean and handsome ship, I passed her smartly dressed officers saluting friends with a brisk "Heil Hitler!" The army of the Reich had just annexed Austria, and dozens of large German families had immediately come up from the farming state of Santa Catarina in the south, and had bought passage to Greater Germany. They swarmed all over, and talked frankly about the economic need to push the Jews out—maybe the Jews could take their places in Brazil; they sang, they danced, they relished the excellent food and the mealtime music, they were incredibly glad to leave Brazil which had provided them home and support for years. They thought Brazil was a brutal, mongrel land; and Hitler had saved them from it.

Need I say that I felt bewildered and unsure? My anthropological inquiry was now stripped of the safety, of the sanctity of the ivory tower. I had left my English-speaking democratic home with its reliable laws that allowed a white scholar to study in all dignity the drawn but stilled battle of the races; I had left it for a dictator's country whose difficult language and harsh customs—because women were as handicapped in their movements as political opponents—made me feel disoriented and helpless as in a jungle; and in addition suddenly—suddenly—I was confronted by people speaking the Nazi beliefs and taking ship to fight for them. My training in pure science had left me unprepared for such events (but I think many decent young Americans were equally unprepared then, even those who insisted upon fighting in the Spanish Civil War), and I wondered in some alarm what these Nordics would say or do if they knew that it was my professor's output of scientific works that had been thrown into the first bonfires at Heidelberg.

The purser checked my papers carefully. I stared miserably at official portraits of Hitler on the walls. That face ground into me a horror of this floating trap, and a frantic longing for the hour of escape into Bahia. Hitler had invaded two European countries by then, but I could not have dreamed of finding his forces and his symbols in the western hemisphere. When the purser finished, he shook hands and said sympathetically, "God, I feel for you, stuck up there in Bahia with all those blacks! When you're through with your business, come over to Germany. We need fine people like you."

It was early on a Sunday morning, hot, brilliant, and the two-tiered city of Bahia—the City of the Bay of the Savior— stretched gleaming-white out of the water. Black stevedores swarmed over the docks waiting for the ship to pull up. I felt completely suspended in space, in thoughts, in time. How far, how far this was from the books in the library, even from the classrooms at Fisk!

II

IT WAS NOT easy to live in Bahia. Let me put it positively and say that nearly everything about it was hard. Like Alice in Wonderland, I had come into this lush theatrical country with no awareness of my own personality, of the permanent difference between it and the others. The modern American woman is a strange, offending phenomenon in those surroundings. In after months I sensed something of this when I watched tourists march through the town.

In Bahia, old traditions sprang into threatening life at my presence. To begin with, there was no provision for housing or entertaining a single, unchaperoned young woman without a family and of independent means. My fair coloring and athletic health were not agreeable in that dark-complexioned, tropical city. My good American clothes were too tailored, too unsexed, too nonchalant. And my shoes! The fact that they were larger than anyone else's did not embarrass me; but their style was occasionally very disconcerting. For example, I had a nice pair of laced black leather and suede shoes, the style that Fifth Avenue shops called "ghillies." I found them comfortable and

Ruth Landes in Bahia, 1938

Ruth Landes and Edison Carneiro

(*opposite*) Edison Carneiro

Sabina in her *terreiro*

Sabina's *festa de mâe d'agua*

Terreiro do Gantois

A *Lavagem do Bonfim*

Mâe Menininha and her household

good-looking. One night, however, about eleven o'clock, a young woman who was strolling down the street in a trailing evening gown caught sight of me, stopped still and stared, and suddenly began to scream. I hurried away. The next day I learned that she was a properly licensed streetwalker who must have known that I was not one but feared that I would be competition for her on her beat because my ghillies resembled shoes worn by her profession!

Upon my arrival I met members of the small American colony that lived a fretful and bored existence on the handsomest and coolest heights of the city. They came from Texas, Oklahoma, Georgia, and had ironclad rules about relations with "natives," "niggers," "trash," and Jews. It was my first exposure to such a group, and it found me vulnerable. The couples were torn apart by infidelities and excess leisure and idleness. On the other hand the group as a whole was bound with the intimacies resulting from the grief, the passions and fleeting affections, and the vital protection that each individual promised against total loneliness. Everyone mattered intensely, no one mattered at all, and certain events later showed that they had no loyalties whatsoever, to family, or to country, or to friends. Individuals told me stories about themselves, sometimes at length, sometimes in fragments, sometimes straightforwardly; and once I was warned that, completely unbeknownst to myself, I was the third figure in a triangle. However, I remember with affection one graceful bright matron of twenty-five or so, who cheered the macabre colony like a morning-glory on a vine. Yet she, too, was sick from tropical ennui, desperately unhappy in Bahia, desperately bored in her marriage, with a desperate feeling of guilt about her wishes to escape. As a way of punishing herself, she told me how she tried to lead others astray so that she would have company in her loneliness. Then she brought me wild flowers to erase the memory of her mood.

None of these people were interested in the life of Bahia, in the great agricultural exchanges, in the busy shipping, in the oil prospecting, in the famous universities, in the buzzing fairs and markets, in the brilliant folk life all about. They had a complete scorn for their surroundings, so bitter and futile that it sickened their very physical selves. One could see them growing wizened from month to month. "I am stationed in this good-for-nothing hole," the young consul from Texas told me, "because of the larger retirement pay. But I just live from one year to the next. I'm living for the day I can retire and get back to civilization. I can't wait till I'm forty." Everyone drank too heavily for the climate; they dreamed of adultery; and except for my charming friend no one cared to learn Portuguese or associate with the "natives." The British colony was somewhat better adjusted, and the Germans actually married and lived among the Bahians.

My countrymen condemned me for not joining the Beach Club and adding to their circle. I could not room with them because that would disturb conjugal peace. There were no houses or apartments I could rent. So I took a room in the best hotel in town.

That sentence should have been studded with stars of crimson and gold. Because decent women—another studded phrase—may not live that way in the tradition-bound regions of Brazil. And thus appeared a faint cloud on my political horizon which in later months blackened and filled the skies. For, as I later learned, it was women of a certain calling, though in the upper brackets, who lived alone in the hotels, who in fact were swarming up from Rio because of the many officers of the federal troops then in the Northeast. People seemed to assume that I was not such a woman, however, and so they expected that I would have a husband, or an official lover, or a chaperone. But in the ensuing months I produced none of these. It was then they decided, it seems, that since I came from Columbia University, and associated with faculty members of Bahia's universities—most of whom had been in exile or in jail at different times for political opposition to Vargas—and devoted my attention to the Negro folk in the jungled suburbs, that I must be a spy, from Moscow. The secret police observed me for months in three details daily, but I did not know of it for a long while, and by that time I had completed my studies. The American consul tended to agree with the Bahia police, so that I was obliged to turn for assistance to the British consul, and that too helped to confuse my old admiring thoughts about citizenship rights under the flag of the United States. Especially when, hearing a Negro on the dock speaking English, I called to him with pleasure, "Oh, are you from Chicago?" "What's that to you?" he snarled. "I'm in Brazil now, and I'm free!"

So I unpacked in the hotel where I remained nearly a year, with the hawk eyes of the suave young German manager constantly on me. If he was not a Nazi, then the dining-room steward was, and bullied him. That feeling grew on me, especially as the plump, rascally-faced steward became chummy with the big, dapper colonel of the federal troops, and the two would watch me smoothly when a Negro would call for me to drive into the near-by country. Eyes were everywhere, tongues were everywhere, fear—yes, fear was everywhere. For occasionally word would come that a university acquaintance had been hauled into the jail near the city plaza, or that a candomblé had been raided under suspicion of concealing a political enemy, and finally mysterious telephone calls came even for me. Maybe this meant that I was now a part of the world into which I had blundered; but it was not relaxing. No. And in a sense it was a wasted experience because it proved nothing about race relations.

Even like simple Alice, I made some friends. Letters of introduction from scholars at Fisk University, and from scholars in Rio de Janeiro, led me in particular to a young Bahian ethnologist named Edison Carneiro. Dr. Edison was only twenty-seven years old, but the number and originality of his studies of Brazilian Negroes and candomblés, and the solidity of his reputation had caused me to expect a much older man. On the other hand, twenty-seven meant a more advanced maturity in Brazil than in the United States, and Edison had already been in hiding and in jail for his opposition to Vargas, and was to be jailed again during my stay.

It seemed significant to me that Edison was a mulatto, of the tan-skinned color called "pardo" in Brazil. It was significant to me because the letters of introduction were from white colleagues who had not mentioned his race or color. To them that was not important. They were taking him at his proven value as a journalist and a scholar. Nor did I ever notice any special consciousness on his part of my own race.

He came of a poor but good family, called "fidalgo." His father, fair in color, was a retired professor of engineering, with a reputation for original work. His aunt looked like an Indian, and owned a school. An uncle was a judge. An elder brother was a well known lawyer. One of his young sisters was reddish-haired, the other brunette, and both were studying to become teachers. It was the kind of family that was sometimes called "white Negro" because it was so respected. By now, Edison has reached the top of his journalistic profession. No, he did not link race with personal or social matters because he was planning then to journey through the South of the United States and study conditions there. When I said, "No, you can't do that," he protested. "Well, why?" he insisted. I had to explain, "There is Jim Crow there, and they'll embarrass you on account of your color." His face twisted as though I had cracked a whip over his eyes. I thought in an agony that an American should not have to do such things to other human beings.

Edison was carrying on his own field studies among the Negroes, gathering material for the newspaper that hired him as a reporter, and for the new book he was planning to write. So we agreed to pool our resources, our knowledge, our time, our observations. Need I state that it was I who was the debtor? True, his company convinced the police of my political guilt; but in this land where tradition locked single women in the home or threw them into the gutter, I should have been unable to move about unless escorted by a reputable man. Now here he was. Furthermore he was the best possible reassurance to the Negroes that I was not an upper-class spy or mere busybody; and to some extent he broke down the discomfort they felt with foreigners. Even if I had not been so obviously a "gringa" ("Her face is white like a sheet," the little children would say in big-eyed wonder, "that's why she talks gringa"), the Negroes would have hesitated to talk with me alone, for my own protection. A woman must be exceedingly young or very old before she can be unchained in those parts of Brazil. But Edison, who had lived among them all his life and described them in the daily press, introduced me and was assumed to be my "protector."

III

THERE IS a joy of life in Bahia, tangible as the young palm trees framing the churches on the hills and rising dark and vital against the glowing horizon. I felt it mornings from my hotel room when the sound of distant music echoed along the narrow streets and roused me to the five o'clock brightness. I felt it as I sauntered around the town and rode the open streetcars, watching barefoot boys in knee pants and huge straw hats calling out for sale the candies and newspapers in their arm-baskets; watching Negro men, barefoot or in clanking wooden tamancos escorting their donkeys up and down the steep cobblestoned pavements; watching Negro women in voluminous cotton dresses walking barefoot or in small slippers to many unknown destinations, stopping often to smile and chat with acquaintances. There was something in the flow of these busy walkers through the sunny clean streets and down the crowded outdoor elevators connecting the Lower City of Bahia with the Upper, something that convinced me, a foreigner, of great good humor. I felt it was fine just to be among them, and I wanted to be of them. The brilliant cloudless sky made a flattering frame for everything, and everything became elegant. Songs blared from loud-speakers over the entrances of shops, and somehow it was good. My eardrums would protest, but my heart declared it was good. I recalled often a wise man's caution: "Beware of a Latin when he becomes quiet. But when he is noisy all is well."

Evenings the contentment became a singing thing, when people visited, and young folks promenaded in large bands, just marching around in fresh clothes and laughing quietly, sometimes taking up the choruses of the latest Carnival tunes. Finally late at night, with most families preparing for bed, some old

Negro women would stroll the dim streets and, watching the low-hanging skies, would intone chants whose clear mournful melodies had come originally from Africa, and whose words were part African, part Portuguese, announcing to late workers the delicacies they had for sale, to eat and to drink. And these very mournful chants were a tender thing to hear, being the lullabies to the city.

I knew I could not study Bahia as I would an art gallery, nor as I could study certain Indian tribes on our reservations where it is possible to hire individuals to sit in a chair for months at a time and tell about themselves. I should have to persuade the Bahians to take me into their life. I should have to force my way into the flow and become a part of it. To study the people I should have to live with them, to like them, and I should have to try assiduously to make them like me.

That was not simple. They are busy people whose every hour must be turned to some purpose, and in a peculiar Latin way—maybe it is also African—they keep outsiders at arm's length. Some people consider them arrogant. I thought their manner was proud but gentle. The women show it in their very carriage, erect as trees while they walk down the principal streets balancing trays of sweetmeats on their heads, the flowered skirts undulating grandly with their wide deliberate steps, their dark faces relaxed and shadowed under the long trays.

Upper-class people, who are usually well educated and in professional occupations, like the Negroes enormously and enjoy showing them off. When they say "Negroes," they mean only the kind I saw in the streets, the hard-working, poorly paid people who were distinguishable by their dress and songs and other unusual characteristics. They never mean merely people of a certain skin color, and in fact they usually say "Africans" or "Afro-Bahians" rather than "Negro," which is felt to be insulting. "Black" is a preferred term. But "black" and "Negro" and "African" are not used in references to persons of that physical type who are in the superior social class. Education or wealth, singly or together, takes a person out of the picturesque group of "Negroes."

One Sunday morning a noted children's specialist, Dr. Oliveira, to whom I had a letter of introduction from Rio friends, offered to drive me about the town to show the "Africans" to me. Up and down and around the narrow streets our car skittered, horn honking as the driver tried to secure traction on the streetcar rails. It stopped suddenly when a skirted padre crossed the road against the lights. The car was a fine new Chrysler, and obviously its designer had never visualized terrain like this. Finally we arrived at the great market on the edge of the bay in the Lower City, adjacent to the cacao warehouses and yards and wrapped in their stench. Negro women were everywhere, in colorful skirts and turbans and white blouses reflecting the sun. Usually they were older women, powerful in appearance and self-confident, and keenly interested in the work at hand. They managed the butcher shops, the vegetable stalls, the candy and flower bars, and the stands selling spices, soaps, beads, and other specialties imported from the west coast of Africa. The trade with Africa had been going on since the loading of the first slave ship. Relations had been so close before emancipation that the trading interests and viceregal court of Bahia had exchanged representatives and titles of nobility with the tribal courts of West Africa. The Catholic Church had even included Bahia within the African bishopric of Angola. Brazilians had sound reasons for considering Bahia as the gateway to West Africa. One prominent Negro woman even called the city the "Negro Rome."

The doctor was telling me: "These are the people you will have to know, so don't be frightened of them. They are very sweet-tempered and will answer all your questions." He pointed to a massive dame seated cross-legged on the ground, her bright skirts spread around her, her head bound in a prettily tied kerchief.

"Aunt Julia," he said precisely, bending towards her, "who are your saints?" He had in mind the Catholic saints, whom these Negroes identify with the African deities of the candomblé cults. Glancing shyly at him, she answered in a remote small voice, "Sir, I have no saints."

"None, auntie?" The doctor straightened up and smiled to me. "She doesn't feel like explaining," he said. "She feels embarrassed." Standing off from her a bit, as though trying to see an object in perspective, he pointed out to me: "Notice her physical type. She is not exactly of pure Gold Coast blood because she is not black enough, she is a light golden-bronze. Maybe she has Arabian blood, maybe Portuguese. She has broad prominent cheekbones and rather thin lips. Her nose has a bridge, but it is very broad."

The woman was listening. "Senhor Doctor, I am not 'quality,'" she said deprecatingly, "but my mother was, may she rest in peace. Her father was a white man. My father was an African."

The doctor nodded, dropped her a coin, and led me on until he caught sight of a tall black woman with close-cropped thick white hair. "Now, go on and ask her a question," he urged me.

"I haven't the courage," I protested. "And besides she wouldn't understand my accent!"

He talked to the woman then. "How are you, Aunt Luzía?" he said politely. "I want to buy two sapotes. I see you are wearing a coral necklace. For what saint is it?"

"For Oxum,* Senhor Doctor," she answered matter-of-factly, in a bass voice.

The doctor turned to me. "She says Oxum is her saint. Oxum is an African goddess, and they say she is also Our Lady Mary."

I was dissatisfied with this excursion. Possibly I was mistaken, but I felt that these Negro Bahians should be approached in a more personal manner, in a manner that conveyed clearer evidence of my regard. Actually, I wanted to see them live their own lives instead of merely hearing them answer my questions. Indeed, I myself could not ask questions before I knew about their lives.

It was afterwards that I met Edison. We had gone to the docks one evening to meet a boat bringing friends from Rio, and we sat on a box and talked. He was amused and also exasperated

* Portuguese *x* is pronounced like English *sh*, so that Oxum=Oshoom.

18

when I described Sunday's experiences. His social views were democratic, and he felt that the Negroes had been patronized because of their poor economic position.

"The aristocratic class always condescends," he muttered in a quiet voice packed with intensity, and puffing at his cigarette. "And when some of them decide to study candomblé, they get their material by calling Negroes into their offices for interviews because they're too proud or too lazy to visit the temples in the country. But *you* will have to go to them. You can't expect them to act naturally in an office or in a hotel. And they will know you respect them if you go to them. I'll introduce you."

During the ensuing months we visited people day and night, eating with them in their homes, chatting through long after-noons about their interests, passing days and weeks at tedious parties and ceremonies. We gave gifts; we traveled endless distances by taxi in the jungled suburbs, and by boat to the near-by islands in the bay; we spent long hours and lost much sleep, and finally got quite sick from the fatigue and the heat. We had to be continually available, endlessly patient and cheerful, always alert, always mindful to take notes and snapshots in an unobtrusive way.

I had to be patient with the Bahians, but Edison in addition had to be patient with me. Not only were my behavior and thinking foreign to him, but as a writer he underwent the daily torment of hearing me mutilate his beloved language. I can imagine what he endured because every now and then I shuddered hearing him attempt some English conversation. But Brazilians are incomparably kind to foreigners struggling to learn "the language of Camões"—as they describe it out of admiration for Portugal's greatest epic poet; and they are so willing to cooperate that "they would even understand Chinese," as my patriotic carioca teacher used to say. I have always been humbly grateful for Edison's patience, a quality which he said was very useful in Brazil and was inherited from distant forbears in Africa.

*　　*　　*

I realized soon enough that my study of Bahia was not a one-way arrangement, which I could limit as I chose, or begin and end at will. I had been instrumental chiefly in bringing myself to Bahia, and after that I was more or less driftwood on the tides of public opinion. Very few people there, I am sure, had faith in my simple intentions. The fact that I was an American immediately cast me into the role of an adventurer. I was a specimen, a curiosity, to the 350,000 or more people in the city and environs. The newspapers had told readers about my arrival and my purpose, and I gathered that they immediately began remembering the "crazy" Americans they had watched in Hollywood pictures. They lauded Americans of the silver screen for having "courage"—but these Latins valued discretion more—and they smiled scornfully at our leggy scandalous girls and noisy bandits. (They adored Mickey Mouse.) As there were only about two hundred Americans in Bahia, and about two thousand lost in Rio's population of a million and a half, the images of the films could not be corrected from rounded experience with the figures of the flesh. In Rio, children found me so strange that they called after me in the streets, "American, American!" and boys in streetcars would clown noisily and try to talk the English they were learning at school. In aristocratic Bahia they were more restrained; but, as I have said, the police summed up the population's latent questions and uncertainties by calling my activities "espionage." They took me too seriously to believe that these were truly for science. The scholars and intellectuals treated me with grave and generous courtesy, sympathizing with my purpose, yet to them I was about as much a novelty as the Negroes were to me.

It is a peculiar experience for an American to find that he does not count. That is the way our nationals felt in Bahia. The people were used to seeing British and German businessmen and their families; when sometimes I was mistaken for a German it added nothing to my prestige to insist emphatically that I was from the United States. The Negroes were seldom sure of the location of the United States; they knew it was over the ocean, but they supposed it was in Europe. Americans were little more known even farther south where there was considerable contact with the wider world, and where there lived many Britishers, large colonies of Japanese, so many Germans that one entire state was dominated by them, so many Italians that another state was dominated by them. Important industries were controlled by these other nationals, though Standard Oil did satisfactorily in Rio.

I fulfilled one popular requirement for American-style conduct by appearing to have ready cash. It was assumed that I was rich, and apart from the fact that all Americans are expected to be rich (and money-mad), this belief was a token of social recognition because no "aristocrat" was supposed to have to work for his daily bread. Actually I had come with only a couple of thousand dollars to cover all expenses for more than a year. But the people, who lived on infinitesimal sums of money, reasoned that any woman who traveled, lived in hotels, and called taxis abounded in money. And indeed I was well provided for, as the purchasing power of the American dollar was high and I used it carefully.

To facilitate my work and introductions, Edison and some others, like the elegant Dr. Eustacio da Lima of the Medical School, started to coach me in deportment in the country among the people.

"Don't wear a nice white silk dress like that," Dr. Eustacio said, looking me over. "It'll get dirty." He himself wore a beautiful starched linen suit, but he really meant that the Negro women wore such simple calico frocks that my own tailored one would make them self-conscious. "And wear very plain shoes," he advised. "The roads are dusty." But again this advice was not so much because of the jungle terrain as because the women walked in very casual footgear.

Edison went further. "Don't talk when you eat with those people," he commented sharply and quietly. "It makes them think you are not enjoying the food. . . . And why don't you use rice powder? It'll protect you against sunburn. After all, our women have been in this climate for centuries and they've learned what to do. . . . And don't go alone to the movies!

Men will get impudent, and you won't be able to defend yourself. If I'm around, I can hit the fellow. Don't be obstinate! This is not the United States of America!" Edison belonged to the vanguard of radicals fighting for women's rights; but he chose not to fight within the bastions of Bahia tradition, and not during the course of social research.

IV

THE FIRST person with whom Edison arranged a formal call was a Negro almost eighty years of age known as Martiniano—his full name was Eliseo Martiniano do Bomfim. He was an institution in Bahia, indeed throughout Brazil; he was reputed to be the wise man of his world. Born under slavery in Brazil of parents who had purchased their own freedom, he was sent by his father, at the age of about fourteen, to Lagos, West Africa, to study the tribal lore of his ancestors in the bush itself, and also to learn English at the mission school. This meant that although Martiniano—like his parents—was a practicing Catholic, he passed through pagan training and ceremonies. He spent his young manhood doing this, and when in his prime he returned to Bahia he was preceded by a reputation as a seer and magician. The bush around Lagos was to his people what Oxford and Cambridge are to the English. His parents had done this for him in the highest tradition of the Negro community of Bahia. Pagan priests were often imported before 1888—the year of the emancipation—to serve needs of the slave population; and black freedmen strained every nerve to finance visits by themselves and their children to Nigeria. The visits were a kind of hegira, and endowed the travelers with permanent prestige. There was a great deal of Mohammedan influence in Bahia through the presence of Hausa slaves, and this helped keep alive the fierce ties with the ancestral land. For Martiniano's world, Lagos was Mecca; he once showed me pictures of steamers carrying Bahia blacks to Lagos. Many people remained there and became leaders of the community. But Martiniano returned to Bahia, where his shrewd intellect, dominant personality, and esoteric knowledge won recognition and sped him to fame among the candomblé followers. Eventually scientists sought him for information, and his name was made famous among them by the greatest of Brazil's social scientists, Dr. Nina Rodrigues.

When we went to see him, as Edison explained, Martiniano was sensing the doom of his epoch. African institutions in Brazil were less popular, were losing their vitality, their leaders were dying out, and to the old man this was a terrible and an immoral thing. He could not appreciate the fact that it was an inevitable consequence of the emancipation of the slaves, when the opportunities and the urge for assimilation increased immensely.

He was a pure-blooded black and was fiercely proud of it; he condemned mixture with white blood, and camouflaging Negro traits like straightening the hair. He denounced indifference to the ancestral languages of the Yoruba and Ewe and related tribes; passionately he condemned ignorance of African morals and traditions. He found it terrible that the new generation did not care much about cult practices, and that present-day standards for these practices were being lowered and cheapened. He felt that he was losing his footing, and he was frightened. Not frightened for himself, he would say, but for his people, for whom he felt responsible, and upon whom he feared would fall the whimsical vengeance of the neglected African gods. He warned the people, and warned them again, and finally decided to retire.

Such was the state of his mind at that time, and five years later he was dead. Vigorous as were his body and spirit, I know that he died because he felt there was nothing more for him in this life. He must have struggled bitterly in his mind during those years because to an African of his beliefs death means the end. The soul or the personality that survives the flesh alarms the Negroes, and for a whole year they placate it, and finally in elaborate candomblé rites they whisk it away into distasteful oblivion. But Martiniano knew in the Catholic sector of his being that his soul was immortal. I wonder if he derived any comfort

23

from this conviction. The two worlds that were warring among his people were no doubt deadlocked within him, and the visit that I am about to describe reflected the disorder, the misery that he felt.

Martiniano was a proud man, even an arrogant one, and the justification that Edison gave him for my visit was that I wanted to meet him as the president of the recently created organization of cult groups called "Union of Afro-Brazilian Sects of Bahia" (União das seitas afro-brasileiras da Bahia). Edison himself was the secretary, and the purpose was to enforce the high traditional standards of conduct and to defend the groups before the police. It was one of Martiniano's last efforts to preserve the glories of the past, and in this he had the enthusiastic support of Brazil's leading scholars, if not of the governing authorities.

It was a sunny afternoon in August, towards the close of the winter season, and it was beginning to grow very warm when Edison and I set out to see Martiniano. Edison was a semi-invalid, having submitted himself as an experimental subject to the Medical School, which was trying to perfect new cures for the ailments of the people; and the experimental treatment had affected his heart. He was a frail man, like most of his class in Bahia, but his intellectual curiosity was endless and his will power amazing. Feeling unsure of his feet now, he called a taxi to take us to the slum district in the Lower City where the old man lived.

Martiniano had no telephone but Edison had notified him of our coming through his aunt's laundress, who knew the grocer on the corner of the street near the church dedicated to Martiniano's patron St. George. As Martiniano often prayed at St. George's, the grocer would be bound to see him.

And he had, as we were informed when we stopped to ask. It was Martiniano's eightieth birthday, the grocer said with some excitement, and to celebrate "catching" it he had surprised his young common-law wife Elena by marrying her in the church! There had been seven years of calm domestic partnership but Martiniano knew, everybody knew, that this marriage would please Elena though it was not binding like a civil marriage. He had invited all his friends to witness it. Elena had been too over-come to move a muscle.

We walked on to the apartment house, pleased somehow. Edison could not allow himself to be sentimental, however, so he observed:

"Do you know why people don't get legally married in Brazil? Because it costs so much! And then they can never get divorced. A friend of mine had to go to Montevideo and take out Uruguayan citizenship in order to get a divorce. Now that costs a fortune!"

The apartment house, a decrepit building of three or four stories in the oldest part of Bahia, was at the foot of a ladeira (steep incline). The ladeira bore the name New Road which it had received in that progressive time generations before when slaves freshly paved it with huge cobblestones. A continuous and heavy stream of traffic, rains, and refuse had passed over the road, and still did, so that the cobblestones had become smooth as satin, and at that angle it was impossible to walk without holding on to something. I clutched Edison's slender arm, and when matters became too much for him I staggered to touch the side of a house. We had to half crouch to the ground. The farmers and laborers who had never known anything different walked slowly and confidently on bare, horny feet which clutched as powerfully as hands, and they guided their mules at the same time. Bare feet certainly appeared to be more effi-cient than my leather shoes (especially designed for "tropical wear"!), which slipped and were too stiff to conform to the character of the paving.

The house itself had once belonged to a plantation owner who used it as a town mansion, Edison said. Whole books have been written about this period of Bahia's development, when the slaves broke the jungle and built the cities. Now the house was decaying, but it would be used until its roof fell in on the tenants. When we stepped into the hall, the sharp odor of urine was strong and ripe. The stone walls were wet, even dripping from accumulated rains and dampness, and the steps of the broad wooden stairway had broken through in vital places. The stair well was black and unlit. It was a feat for us, a feat of balance to move up the three flights to Martiniano's apartment.

Edison was amused; he said that it was of tremendous advantage to the old man to have the stairs squeak and cry under the slightest pressure because they told him if people were coming or going. Because he was a practicing sage and seer, to whom people of every class and complexion came for advice on any problem, the police regarded him as a sorcerer. This was —and is—an illegal profession in Brazil, and they sometimes came after him. (The opinion of the police was in this instance in accord with that of the scientists, not to mention the clients.) His stairs gave him warning, and so he had time to prepare an explanation.

Reaching our floor after a tortuous climb, we knocked at the door. The old bridegroom opened it, smiling heartily, his red eyes striking in his dark face. Standing erect and vigorous, he was dressed in a black suit that he usually kept for funerals, he later explained.

"Dr. Edison, what a surprise!" he exclaimed with great affability, embracing him in the Brazilian way. He seemed to engulf Edison because, though he was not tall, his air and his barrel chest made him seem like a giant. I liked him immediately, though I instantly thought, What a rascal! My, what a rascal! There was something wily and calculated about his whole expression.

"Meet Dona Ruth, Seu* Martiniano. She brings greetings from friends in Rio," Edison introduced me stiffly.

"A great honor." Martiniano appeared to increase his output of affability, and kissed my hand. "Sit down, sit down." He brought up some dusty chairs. "A great honor for a lady to visit the house of a poor black—an old *africano!*" He spread his hands, long and powerful ones, in a gesture of mock deprecation.

"I have heard about you and read about you for a long time," I answered.

* Colloquial for "Senhor."

"You can have confidence in Dona Ruth," Edison said carefully. "Complete confidence. And she wants to learn more about the Africans."

Martiniano listened and nodded, smiling in a determined way, watching and wondering behind the smile.

Edison tried to make conversation: "What a house! What a staircase! Must you live here, Martiniano?"

"What's a poor black to do, Dr. Edison? People seem to think I'm made of money, but since Dr. Nina died I have not had any regular employment. And these blacks here are always asking me for things! I must have hundreds of godchildren, and they all visit me and they all expect presents from me! I've got one living with me now, the little Carlinho, a spoiled little fellow who won't study. But what am I to do? His father cut up his mother with a knife, and now he's in jail and the mother is sick. I'm just afraid that that little fellow will grow up with his father's temper, and he's only five years old—and he won't study!"

Martiniano was clearing a large table as he spoke, pushing books and pencils to one side, and dusting and arranging chairs for us. The hot sun poured in from the windows opposite, and we moved as far away from them as we could. As I learned later, the apartment was large for a poor man with only a wife and the child, but no casual visitor could guess that it contained five rooms, all leading into the huge bare living room where we now sat, and which in turn opened by a window onto a vegetable garden planted on the incline supporting that side of the house. The furniture was completely shabby.

"Did you know that the old Africans used to live in this part of the Lower Town, Dr. Edison?" Martiniano continued, as his wife came in to help him remove his black jacket. No one introduced Elena and she left immediately. "After my father bought my mother's freedom, they came to live in this neighborhood, where there was a whole village of blacks, both slaves and freedmen who stayed in town to do special work for their masters living in the country. I remember the stevedores used to congregate on certain corners on Sundays and holidays, the

27

free ones wearing frock coats and silk hats!" He laughed. "But they were true Africans," he said seriously. "No white was mixed with them, and they knew their religion."

"You ought to tell Dona Ruth about it, one afternoon," Edison suggested, "about the African beliefs—"

Martiniano spread his hands again. "I teach? What do I know? They call me a babalaô—you know a seer, an olhador. Such nonsense! All I can teach is languages. They blame me for things because I was a great friend of Dr. Nina—may he rest in peace!—when he was studying the candomblés forty years ago. Why should I be a babalaô? Just to get into trouble? I don't even visit the temples since Dona Aninha—may her soul live in peace!—passed on. I consider her to have been the last of the great Mães.* She really tried to study our ancient religion and reestablish it in its African purity. I taught her a lot, and she even visited Nigeria. My mother too was a great Mãe and I still sacrifice to her gods. Aninha's temple was dedicated to Xangô; Dr. Edison, you recall, you wrote about it for the papers. I miss her now. I guess all of Bahia does. I don't care to step into any of the other temples even though they invite me. None of them do things correctly, as she did. I do not believe that they really know how to speak to the gods and bring them down to dance with them in the temple grounds. I think many of them are faking—especially that Sabina!"

Martiniano was agitated, and he sat up stiffly, craning his neck to see out of the windows. Suddenly he called out, "Carlinho!"

"Senhor?" a resonant contralto voice, sweet and deep as a woman's, answered from right under the table. The boy stood up, a beautiful stocky child with bronze-colored velvety skin, curly short hair and enormous dark eyes shining under long lashes that cast blue shadows into the whites. He glanced shyly, flirtatiously at me, and I in delight smiled back. He had small sharp white teeth in a full mouth of lovely shape. I thought, that round face belongs to an angel of the Renaissance, and already he knows it! He wore ragged white pajamas; suddenly

* Chief priestesses of candomblé.

28

Martiniano cuffed him on the head to remind him to hold up his falling pants.

"Take your alphabet book and study!" he ordered sternly.

"Yes, sir," the boy answered obediently. He picked the torn book up from the floor, trotted away in bare feet and crouched in a corner like a plump puppy. He stared at the book, and then stole glances at Edison and me until finally Martiniano asked him to read a bit. "What an excellent memory the baby has!" Edison remarked, and grinned because Carlinho was "reading" the verses correctly in spite of the fact that the book was upside down. It was impossible for me to resist going over to him and picking him up in my arms. He was strong and heavy, but I tossed him until he laughed, shyly and in deep tones. He had an extraordinary charm, and such mischievous looks! I thought that he must actually be content with this seemingly severe old man, this canny old African sorcerer. But what will he be like in Bahia of the 1950's, with universities, moving pictures, the radio and the candomblés all clamoring for his attention? What will happen to his inheritance of African tradition and thinking which obviously Martiniano would stuff down his throat? I should like to see him now.

"You ought to put him down, Dona Ruth," Martiniano cautioned me in a displeased way. And he continued to talk in the labored English he had learned more than half a century before in Lagos. "The boy is bad! He does not want to study his lessons! All he wants to do is play with the children." Glowering at Carlinho, he continued in Portuguese, "I have ordered him to stay in that corner and study." Torn between the two, I let the boy down and watched him trot back to his corner.

No sooner were things quieted than Martiniano again called sharply, "Carlinho?"

"Senhor?" Deep, resonant, polite.

"Stay there and study!"

Clearly Martiniano was uncomfortable. Edison did not aid him with small talk, and I was deliberately quiet and inconspicuous. The old man began rummaging among some worn books on the dusty table until he found one containing pictures of Negro families in Bahia and their distinguished relatives in Lagos. "Look at these, dona," he said to me, and he listed their names. Unexpectedly a boy skipped in to visit Carlinho, and the two scampered around the great room; chicks escaped from their pen in one corner and wandered underfoot. Suddenly Martiniano straightened and shouted, "Carlos! Oh, Carlinho!"

"Sir?"

"Come here, child." The boy materialized, holding up his pajama pants.

"Didn't I tell you to study?"

"Yes, sir."

"You'll grow up to be as useless as your father, and you'll make your mother cry. . . . Go on, now!" Martiniano turned to me and said, "Sometimes I fear he's going insane."

"Carlinho's glowing eyes glanced at us, then he picked up his book of shreds and set himself to "study." Yet once again Martiniano called sharply, "Carlinho!"

"Sir?"

"Go tell Dona Elena to bring drinking water and manioc."

"Yes, sir." And the boy picked himself up like a ball, glad to be restored to the old man's graces. I felt like sighing with relief.

Martiniano resumed his conversation. "Times have changed, Dona Ruth, as Dr. Edison knows. They are crowding the old Africans out. These young ones don't want to know the truth. They are after show and money and noise. But the important truths are to be kept quiet and secret. I don't feel as though I belong here any more. The young ones blaspheme—it all shocks me."

"I think many people get to feel that way as time goes on and their friends die," Edison tried to reassure him. "My own father has begun to complain."

"Ah, Dr. Antonio." Martiniano nodded respectfully to show he remembered Edison's father.

"It may be that you don't know the younger ones well enough," Edison suggested. "Why don't you visit around with them and maybe teach them things?"

"No, no!" The old Negro rejected the idea testily, and waved his right hand rapidly in an impatient gesture of refusal. "No, I know them all, I've known their parents and grandparents. There was only one woman who knew how to do things and she has passed on. I was brother to her in the temples, and so they called me 'babalorixá.' Do you know what that is?" he said proudly. "In the Yoruba tongue it means 'father in sainthood.' Aninha was the 'mother in sainthood,' the *iyalorixá*. Didn't you put that in your book, Dr. Edison? I was her equal and worked with her, but now I'm going to give up candomblé. There's no place for me any more. They are all pretenders!"

His dry husky voice was angry and despairing. In a final gesture he slapped his hand on the table, and I was startled to see his long, strong yellow nails. In Africa, as in old China, Edison said later, they were a symbol of leisure and authority.

"They garble things," Martiniano went on, turning to me with a harassed look. "I can't bear to see it. Take Maximiana—Tia* Massí, they call her. She's head of the oldest temple in Brazil, Engenho Velho—it must be nearly a hundred and fifty years old. Yet she gets everything wrong, and worst of all she tries to call the souls of the dead into her temple! Now, that's sacrilegious!" he shouted, truly horrified. "Only men should look at the dead! But at Engenho Velho *women* look at the dead—and ask them questions! . . . So I left."

Edison tried to comfort Martiniano, and I listened to everything in great confusion. I had never seen a candomblé performance, and the regulations of the cult procedure were as mysterious to me as those of the Catholic Church. Edison was saying: "What about your son? Can't you teach him?"

"No, no use," the old man sighed. "He just can't learn. He won't apply his head. Since his wife's death he moves around from one temple to another, and that doesn't go among the African people. Nobody trusts you if you keep visiting around. They think you're snooping on secrets, and evading responsibility to one temple. You're supposed to be loyal to one temple.

* Aunt.

31

It is like a mutual aid society, you know. The *terreiro* * is yours, and the people will help you if you work for it.

"Anyhow, I don't believe much in these young women who run the terreiros nowadays. They want to make money, and they want to get men. Most of them are too young to be dedicated to the gods. After all, Menininha is only forty-two or -three, and the blood is hot in her! Yet her experience is of the best because she was trained by her aunt, Dona Pulcheria, who made Gantois temple famous. That was where Dr. Nina did his researches, you know, and he thought there was no one like Dona Pulcheria. But nowadays in the middle of their services they are thinking of other things: the man they saw last night, or the one they will see next night, or the men who are watching them dance. That is hardly right when they are supposed to be praising the gods! And these new temples of the caboclo 'nation'—my God, they are crowding everything else out, they are throwing our traditions away! And they allow *men* to dance for the gods!

"No, I've got nobody to teach. I have a godson of sixteen who helps me collect herbs, but he's not interested in the ways of the Africans." He dropped back in his chair sadly. "I'll die with all I know. I'm out of everything now, though they do call me 'king of the candomblé.' I haven't even money enough to live on. You see how I am." He waved his hand towards the room. Then he smiled in a rather unpleasant way as though he were forcing himself to be deferential, and remarked, "I'm just a poor black of low quality."

It suddenly occurred to me that he was preparing to ask for a loan of money.

He pushed his chair back. "Well—Oh, Carlinho!" he yelled suddenly.

"Sir?" the lovely voice intoned from almost under his feet. "Senhor?"

"Did you speak to Dona Elena?"

"Yes, sir," the baby replied. And immediately afterwards the woman's voice called, "Coming, coming."

* Temple grounds.

32

She walked into the room, holding a silver water tray by its wrought handle which rose as a slender pole from the center, and around which rested cups and spoons in little compartments. They introduced her to me then, and she acknowledged the presentation with a painfully shy glance. Always afterwards I was struck by her great shyness, which walled her off from others as though she were sorrowing from some profound hurt, and which acted like hands pushing other people away. She was a tall stout woman with a morose expression, but I knew that she was generous and gentle; and I came to feel sorry for her in her marriage with a man who was twice her age or more, because apparently she had accepted her husband's opinion that she was unworthy of him and lucky to have him, and she served him hand and foot. Elena never conversed in her husband's presence, so she barely acknowledged our thanks and left as soon as she had set the salver on the table before Martiniano.

He chuckled, showing his healthy yellow teeth. He rubbed his hands together and viewed the materials before him. There were water, manioc flour, lemon, and sugar. "People don't know how good this Brazilian drink is," he gloated, "especially for a hot day. They think they must have ices and ice creams and soda waters! But *this* is the thing for cooling the stomach. Now watch." And he proceeded daintily and precisely like a cook over a rare dish. "Watch. First a tall glass of water, filtered. Then, a tablespoon of manioc—see how white it is, and each grain so fine. Third, a quarter of a lemon. Now, sugar!" And he poured in a heaping tablespoonful. Stirring the mixture in the glass, he crooned, "Drink this, my esteemed friends! Drink this! I want to hear you say, 'Ah-h-h!'"

He filled a glass for each of us, and in fact it was bland and cooling. Now he prepared his own drink, slowly, carefully, and finally he saluted it, "Ah-h-h!" smacking his lips and smiling. "It hits the spot, eh? Now, watch how I do, and eat the manioc at the bottom." As we all ate, Martiniano observed to me, "Somebody could make a fortune selling this drink in your country, couldn't they?"

I looked startled.

"Well, I'll be glad to help you whenever you desire my services," Martininano offered, speaking carefully in English to indicate affability. ". . . I wonder if you could trust me with a small loan, Dona Ruth, just a little since we will be friends and I will teach you what I know." He needed sixteen dollars to help him fulfill certain ritual obligations, he explained. He could repay the loan after a month because he had been sent for concerning some "business" in the great city of Recife, Pernambuco.

Greatly embarrassed, I gave him the money as a wedding present.

"My lady," stated Martiniano, standing up and bowing with dignity, "I thank you and am always at your service. You have the heart of a Brazilian. I and Elena will always remember this occasion."

We shook hands, and after demonstrations of affability, Edison and I picked our way laboriously down the stairs. Martiniano stood at his door calling blessings and goodbye in the Yoruba tongue of his deceased father's tribe. Reaching the street, we braced ourselves against a rusted iron-grille railing and looked up at the windows. There the couple stood watching, and they waved to us attentively, as people wave to voyagers.

"They are guardians of the old times," Edison said sentimentally. "But watch him," he smiled. "He's an old fox."

V

WE HIRED an open taxi that evening and rode along the bay. The chauffeur was a favorite of Edison's because he knew the temples of candomblé and their elaborate calendars of ceremonies; he knew the people who visited them and the people who participated in them, but he never confided his knowledge to the police. He seldom entered a temple himself, and so he could not be called a devotee; but the blacks relied on his discretion. Police raids occurred so unexpectedly, and could be so serious that it was vital to the temple worshipers to have friends in many places. The chauffeur's nickname was Amor (Love), and he had a gentle good-looking face atop a tall neat body. He talked little and was very shy. Sometimes for company he took along his gentle ten-year-old daughter, and the two would enjoy long pleasant silences together. But tonight he was alone, and Edison simply said to him, "Drive where it is cool."

I settled back; it was refreshing to be in the wind of damp ocean air, and Edison began to sing a new song in a charming "march" style: "O flower girl, why art thou so sad? What has happened to thee?" He always sang songs of Brazil, and talked about the folk of Brazil; I do not recall that he ever asked questions about the United States, and I suppose he felt, like other intellectuals, that he had nothing to learn from us. Brazilians said that their spiritual life was nourished only from France, and they were scornful, yet also admiring, of our mammoth automobile and film industries. They thought of the United States in terms of these two industries, though Edison's father, who was a scientist, had named his son in honor of a great American inventor. Edison, I am sure, found it natural and laudable in me to have made a long and costly journey for the sole purpose of observing life among the Negroes of remote Bahia. I was an intelligent American.

"Edison," I said, "how am I to understand Bahia if I do not learn about candomblé at first hand? And how am I to do that if I do not meet some of the women Martiniano talked about? Aninha is dead, unfortunately."

"Dona Aninha could have explained everything," he assented gravely. "And she died less than a year ago. She was very intelligent and impressive. Did I tell you that she made me an ogan?"

"An ogan?"

"That is an honorary post of candomblé open to distinguished laymen." He chuckled lightly, "I share that honor with many prominent people, as well as with some humble blacks. We are supposed to give protection to the temple, in the form of money and prestige. Aninha discovered that my guardian saint was Xangô, the god of Thunder and a deceased king in the Yoruba region; so I was created an ogan of the court of Xangô.

35

Naturally I was a pallbearer at Dona Aninha's funeral. You can't imagine the size of the funeral."

"So many people?"

"I think everybody in Bahia was there, and in addition visitors from Rio and Recife. Only a few of them could fit into the church for her mass. The newspapers carried stories all the time."

"She had so much influence?"

He nodded. "She was a powerful personality. And at the same time motherly and sympathetic. She was great," he concluded simply.

"Didn't she have a family?" I persisted.

"I've often wondered," he said with an air of curiosity. "She was so much older than I, possibly forty or fifty years. She never talked about herself, but we think she has two sons in Rio. She left such a large estate that they may appear to claim it. I don't know if she ever had a husband. She was very handsome when she was young, as you will see from pictures at her temple."

"Isn't it unusual for a woman to be so recognized in Brazil?"

"Not in Bahia," he smiled. "Not in the world of candomblé. The shoe is on the other foot here. It is almost as difficult for a man to become great in candomblé as it is for him to have a baby. And for the same reason: it is believed to be against his nature.

"Candomblé," he expounded in his hurried quiet voice, "is a system for worshiping gods, or saints. The word is from the Yoruba language and means mysteries or ritual. The system comes from Africa, and so do the gods; but, as the people are all practicing Catholics, the African gods are blurred with the Catholic saints. You will be amazed to know how easily they blur together. Even Jesus is there, identified with their aged god Oxalá. Mary is blurred with the loveliest of the young goddesses; and the Father of all is remote, remote, in both beliefs.

"A great difference between candomblé and Catholic practices is that the Africans try to bring their gods down to earth where they can see and hear them. And that is the most sensational job of the women who are priestesses of a temple. A temple woman becomes possessed by a saint or god who is her patron and guardian; they say he—or she—'descends into her head and rides her,' and then through her body he dances and talks. Sometimes they call a priestess the wife of a god, and sometimes she is his horse. The god gives advice and places demands, but often he just mounts and plays.

"So you can see why the priestesses develop great influence among the people. They are the pathway to the gods. But no upright man will allow himself to be ridden by a god, unless he does not care about losing his manhood. His mind should always be sober, never dizzy or 'tonto' from invasion by a god.

"Now, here's the loophole. Some men do let themselves be ridden, and they become priests with the women; but they are known to be homosexuals. In the temple they put on the skirts and mannerisms of the women, and they dance like the women. Sometimes they are much better-looking than the women.

"But this could not happen in the great Yoruba temples Martiniano was talking about. Not in Aninha's, or Massí's, or Menininha's. It does happen often in upstart cult groups called 'caboclo' which have been mushrooming all over. Martiniano mentioned them. 'Caboclo' refers to the Indians of Brazil, and these cults worship Indian spirits which they have added to the roster of African deities. By the high standards of Yoruba tradition, the caboclos are blasphemous because they are ignorant and undisciplined, because they have created new gods at will, and because they welcome men into the mysteries. . . . Personally, I think their music is pretty and gay! You'll find that Yoruba ceremonies are very solemn affairs."

"Hard on the men, isn't it?" I asked, thinking of the Catholic Church's hierarchy.

"Well, they have a place, you know. They support the terreiros financially. They play the musical instruments for the sacred dances, they slaughter the sacrificial animals, and get herbs. They do many things, but they must stop short of be-

37

coming tonto. They can even dance, but they must dance soberly and alone, never with the women. The women are sacred to the gods when in the temple, you see, and the men are supposed to be profaned by their dealings in trade and with other women. The blood of the men is supposed to be 'hot,' and that is considered offensive to the gods for whom the women have been preparing themselves."

"Didn't Martiniano complain about the hot blood of the women?"

"Of the younger women, yes. He thinks women should be chief priestesses—'mothers,' as they are called—only when they are old and all desire has left them."

"Is it hard for men to remain sober?"

He laughed. "Sometimes—you'll see. Some men really have an urge to become priests, and they set up cult organizations according to traditions of the Angola nation or of the Congo nation. There is one Angola priest who conducts his own temple. He is Father Bernardino, and the cult people respect him because his work is good. He is a big powerful man who dances wonderfully, but in the style of the women. There is a handsome young Congo father named João who knows almost nothing and is taken seriously by nobody, not even by his own 'daughters in sainthood'—as they call the body of priestesses; but he is a wonderful dancer, and he has a certain charm. People know he is a homosexual because he straightens his long thick hair, and *that* is blasphemous. 'What! How can one let a hot iron touch the head where a saint resides!' the women cry."

"But how did Martiniano fit in? Surely he didn't dance?"

"Such an idea! No, of course not! He learned how to be a magician and a seer in Africa. So he divined the future for Aninha and other mothers, and for anyone else who would pay him. He still does it, but it's all very secret and sacred; and that's why he denies it. He does it by tossing consecrated beads and cowrie shells which he reads after they fall, and he uses special herbs that he orders his godson to collect; he used to direct the ritual slaughter of sacred goats and cows, and I think he divined by reading their entrails and shoulder bones. He knows all kinds of magical formulas and rites, for good and for bad, I've no doubt. In Aninha's temple, where she had organized a court of ministers of the god Xangô, he was the highest officer and was called the 'mother's brother.' That was more significant than being called 'father'; in fact every ogan is addressed as 'father.' . . . Now Martiniano is free-lancing. He is a religious man and would like to join a new temple, but his prestige is so great that he would overshadow any of the remaining mothers, and trouble would develop. Besides, there have been so few trained magicians like Martiniano that the mothers had to learn to do these things for themselves, and they don't really need a babalaô any more. They aren't like Aninha; she wanted everything correct and on the grand scale."

"Can we see a ceremony soon?" I suggested.

"Fine," he nodded thoughtfully. "The season opens at Engenho Velho in a few days. We'll go there."

We got out then for a stroll. We were at the beach on the bay, in an outlying district of Bahia. It was early in the evening; but night falls heavily there, and the sky always seems near and black. The atmosphere was clear, and a bright lamp burned in the street. We walked out onto a narrow concrete ramp and, looking over the quiet inky bay, saw an old abandoned fortress.

"It is beautiful," Edison said quietly. "But it's a land that even the devil has forgotten."

His neat dark head and face, his brown childlike eyes, his small fine hands always playing with a cigarette concealed a tremendous intensity. American young men I knew did not care that much about the life of their times. He noticed my puzzled expression, and chuckled.

"You Americans are so rich in goods—you can't understand our poverty. . . . But we have gold of a kind: we have the Negroes and the music of samba! I am going to write a poem and call it 'The Land of Gold'!"

VI

WE DID GO to Engenho Velho one Sunday afternoon when the temple was to open the ceremonial season by worshiping Oxalá, the old father of the African gods. Oxalá was also Jesus "in the Catholic life." We took the streetcar in town near my hotel on the fashionable Rua Chile and rode out into the suburb called Mato Escuro (Dark Forest). It still looked like a forest, and when the car stopped at the foot of the tall hill on which the temple stood, I could see only immense cotton trees reaching up, up into the white skies. We located a stairway cut out of the soft red earth with a wooden railing on the right side. Walking up it slowly while I took pictures of the scenery, Edison remarked, "This is believed to be the oldest temple in Brazil; it must be a hundred and fifty years old. When it was built, in slave days, the mato was a jungle and the temple was well hidden. But now freedom and civilization have caught up with the blacks."

"They are poor people, Edison?"

"Poor! You will never understand how poor. You see how rough their skins are, how decayed their teeth? They have not had enough to eat for decades. The average earnings of a candomblé woman, if much, are a hundred milreis * a month. That has to take care of the woman and her children and also of her obligations to the temple." His tone became drier and quieter, as though he had to throttle his indignation.

"But their husbands, Edison?"

He lit a cigarette and shrugged faintly. "Husbands? There aren't many of those, not reliable ones anyway. This is not a comfortable bourgeois society, dona. Nowadays there isn't enough work to go around among the men. They don't earn enough to support themselves, let alone a family."

The old house that was the temple came into our sight and I saw that it was not at the top of the hill but only at the top of one rise in a series of rises which might be steep landslides.

* Five American dollars.

40

The temple was like any dwelling of the people, only larger; it was an oblong rude affair of local clay painted a white color, with a roofing of clay tiles, and the whole was in good repair. After the three hundred and sixty-five beautiful pretentious churches of Catholic Bahia, this was a letdown; yet it was not merely the poverty of the worshipers that kept it in this style. I think it was regarded as a deliberate connection with the humble past. The blacks have always been proud of their slave record, and candomblé was a creation of the slaves. There was reason for pride since it was Negroes who made the jungles and the mines productive; besides, they led regiments in the army and even fought powerfully against the ruling authorities to secure freedom for themselves. The appearance and the character of the temple kept green the memories of those accomplishments.

The main building was surrounded by subsidiary ones of mud and twigs climbing up the steep inclines, and it was shaded by massive cotton trees towering into the skies. I learned later that every tree had a sacred history, every little shack was dedicated to some god. How much of living had been going on there! For a century and a half there had been a succession of women, the mothers of the temple, who ministered to all the needs of the people and regularly entertained the gods in their own flesh. Edison said that according to one school of thought, the first mother had been a free woman especially brought over from West Africa. But according to another school it had been a slave woman of Brazil whose freedom had been purchased by a fraternal organization of freedmen.

"We've got to tell one of the daughters that we're here," Edison observed, "so they'll give us a good seat when the ceremonies begin. . . . Oh, Jilú!" he called out as a tall scrawny woman walked hurriedly from the rear of the house. "Dona Jilú!"

She looked up. "Dr. Edison—Father," she said in a greeting of courtesy, and came over. Her air was rather distrait. "You must excuse me. We're so busy preparing for tonight—and I have to heat water for the baths!"

"I want you to meet Dona Ruth. She's a friend from North America, and she is here today to do homage to Father Oxalá. Here are white roses she brought for the altar." He handed her the small package we had been carrying in the wilting heat.

"Oh, thank you! Naturally everyone wants to honor the old father!" she said in a rush. "And now will you excuse me? I must help the others, and then bathe myself. Tia Massí is all stretched out with her saint. I'll see you later." And she dashed off.

"Well, she knows you're here, and she'll tell the others. That's all that matters just now. So they won't think you're a suspicious character."

"Jilú! What sort of name is that?" I wondered.

"The baptismal name is Januária; Jilú is a nickname. Most people have one. Maximiana is Tia Massí's real name. Even President Vargas is known by a nickname: Gêgê."

People were drifting onto the grounds now. Edison said they were the women who helped around the temple at various duties. Each had special functions depending upon her place in the hierarchy. Jilú, for example, was an ekedi, the kind of temple woman who never became a medium for a god; she was a sort of "slave" helper to the women who were mediums. (When she came to know me, she spoke rather scornfully of the women who "fell tonto—who couldn't control their heads.") Children came with their mothers, and after a while men arrived from town and waited for things to begin. Everyone was dressed in white, because that was the emblematic color of the day's god, of Oxalá who was too aged to sense any desires; and that was why my altar roses were white. Children hopped and teased around us, and finally a couple pulled at Edison's hands and led us to the little houses which were each dedicated to a different god and were sometimes built around the huge trunks of the sacred trees. They teased Edison, who pretended to hold back from them and called them funny little names; they chattered shrilly, irreverently about the coming function, about the priestesses' costumes and their own guardian saints. Adults seldom paid them any attention, and so Edison's docile submission was a treat. In their white dresses and shirts they tumbled around him while he stood still as a pole in his dark gray suit and felt hat which he had neglected to change for white.

He looked at his watch and said to me: "It's about five o'clock now, and they're going to do a special ceremony called Padê. It's to send the devil off to the highways, to keep him out of the way of the gods tonight! His name is Exu, and he's a pleasant sort of demon, like a relative. The ceremony is quaint. Let's go in and see."

So we entered the main doorway of the temple, over which was painted a white cross in honor of Jesus who is Oxalá. Behind the door was a large cage containing a lump of iron, and this was Exu, who must not be in the room at the same time as the gods. Only a few women were there, and we heard some ekedi in an inner room calling for the "little mother" to come out. Soon she did—a big impressive woman named Luzía who was the second in command of the temple. Her manner was tired as she acknowledged the women by extending her hand in a most indifferent fashion for their kiss of salutation. "A blessing, my mother?" each asked. "Be blessed, my daughter," she granted in a deep, hoarse voice, not the voice of a man or of a woman but the voice of a sibyl.

She talked and moved slowly and majestically, strolling over to a low curved bench which was painted white and encircled a white pillar in the center of the room. Edison said that she was considered handsome because she was strong and well fleshed. Her skin was so black that the rims of her eyes and the inside of her mouth looked bloody coral by contrast. Her hair, a real Negro carapinha, had become almost white, so white it sometimes caused her black skin to appear ashen. Consequently she was not young, because the folk say, "A Negro when he grays, three times thirty is his age." But she seemed vigorous and confident, and I learned that she had made a good deal of money, for a Bahian, selling meat in her stall in the market of Santa Barbara in the Lower City. Just now she was sorrowing over the death of her husband, and she was in her mourning retreat in the temple. She had removed her heavy gold orna-

43

ments, and although she was dedicated to the young goddess Oxum, who is one of the Virgin Marys, and was therefore obliged to wear her colors of coral and gold, she was actually today dressed in mourning drab.

She sat down on the bench, spreading her thighs like an eastern potentate and leaning her elbows on them. Her flowing skirts made a huge circle on the floor. She began to intone the chants, and the old women near her got up and danced in bare feet. She intoned further, and they lifted up offerings of oil, rum, and popcorn, offerings which were to buy the good will of Exu and compensate for sending him out of the house. She intoned more, and an old dancing woman took the offerings, one by one, and poured them down the stairway up which we had come that afternoon; Exu was to follow the offerings. Watching Luzía, I would have said she was not the least interested in this routine, for her deep monotone pulled the songs lazily and her sad eyes were shut. But I cannot know, for they had roused her from a nap, and after all she knew her gods so well, as had her mother and aunt and sisters before her. How many numberless times had she chanted the Padê, bargaining with the docile demon to leave the gods in peace and carry mischief to the crossroads?

When I left much later that evening, I slipped on the clay steps that curved steeply from the temple door to the streetcar line, and I twisted my ankle badly because the libations poured out for Exu had converted them to greasy mud. Luzía in distress told me I had stepped right in the middle of the evil that was to have been carried away by the demon, and that instead it had now all been transferred to me. My ankle indeed did not heal until long after I had left Bahia. The priestesses dusted me off regularly with magical leaves, but I was a difficult patient; and they concluded that someone had put the evil eye on me. I used to wonder about it.

The Padê over, I was introduced briefly to Luzía, and then Edison and I went out of doors to wait for the principal ceremonies to begin. The tropical night had fallen suddenly, and lights sparkled through the velvet warm darkness, shining from

44

the houses of the terreiro. Numbers of people were now arriving, and voices and other tones seemed to move slowly, as though they cut through the heat with effort. People crowded around the head of the stairs. Priestesses and ekedis rushed distraught back and forth. Someone warned Edison to avoid the kitchen and dining room in the rear of the temple because women were bathing and dressing there. In another room, Aunt Massí was still stretched on her bed possessed by her god Oxalá, while assistants watched. We could hear a woman garumphing through the corridors: "Folks! It's late! We've got to begin!" Suddenly at the side of the temple we saw a little girl lying sound asleep on a box amidst all the noise. "She probably hasn't eaten all day," Edison noted pityingly. "The women are too busy. Brazilian children are the most neglected in the world."

But I was still thinking of Luzía. "Was she really married?" I asked Edison. I had not yet learned that this was an unimportant consideration. Well, he said, probably they were never really married in the eyes of the government or of the Church though both were devout Catholics. But they were married in the eyes of the people, and were faithful and good to each other. For untold years they had been selling meat at their stall. The meat was blanketed with flies as in every other Brazilian market, but after all people must eat meat. In addition, some time ago, they had bought a little store where Luzía sold finery and foods sacred to the cult. Because of her excellent reputation in business and in religion, she enjoyed a steady flow of customers. After her long busy life with her husband, it would be hard for her to go on alone, Edison thought.

But actually, he reflected, these people of candomblé never find themselves alone. The other priestesses make much of them. Besides, there is warmth in the constant flow of patrons and clients bringing their own special problems, clamoring for prescriptions, advice, and the simple friendliness of a listening ear. It is right for a priestess to lose herself in these matters. It must be forty or more years since Luzía was made a priestly "daughter." She could not be the second in command at Engenho Velho if she were not the oldest in service, or the next to the oldest.

45

"Has she special duties?" I asked.

"Almost everything rests on her shoulders," he answered. "Together with the mother she makes every decision of consequence affecting the temple. In addition she hears the complaints of innumerable clients and settles their cases. They pay her for the service, but she contributes a good deal of the money to the support of the temple. Lately she has had a little chapel built to Oxum on a near-by slope."

"Has she any children?" I asked.

"People know only about her husband," Edison answered. "Now she is paying for masses for the safe conduct of his soul at the church of her patron saint and goddess, Our Lady of Conception of the Beach." Luzía and her husband were such good friends, he commented, that it must have been hard for her to face "sending him away entirely" in the African style, burying even the memory of him.

A lovely-looking light-complexioned woman in her thirties came out of the temple then, and greeted Edison. "Dona Ruth," he turned to me, "will you meet Mother Totonia?" She was unusually fine in appearance and the only woman I had ever seen in such circles who was not in the lacy Bahian costume; she wore a tailored gray dress like any upper-class woman.

Edison guessed the questions in my mind. "Yes, she's the mother by right of inheritance," he explained after she had gone. "But obviously she doesn't quite belong, and her story is pathetic. Her true name is Antonia, and the aunt who raised her gave her the nickname. This aunt was the mother of Engenho Velho, and she hoped to train Totonia to succeed her. But the girl came from different surroundings. Her parents were respectable mulattoes who objected to candomblé life and would not allow her to complete the novitiate as a priestess. But the aunt was determined, and it was common knowledge that she was passing her leadership to her niece.

"Suddenly the aunt died. Totonia was unprepared in every way, and harassed still by her own family. She had been over-sheltered at home, and she did not seem to have the resourcefulness or ambition necessary in a mother, especially the mother

46

of the most noted temple of all Brazil. And she couldn't develop. At one time Martiniano wanted to marry her, and that would have been a great help to her; but her socially superior family forbade it.

"Well, the girl was the mother by her aunt's dying command, so she went into the temple to train further. Not long after, while still in retreat, she was discovered in a relationship with another priestess. The women were very disturbed, for they considered this an abuse of the sacredness of the temple and of her office; but they couldn't or wouldn't discharge her, so they appointed their senior priestess to be an acting mother. This is Maximiana, or Aunt Massí as they call her here. They gave Massí three advisers: one is Luzía; another is Eugenia, who generally lives in Rio but comes here for important ceremonies; and the third is Totonia."

"Poor Totonia!" I said. "She doesn't fit into either world, does she?"

"Well, she's a simple, gentle woman, and they should have allowed her to marry and not have forced any responsibilities on her. I guess they've remedied matters now. Everyone likes Massí and her advisers, and Totonia is just a gracious lady without any worries now."

I thought how frightening it must have been to her to receive the temple as a gift, with its fifty or so priestesses, its hundreds of followers and clients, and its terrific calendar of ritual obligations.

We walked indoors again, and a priestess named Juliana greeted Edison and gave us white chairs in an advantageous spot. "Father!" she exclaimed in greeting and kissed his hand. She said she was living now in Ilhéus, in the southern part of the state, with her son who was a policeman; she had come up just for the ceremony. I began to feel that this was indeed a temple of matriarchs, and that men, though wanted and necessary, were chiefly onlookers.

The large room was bright now with electricity; pretty strips of white crepe paper festooned the roof and also the wires, framing a half-dozen hanging lamps. Our white chairs were near the orchestra of male drummers, who sat at the rear of the room facing the entrance, and concealed behind a pole painted white. These chairs were seats of honor, and the only ones in the room.

The men began to beat the drums and a few old daughters straggled out to dance in honor of the god of the evening; they were dressed in his prescribed white lace, and danced in a wide circular path before the drummers. The women were black-skinned, strong and big, and had none of the mincing ways that the upper class considers feminine and alluring. In fact, they seemed to me like men dressed in the skirts of the Bahian women.

Suddenly I heard a woman's strident voice pulling songs for the drums to take up. This was Eugenia, who had come from her dressmaking trade in Rio to celebrate and lend a hand. She was a pretty, middle-aged woman, fair and plump, and she dressed elaborately. Energetic as a cheer leader, she sang like a shouter and danced in all directions with the speed of a skater. She pulled one song after another, in a fixed order that answered to the hierarchy of the gods. On the white bench built around the center pole, there crouched unperturbed a sleepy old priestess with a snowy head. To my inquiring look, Edison answered that she was a former slave who had been brought from Africa more than a hundred years before. Also a priestess, she was dedicated to Oxalá, and because she was so old they called her, like the god, "Papa." A slim little girl of nine, already dedicated to the goddess Oxum, joined the dancing file of women, and when she passed the Papa she stooped for a moment and kissed her hand in greeting.

The drummers now prepared themselves for an evening of enjoyment. Drummers had to be men, and it was they who summoned the gods with the voices of their drums to descend into the heads of the women. The voices of the drums were the active agents, and the women moved in accord with their commands. There were three drums of different sizes, with traditional names and characteristic tones, and each had been "baptized." The drummers were prominent temple officials called ogans, and were led now by an ogan visiting from another temple with which Engenho Velho had friendly relations. (Among certain temples a great bitter rivalry existed, to the point where they accused each other of serving poisoned food.) This ogan was black and fat and amiable, reputed to be a versatile and dramatic singer of cult songs.

I watched the drummers intently. How those boys beat and tapped! In exuberant patterns sharply struck and phrased, they forgot themselves as completely as did the dancers who later fell into holy trance. They bent over their instruments, tapping at a speed possible only to those who are deaf to other concerns. It seemed like spying on something intimate to watch them. At times there was a rapid change of hands when an eager youngster after much begging was allowed to take over the drumsticks, or an experienced older man pulled the sticks away from him to demonstrate technique, not even troubling to sit but standing bent over the drum and the seated boy. One man sang accompaniments in a voice so hoarse from prolonged use that it cracked; but somehow it carried conviction. The daughters sat together on the floor to the left of the drums, near my chair, and following the drumbeats they would come in with chanted responses. Watching the orchestra with the attention of a seasoned colleague was an old ogan who sat near by; he was dressed in immaculate linen with a red satin sash across his chest; he too was visiting from another temple, and the sash was his temple's badge of office. Lay visitors dressed in white crowded the uncomfortable benches and the limited standing room, leaving hardly enough space in the center for the ritual road of the dancers; they all were intent on the drummers.

Eugenia greeted a man at the doorway and escorted him up to the orchestra. Edison touched my arm, "That's Felipe Néry," he said in a low voice. "We're to visit him soon." Felipe was Martiniano's cousin, the son of the old man's mother's sister— a kinship that was very close in the African mind. Twenty years younger than Martiniano, he was robust, black, and handsome; his crisp white hair and mustache somehow created a resemblance to Teddy Roosevelt. His eyes were unusually large and heavy-lidded, and his facial expression was sweet. "The people call him 'a son of Africans,' " Edison explained, smiling, "and there is no higher compliment they know." His mother had been a famous priestess, and when she found that her young son had a patron saint or deity—Martiniano must have divined this—she decided to placate and tame the deity by a cult ceremony called "seating the god." It appears that a god is wild and disturbing to its protégé until brought to order by a priestess. Consequently they "gave food to the head" of Felipe, that is they went through ceremonies of feeding the African orixá whose human lodging is the brain. And Felipe's was a stormy god. It was young Xangô, who was also called "golden Xangô." But Felipe never encouraged his god to descend, even though he sang at temple rites in an extraordinary repertoire, beating all three of the African drums like a demon in the intricate rhythms of the calls. He also danced superbly, though only at home functions. He would never initiate a priestess, and he never joined a priesthood. "He's a real man," Edison assured me, "he's an honest man. . . . But, Dona, wouldn't it be wonderful if we could let go like those women do? What an exhilarating time they have!"

No sooner had he spoken than a spark seemed to jump out of the air and shock everyone. The gods had struck! I too felt keyed up and restless. Voices called, "Make way! Make way!" And the standers-by parted their ranks to clear a pathway to the door. The drummers beat on in a frenzy and sang, the daughters were dancing solemnly and heavily—when from among them rushed a woman in the direction of the doorway. She was driven by her god who had descended and was possessing her, and he grunted with her voice. She tore down the stairway slippery with the offerings to Exu, and out she scampered into the warm dim night. Observers said she tried to climb the smooth trunks of giant jack trees, then she tried to throw herself into the stream that flowed by the well at the foot of the incline. An ogan pursued her, trying to seize her and keep her from injury. Then a laywoman began to dance in place before Edison, bowing, and grunting like a Victrola needle at the end of a record. It seemed that his chair was in her way, and she wanted to pass and follow the first woman. But Eugenia bounced by in the circuit of the priestesses, and she put her strong hands on the possessed laywoman. "No more are to leave the building!" she ordered loudly, fearful that people would fall down the stairs. The first one had already sprained some toes. The people showed enormous excitement.

And then! Then the unlooked-for happened! It seared the souls at Engenho Velho.

The drums were working out a fantastic pattern in subtle syncopation, the men crouching over the drums, balanced on the balls of their feet, beating orgiastically. (The basic beat was usually two eighth notes followed by a quarter, or a quarter and a rest, the African melody being a simple monotonous chant which sometimes acquired a racier Iberian character.) Eugenia was hopping along cheerfully.

Suddenly a white man, young and thin, staggered into the double line of dancing women. Massively the black file moved on, ignoring him. He showed that he was possessed because he made the rigid contortions of a horse of the god Omolu, and developed these dramatically into the horrible representation of a chorea sufferer. I glanced at Edison, and saw that he was fascinated. The young man tried to race through the door but was blocked by two old ekedis. They wished to expel him from the dance ring, but unheeding he returned to it, staggering extremely, pressing his palms against his ears in the cult trancer's manifestation of possession. People craned their necks to see. The ogans ridiculed him, amazed: "I never saw the like of this! The impudence!" Eugenia chugged by in the sacred circuit and stormed to Edison: "I know him! He's from the house of Procopio." * Finally, as he twitched badly all over, the ekedis gave up the struggle and allowed him to dance with the women. They removed his shoes and socks—as only the bare foot may touch the floor in dance—loosened his tie and collar so that he would not choke himself twisting, removed his jacket and wrist watch, and rolled up the cuffs of his trousers.

* A father who encouraged a few men.

51

So he danced, charging like an animal let loose from confinement. He was the god, he was Omolu and St. Roque, he was the master of lesions, sores, and pests. He danced alone in the circuit now, preceded and followed by ekedis watching that he did not injure himself or anyone else. His eyes seemed closed; but he could guide himself, and he knew when to stop to bestow upon favored persons the embraces of the god. The room was hushed except for the drums following his faintest command, and the songs he hummed in the cracked small voice of a somnambulist. At moments his lids were torn wide open, eyes fixed and staring. He danced like a genius, though in amazing strained postures, crouching with his right leg bent behind his left. He did the Victrola-needle grunt occasionally—ugh! ugh!—especially when the drumming and singing paused. It seemed to me as though these blank intervals induced crises within the dancer's soul, during which he stood still, excited, with nothing to support him. Once at such a time, the youth tried to sing a song; but his throat was so contracted that the tones escaped even those straining their ears to catch them. When finally someone did, and the drummers took up the beat, he danced with abandon.

After seven long dances, the prescribed number for a horse, the women led him backwards into a rear room to restore his normal state—by ingenious techniques that were supposed to be secret—and to dress him. They were not the least in awe of his divinity. Eugenia, for example, waltzed by us and, pointing disdainfully to the floor, remarked, "There is his precious watch." Then she held up a tiny withered rosebud, "And I'm bringing this for his buttonhole." Hours later the lad came out and ran away, his hair upset, his tie awry, his eyes disturbed. When a week later he returned, his attention was drawn to this sign posted on the central pillar:

This notice begs gentlemen to observe the greatest respect. Their sex is prohibited from dancing among the women celebrating the rites of this temple.

From then on, for hours and hours, different gods descended

in various priestesses, who were thereupon led to the rear of the house to be arrayed in special finery. Eventually all were lined up in a gaudy parade walking like somnambulists, rocking uncertainly, occasionally jerking violently, and guided at every step by the sober ekedis who kept them in order. Eugenia quipped that "everybody" of importance was there except Exu!

Everybody indeed! The gala atmosphere was so infectious that for the first time in the people's experience Felipe Néry was forced to run out of a temple!

He was leading the drummers, who seemed in a frenzied condition, and he had pulled a dozen fiery songs for his god Xangô while he watched the deity dance in the person of a charming priestess, when suddenly he clapped his hands hard over his ears and rushed from the room as though for his life down the oily stairway! This could mean only one thing, as Edison explained excitedly. He had felt the god-impulse so strongly that he feared he would yield to it. But the women laughed admiringly that Seu Felipe had proved his manhood. For he had kept himself from dancing. He would not return that evening, and his young wife followed to steady him.

Now the drums beat out a song of goodbye to which all the gods danced. Departing guests kissed the hands of favored priestesses. Many times I heard Luzía's sleepy resounding voice say, "Be blessed, my daughter." Near me a sweet-faced middle-aged woman exclaimed: "Isn't it wonderful to see them! I wish *I* could dance with a god. . . . But I can't, I never could. . . . My daughter does. . . . What is it like to feel a god coming into your head? . . . But the god did put his arms around me tonight and told me all would go well."

Not till long after did I learn that activity in the temple continued far beyond our departure. The women who were possessed by gods had to be restored to normal, by despatching the gods from them. I never saw this procedure as it was open only to women advanced in the hierarchy—though possession itself was discouraged among the senior priestesses of the Yoruba, who liked to think of themselves as mastering the deities instead of serving them—and was one of the great secrets of temple practice. But I was told about it by priestesses I came to know:

The possessed woman herself was unaware of everything. She was taken by her god against her will, and so when the god first started to ride her, she bucked like a wild horse. Her face set rigidly, her body jerked wantonly, she lost her balance, and she conveyed a general atmosphere of tension and pain. It was now that the ekedi (who never fell possessed) had to guide her, to see that she did not injure others inadvertently, or herself when her head began to flop as though dislocated. But soon the horse was tamed and began to execute superbly, in deep trance, the dance of her god. And now, animated by the deity, she *was* the deity, and the ekedi led her off to dress her in the luxurious clothes of divinity. For the next twelve hours or so, as on this evening at Engenho Velho, the woman lived in a trance, harnessed by the injunction to dance for the drums, forbidden to eat, drink, or relieve other wants. I never saw one cough or scratch, yawn or stretch, or go to the closet. The entranced creatures responded only to signals from the mother and the drums.

Consequently, despatching the god was regarded as a very delicate matter. As anyone could see, women treated carefully emerged fresh and relaxed, but those treated carelessly, like the white boy who "fell," emerged bewildered, quivering, and unhappy, and ready to return to their previous state. Laywomen were often treated hastily, like men, and so were priestesses if the trance state was brief. But on the whole there was great concern over the technique of despatching. A mother forbade her women to visit other temples, fearing to have them fall there and be despatched inattentively by the other priesthoods, and even warning them of being fed poison there.

Despatching took place among the Yoruba in a special room called by the African term "roncô." The gods were seated there in a file of chairs. Assistants laid rush mats on the mud floor, brought in a pile of handkerchief cloths, and filled jugs with water. An assistant mother called an ekedi to help her strip the gods of their finery and, beginning with the eldest in the temple hierarchy, they left each one dressed only in a petticoat (called by the secret name of "tails"). Then they laid each nodding god on a mat in the position a priestess took when saluting her god: on the belly, called a dobale salute, if the god was male; but crouched on a side, called an ikâ salute, if the god was female. The ekedi, having dipped her fingers in clean water, marked a cross on the back of each hand of a god, then on the forehead and insteps, and then, sharply and suddenly, she pulled the hair on the crown of the head and at the nape of the neck (for the god resided here). Then she covered the entire body with a white cloth. Suddenly she whipped off the cloth, cutting the air so as to make a wind, and calling the name of the god. Three times she whipped the cloth over the body. Then she seized the two arms, pulling them up and down together with increasing force three times. And finally the entranced woman was given water to drink, her first drink in many many hours.

The attendant hauled her up, shocked and unhappy, and seated her in a chair where she waited for a sponge bath. The bath water, called abo, was sacred and secret, prepared from an herbal brew, and from the sacrificial blood of an animal, aged for a few months, with an indescribable foul odor. But the odor was removed from the body by a special soap, imported from West Africa and famous throughout Brazil. Then the body was dressed, although not dried. If the woman was to remain in the temple, the ekedi dressed her only in a long skirt slung across one shoulder.

For now the god had left, had been despatched. In his place had come a mischievous imp called êre. The êre were always children, like the saints Cosme and Damião, and were supposed to be the offspring of Xangô and Iansã, the gods of thunder and lightning. This was really a secondary state of trance, lighter and happier than the first, and the women with êre could do fairly normal things. They talked now, though it was a special language of baby talk and gestures, a mélange of pig-African and pig-Portuguese. They were fed the simple, tasteless starch dish called acaçá, their first food in long hours: it was fed to them dissolved in cold water. Then they remained playing on the mats like children.

The êre could be amusing and harmless, but sometimes they used indecent language and gestures and had to be scolded sharply by the mother. They would steal things from one another and from passers-by, and would run around the temple spanking people (theoretically a mother could spank a refractory priestess). It was said that one of them, not long before, had attacked a peddler passing the temple, and upset his cart, causing him to lose his entire investment. Some of them would rush into the surrounding woods and climb trees, some tried to eat stinging nettle (this was once considered a test of true possession), others tried to tear dogs to pieces. One might steal a pot of chicken and eat it all up, tough though it was from the temple style of ritual slaughter and cooking; she would go off with it in a corner, hiding it in her bosom. Women might drink whole bottles of oil or honey. "But they never seem to get sick from this," people said. "It seems to do them good."

"What about the ogans?" I asked.

"Oh, they stand around and laugh," the priestesses told me.

All the normal people would be busy getting things out of the way of the êre, or setting them to rights; some mothers considered it necessary to lock the doors and windows. Despite their impishness, the êre never asked for or sought food that was taboo to them as priestesses, like bread and tea, and they remembered to use the special secret words like "black water" for coffee, and "the deceased" for cooked meat.

Around three o'clock in the morning, the mother would call a halt. "Enough!" she would order. "Go to sleep, or leave!" An êre might complain of hunger, "I've got a wide-open hole!" and she would be fed for the last time. Or another would want to urinate, and announce it like a child, saying, "I want to cry-cry-cry." If one wished to sleep, she would say, "I want to curl up to sleep in a dark hole!" Finally all of them would be put to sleep in the small dark room reserved for novices, while the sober priestesses slept elsewhere.

The êre slept for as long as they liked, sometimes lying as though dead to the world for twenty-four hours. When they wakened, sober, they could not recall anything, were irritable, and refused to tease and joke. An "elder daughter" would take them into the roncô room, to wash the privates and mouth of each with soothing lukewarm water. After drinking acaçá water and playing a little, the women became more relaxed, and were told of their antics.

"But some of them remain cranky," a priestess told me. "This god business is a mysterious force which sweeps over you. I don't like it. You become a slave to the saint, and some- times you go around possessed for three days! You have no wants, your body is dead, you don't feel anything at all until êre comes."

Confusion could come because êre was not always "called" when possession took place only in a private ceremony. They made the short cut to normality by calling the baptismal name of the daughter instead of the name of the god. A laywoman won even less attention, because she was "pagan." The attendant merely struck her three times on the nape of her neck, and on the soles of her feet, called her by her baptismal name, and sent her out even if she appeared dizzy.

The day after the despatching was a holiday. The public function over, everyone was relaxed. Friends of the women visited on the temple grounds, and they loved in particular to play a game of forfeits. The purpose was to trick the priestess or ogan of a male god to behave like a woman. This crossing of the sex line was taboo, and the tricksters levied a fine on their victims, obliging them to buy beer and other refreshments for the crowd, which stood by and laughed at the chagrin of those paying the forfeits. For example, the horse of a male god asked the horse of a goddess for a sip of her beer. When the latter thoughtlessly handed it to her, the first dashed to the mother complaining that a woman had made a gift to a man! Or a woman, passing a male god, unobtrusively set a flower in his hair. Then she too would complain of the outrage to the mother, and the whole priesthood would march protestingly to the male god. "What is this?" the god would exclaim. "I never wear flowers in my hair!"

"Just feel your head and pull it out!" they would urge.

In another type of "joke," sacred taboos were involved. For instance, someone spilled oil on the white dress of a votary of Oxalá cooking in the temple. The mother was summoned again, since Oxalá's food must be prepared without seasoning, and the innocent offender had to buy a nanny-goat and beer in penance.

In paying the forfeit or ransom, the offender was led to a throne in the ceremonial room. Officers, priestesses, and neighbors were summoned. The mother named the levy, and a dish was placed on the floor before the guilty one into which she threw what amount of money she could. She might toss in fifty cents. "But a woman is worth more than that," the mother would protest. Then all the women and ogans serving gods of the same sex as the offender's god would throw in additional coins, freeing the woman by covering her shame. The smiling mother then led the redeemed offender from the chair, the drums beat loud for the restored god, and the women danced in praise! The mother divided the prize only among those serving female saints, because only women were supposed to receive gifts in Bahia! Edison told me that he had once witnessed such fun at Engenho Velho, and noticed that the votaries of goddesses cleared a small fortune since the majority of the women there served male gods!

And so the trance state was ended, and a woman was restored to normal, two days after she was seen possessed, and a god, at the public rites.

VII

THE CLASS sentiment of Brazilian society is something to which I never grew accustomed. I suppose I never took it seriously. It has only an indirect association with race or income and is more closely bound up with ideas that are sometimes as distinguished as *noblesse oblige* and are sometimes merely very snobbish. In Edison I met one of the best examples of the so-called "upper class."

He was a liberal, and was even considered as a radical in some quarters; but he was distinctly not a man of the people. His class nature belonged to a system of thought that was different from his social and political ideologies. It showed in his dress and in his speech, in the very interest he had in the Negroes, and it came out of the society in which he had been reared. He was totally unconscious of it, and he might be amused at my opinion.

I never sensed this special quality in his relations with me or with his Brazilian friends. We were the same in our education and in all our standards; some of us had more money and some less, and Edison was among those who had less. The quality came out in his relations with the blacks. He was their patron, and they wanted him to be their patron. By their mode of address and flattering ways, they set him above themselves. They were courteous to everyone, but they were more robust and humorous with their own than with him. Women of all ages liked him for his fineness of manner, for his pale skin and "good" hair and boyish body. He never took liberties with them, and in fact always had to resist advances because some of them thought that they would like him to set them up in an unofficial ménage. They liked him because he was an aristocrat.

In that country an aristocrat never appears informally dressed in public, no matter how high the thermometer shoots up. In the year that I knew Edison, seeing him almost every day, he never appeared without a hat, jacket, collar, and tie. To have appeared in lounging clothes would have been disrespectful to me, and would have compromised the respect of the blacks. He had his own pride in the matter too. The blacks on the other hand dressed as the weather dictated, and during the fearful humidity of summer, men of the poor white-collar group walked around in pajamas.

An aristocrat never allows his womenfolk to walk alone after sunset, though the black women always walk alone, even when escorted by a man. Hence they thought I was related to Edison, and since we were obviously of different races some of them assumed I was his wife. Unlike the customs of the English-speaking world, the fact of dark race did not preclude him from aristocracy nor from marriage with a white. In fact, the people knew of blonde German women married to Negro Bahians. When Edison could not accompany me, he arranged for one of his friends to do so, usually a young poet named Aydano, son of an old white family of Bahia. He did not trust the blacks nor the military nor the very dandified aristocracy. I presume he had his reasons. I know he became very angry indeed one evening when I planned to go to the movies alone, because my unseemly behavior would have reflected upon my aristocratic friends. Even his aunt, who was the matriarch of the family, was relieved upon meeting me to feel that I was feminine and conventional, "not like the English." But I never felt the aristocracy thus thrust upon me, the way Edison did.

In our country, we expect all persons of color to feel a mutual bond. We ignore the fact that this does not happen to be the case, and that on the contrary there are several mutually indifferent, even hostile, classes within the Negro group. In Brazil no such assumption is even dreamed of. Everyone knows that the differences of education, occupation, and family distinction create a gap as yawning as the American one, which is based solely on color.

Consequently Edison viewed the candomblé people as from across a gap. To him they were specimens, although of course human beings with an inalienable right to live as they chose. All Brazilian intellectuals hold this position, which is surprisingly romantic in view of their democratic convictions. Nineteenth century Russian intellectuals felt similarly towards the peasant serfs. Somehow this distant, patronizing attitude, passionate as it can become, is distasteful to an American reared "north of the line"; it quite denies the common humanity proclaimed in the beliefs of Jeffersonian democracy. However, the people understood Edison's attitude, which was their own, and not mine, which came out of another scheme of living. And they respected Edison, knowing the risks he ran at the hands of the police, while they merely tolerated the good intentions that Edison told them I had. When it came to trust and reliance, he was their man.

Like so many young intellectuals of Brazil, he had a passionate sympathy for peoples all over the world who were oppressed economically and politically, and he had become known as a political crusader. Among other things, he worked to help the people of candomblé live as widely as they desired. Before the dictatorship of 1937 he was active in planning a successful strike of public utilities workers, and in arranging collective bargaining. After 1937 this was no longer possible, and in fact the government had rendered him *hors de combat* by suddenly clapping him and many university friends into jail in 1938 for ten days or so on the first anniversary of the dictator's coup. Now all that Edison could do was to insist that the blacks be allowed to worship their gods—who were also the Catholic saints—as they chose. But this too was dangerous because the municipal police (whose own relatives supported candomblé) were ordered to make sudden raids.

At this time, the cult groups were accused of being nests of communist propaganda. I often wondered at the charge, which was made to me gravely by the handsome colonel commanding the federal troops in the area. For the most part, the blacks could not read or write and never went to the moving pictures, but passed their lives between their places of work and the temples. Fear of communist propaganda was widespread, and my own consul, whose American insouciance was quite intimidated by the facts of life in Bahia, advised me that he was not prepared to protect me in case of difficulty. I saw as little threat to the political life of the Republic as I did at home in the United States. Certain it was, however, that the blacks and the intellectuals were being made scapegoats of the administration's anxieties. And willy-nilly I *was* dragged into it. Some six months later, while waiting one sweltering night in February for the streetcar into the jungle, Edison said in his careful English: "I think a spy is watching you. He is dressed like a black worker." I turned to Edison in amazement because I did not believe him.

"It's true," he smiled. "I have long experience in recognizing the secret police. They are very clumsy at it. Now, when we get on to the car, let us take the rear seat, so we can watch him in front." And so it was.

When we reached the home of the priestess we were visiting, and I told her in astonishment, she answered quietly: "We've known it for a long time. We didn't say anything because we didn't want to frighten you."

Edison was amused. "Well, now you know you are dangerous. You are friendly with the wrong people; you must not be seen with blacks or with university men. Or you'll end up in jail with us next year! Esteemed colleague, you are now in the Republic of Brazil."

I am ahead of my story, but this is the atmosphere in which I found myself shortly after reaching Bahia. One did not sense these things so sharply in Rio because that was the seat of the central government, and the federal police was strong. Even the abortive attempt to assassinate Vargas, which occurred soon after my arrival in Rio and only a block away from my hotel, had no repercussions in the city. Nor were the Rio blacks notorious as "communists"; rather they were feared as magicians, and glamorized as street vagrants, since they were very poor. But in Bahia they were taken seriously in all ways—and, if the intellectuals were communists, why not the blacks with whom they associated?

VIII

CONTINUING his program of introducing me to Negroes who were good examples of their way of life, Edison took me to visit Martiniano's cousin, Felipe Néry. We were going to celebrate Felipe's sixtieth birthday as well as his patron saint Jerome, and we set out that afternoon with Martiniano to the Néry home in a distant suburb. It was a long ride by streetcar to a poor workingmen's neighborhood, and the terrain was unusually flat. Martiniano and Edison talked; I, being a woman, just listened and observed.

When we arrived Felipe, who was a stevedore, had just returned from work. A steady, reliable earner, he provided a nice home for his pretty young wife Victoria and her four-year-old twins, who, however, were not his children. The house was like the others in the street, cramped and narrow, made of local clay tinted pink, with a roof of baked clay tiles that glowed delightfully in the sun. The furniture seemed new, in the narrow fragile style found in the houses of those workers who could afford it.

Martiniano ushered us in through the unlocked door and, while we waited in the front room for Felipe to wash and change to fresh white clothes, told us about him. The old man's manner was gay, and he meant to be complimentary. "He's a good man, a very good man. And what a dancer! You must get him to dance for you. And how the women take to him! All the children in the neighborhood are his, forty of them if one, and he admits to them all. A woman simply walks up to him saying the infant on her arm is his, and he says Yes. They all take his name."

Felipe heard these remarks as he came into the room, and he smiled a little. I gathered that this was a familiar method of teasing.

"What about Martiniano's children?" he asked Edison. "At least I admit to mine. I'm glad to see them." As two of the alleged forty sons entered with Victoria's twins, he glanced at them with pleasure and remarked, "I'm teaching them to dance, and they are learning fast." He stood up and addressed Martiniano. "Well, old man, let's go back and see about the fixings. Victoria and the children will entertain our guests."

They walked out of the room together, but Felipe popped back now and then.

Victoria delayed, and while we were alone Edison told me about her. She was only his own age, he said, twenty-seven; but childbearing and hard work had thickened her body so that she appeared older. She had confidence in him because he had once taken care of a friend of hers, a girl who had wished him to "make her happy" permanently.

When she was young Victoria had inherited a little money; but her stepfather had squandered it, and thus had gone her hope of an education and ambition to be a teacher. But she took pride in herself, and had a fine appearance with her dark-brown color, small features, perfect teeth (so unusual in Bahia), straightened hair, and rose-painted fingernails. She supported herself by taking in washing, and for years she tried to study while she worked. She observed strict moral standards, unlike some white girls of respectable family who, poor things, had ended in the little houses of prostitution that sheltered "women of that life," earning barely enough for a hand-to-mouth existence. Finally her teacher advised her that she could not study profitably while she was working—who could in the sweltering climate of Bahia?—and it was then that she felt the need of consolation. So for the first time she gave herself to a lover. Only afterwards when it was too late did she realize that the man was a thief and a rascal. He was the father of her twins. She fell so ill at childbirth that she was removed to a hospital, and from that time she had been sterile.

She had set up housekeeping again with her stepfather and returned to work when the revolution of 1930 broke out, in which Vargas contested the presidential elections and won by the force of his military. Bahia then found itself in a state of martial law. The soldiers were disorderly and cruel, looting and raping. As she was returning home one day with a basket of clothes on her head, walking alone through a well populated neighborhood, two soldiers stopped her and demanded that she yield to them. Not long before, a friend of hers had been abused in this way by three armed police. So now she refused; and, being a husky woman, she held the soldiers off until they stabbed her. She dropped bleeding in the street, and they took her as they wished. Afterwards neighbors dragged her home and cared for her.

In her long convalescence Victoria met Felipe. Bitter over

her story, he came to visit her when he learned that she was destitute. He was more than thirty years her senior and was already domiciled with a woman, so in all innocence he appointed himself her protector. For two years he visited her daily and always left money for her and her stepfather, even renting a tiny house for them. She was still unable to work, and so they passed a lot of time sitting and talking together while she mended his shirts. He never mentioned love and seemed to regard her only as his protégée, a pathetic young thing.

Then (she had told Edison) one night the woman with whom he was living locked the door on him, shut him out of his own house. Tired as he was from his labor of transporting loads all day, and at a loss as to what to do, he paced the slippery streets of the Lower City until eleven o'clock that night. Eventually it occurred to him to go to Victoria's house. When he told her his story and asked to be allowed to sleep there, she told him, truthfully, that there was no room. He answered, "Well then, let me sleep in your bed." She agreed, and he fell asleep immediately.

After that, he stayed on. He told Victoria that despite his numerous offspring he had never had good luck with women. They always betrayed him; sooner or later he would be supporting not only a woman but also her secret lover. This touched Victoria deeply, and, moved by gratitude for his kindnesses to her, she determined to prove to him that she was "serious," capable of steady affection. They made a comfortable home and lived together in harmony.

She came into the room at this point in the story. She appeared young and fresh, with an air of content, and I should never have suspected that she had seen trouble. She sat down on a fragile settee, too shy to utter a greeting, and began to arrange the dress of a large doll made in the image of the white race.

"So you're going out to compete in the parades?" Edison asked playfully.

He was referring to the januaries—festivals reaching from December through January to the Carnival in which people of all classes in the coastal cities, black and white, Catholic and pagan, educated and illiterate, sing and dance and go on pilgrimages in fanciful costumes. The janeiras are supposed to be rehearsals for the three days of Carnival; but the Brazilians, especially the Bahians, throw themselves into it so fervently that they actually make it an anticipation of Carnival, converting Carnival itself into the wild climax of a crescendo of glorious play. Friends organize into groups called "ranchos" and "ternos," and are supposed to stage incidents from the birth of Christ. But usually they forget about the Nativity, and concentrate on playful ornamental lilies, fish, wolves, nonsense figures, or upon incidents in slave history, always dressing extravagantly and performing the music and dances of the folk. Business and social organizations offer many prizes for the best performances, and the big competitions are always held in the squares of the largest churches. Some groups make the rounds of houses, like the English carol singers, and the countryside is then very gay.

"Yes." Victoria answered Edison's question quietly, absorbed in the plump, full-breasted doll which she held up to show us. She explained proudly, in her stiff, almost sulky way: "She is to be the water goddess.* She is our Janaína. I wish I could comb her."

Edison gave her his pocket comb, and lovingly she arranged the doll's flowing brown tresses. Then she pinned long "diamond" earrings in the neighborhood of the doll's ears, saying:

"These were offered by Felipe's cousin, Dr. Edison. Don't you think she's beautiful? But she has no name of her own, and Padre João is coming tomorrow to baptize her. Will you be her godfather?"

Felipe passed by the doorway just then and heard her request. He stopped to remind her in a rebuking whisper that she had already asked Martiniano: "Woman, don't you remember the 'professor' is making the despacho for her tomorrow?"

I was surprised to hear this because a despacho, according to the newspapers of Rio, was simple black magic. According to Luzía, it meant invoking Exu and often too the gods Ogum and Omolu, who saw to it that evil was kept away and that only good fortune attended. Apparently a despacho could be made in

* Mãe d'água. Janaína is one of the names given to this goddess.

the midst of praises to Jesus, Mary, and Joseph. Yet surely it was no stranger than the heat I experienced in January, the African rhythms and the fanciful songs I heard for Christmas, and the blessings extended over most of these things by the Catholic Church and at intervals by the police power of the state.

Victoria was not disturbed by her husband's remark. She continued to fuss with the doll. "She needs a necklace and bracelet to match the earrings," she said. "Would you care to offer these, Dona Ruth?"

I promised, and she made no comment. She knew that the doll was about to become the dwelling place of a goddess, that the padre's blessing would make of it a mystic fetish; and anyone should feel honored to make a gift to the fetish. She pulled a piece of red velvet out of a basket, beginning to embroider green flowers on it, and she talked about the costumes she had been sewing during the past month for the dancers of their rancho.

"I've been working so hard," she said, "I've not had time to sleep, and I fell sick last week with the grippe."

Why, I thought pettishly, don't they throw all this energy into work? Why don't they move faster in health and social programs? Why does so much of it go into fun and god-imaginings? Why? Well, I answered myself, one reason naturally was that they were not instructed in these other saner pursuits. Another was that they were very, very poor, very, very little educated. And another was that they found something real in the janeiras, deep personal satisfactions they could discover nowhere else.

Felipe, for example, was a stevedore and a good one. But how far could he go in his work? Before the dictatorship there had been a free union in the craft, and then the men had enjoyed improved working conditions. But the scope of union activities was limited now by the general economic situation, which was depressed and stagnant. Felipe did not care to be a union official, and did not care for power over others. He was an honest man, uneducated, and he saw no way to get rich. However, he had never been destitute, which was saying a good deal. He had always been able to eat and dress, to take care of his women, to give gifts to his children and friends, to contribute to the terreiro of his worship. There was no great place for him in candomblé since he avoided possession by his Xangô and would never dream of becoming a "father-in-sainthood." The care of the cult belonged to the female sex. It was enough that he was an ogan, giving money and advice when requested. His great virtue was in playing the drums which gave out the sweet luring voices of the gods.

All drums, all music and dancing interested him; he loved their patterns and their beauty. He cared nothing for dominating the gods, and he avoided trouble with them. Instead, he went into the secular and joyous activity of organizing a rancho! He put a great deal of work into it, and the members chose him president. To him this meant artistic recognition and opportunity.

These things came out in remarks by Edison, and by Felipe at times when he stepped back into the room.

Finally Felipe called us to the back of the house for supper. It was in the kitchen-dining-room. The people were obviously not at ease with us, and their expressions and gestures were the wooden ones they assumed to indicate respect and good manners. Edison as usual was quiet, and simply sat himself down ready to eat. "No farol here," he commented to me, and I smiled at the slang because "farol," which here meant showy display, properly means a lighthouse. The Negroes were always subdued, and even by themselves they were not noisy and extravagantly active like American Negroes; their good humor and sociability came only through smiles and gentle expressions of the face. Their moods were restrained and subtle, and by my American standards our hosts were wanting in warmth. But I know I was mistaken.

It was a poor man's meal, and so it was ample but monotonous. It consisted largely of vegetables prepared in oil, with some hard-boiled egg, and a lot of toasted manioc flour; meat and fish simply cost too much to buy. But it is amazing how good manioc will taste when you are hungry and unconcerned with luxurious considerations like calories and vitamins; and

Bahians mix manioc with everything. Sometimes balls are made of the starch, unseasoned and unmixed with anything but water, and people eat them like apples. In colonial and slave times, when Bahians were richer, they used to eat sugar in the same way; historical accounts, diaries and paintings reveal the enormous intake of pure sugar, presumably because there was so little variety in the food. And this sort of diet shows itself in the people's ravaged skins and teeth, though, as in other slaveholding areas, the Negroes have a better inheritance than others because of their rougher life and diet. Felipe, Martiniano, and Victoria were big and strong with sound glistening teeth. When you looked from them to Edison, you knew that he was very far removed from their blood and their history.

We adults sat at a small round table, and the children crowded among us, to be served by Victoria. There was silence during the meal, but Martiniano created some diversion by walking in and out. I learned later that he was attending to secret business concerning the despacho for the doll. The room was lit only by a small bare electric bulb that hung over the table.

As we were finishing the meal, some girl dancers of the rancho, returning from work in town, passed by the house to discuss details of costume. Victoria grew animated then, discussing designs for slippers of red and yellow velvet. Edison teased her, and began to sing in his true, lilting voice, "Oh, they announced and they guaranteed . . . that the world was going to end . . . that the world was going to end . . ." She ignored him, and then he tried to persuade Felipe to dance for me. "No, doctor," Felipe answered slowly, smiling as to a child. "No. I've got to save myself. I led a rehearsal last night and did not finish until it was time to go to work this morning. And I have another rehearsal this evening!"

Edison laughed and said, turning to me: "There, you see! Nothing tires that black race! Amazing! I've known washerwomen to walk miles after their work for a dance, then dance till the dawn, and when they left they were pouring perspiration. They should have died of pneumonia, but they never do— The gods save them."

69

Felipe smiled again. His quiet manner suggested great physical reserve. "Doctor, too much study taxes the mind. But hard labor keeps us strong, and hard fun keeps us young. In Bahia everything is glorious! How does the saying go? 'The splendor of Brazil lies in the path of the drum.' * So, let us dance!" He slapped the table and smiled.

"It's a land of gold," agreed Edison.

"Come to our next rehearsal," suggested Felipe. "It will be announced in the papers. Our rancho of the robalo is bound to win this year although we have stiff competition to face. I've been drilling my people for weeks. We have costumes and dancers and acrobats of a very special sort! I don't believe their equals are to be found anywhere. Only the Marionettes Club might threaten us because they are rich, and since their members are aristocrats they might carry influence on the board of judges. Though actually I don't think anyone stands a chance against us. Everybody seems to have turned out this year, in spite of the pope's death! Even the ogans and women of Menininha's temple are rehearsing secretly though they are still in mourning for ogan Bibiano. I hear the prizes are something exceptional! Come down, Doctor, and give us a talk! We need inspiration from men of culture."

"Viva Robalo!" Edison cheered humorously, jumping up. "And what's your theme song, Seu Felipe?"

"Come see us when we parade at one o'clock in the morning of January 6th, in the great square before the Lapinha Church, in honor of the Three Wise Kings. You will hear then, and you will see."

"If the police don't forbid it," Martiniano came in with this mournful warning, having completed the despacho outside. "People say they are going to shut up the candomblés again."

"The businessmen have put up prizes—" Felipe objected mildly.

"The Church wants to celebrate the day of the Kings," Edison settled the issue briskly. "They've already strung electric lights around Lapinha Square and the façade of the church, and

* A riqueza do Brasil está na roda do tambor.

they are now building scaffolds to show off the ternos and ranchos, and platforms for the premières danseuses to perform. Don't worry."

"You see, cousin," Felipe smiled to Martiniano, who was bringing a chair to the table.

"Doesn't anybody like the food?" the old man answered humorously. "So much talking going on, the food must be terrible. Now, Dona Ruth, see this oil sauce seasoned with shrimp. I myself showed Victoria how to make it. Eat it, and you'll live forever."

"If God wills," Victoria echoed piously, helping him to it.

We left soon after because the Nérys were so preoccupied with their duties to the rancho that it made us uncomfortable to watch them sit and fidget in the polite idleness which our visit imposed upon them. And I am happy to report that the chief of police delayed the proclamation closing the candomblés until January 7th.

IX

ALTHOUGH Mother Menininha was young by Afro-Brazilian standards, since she was in her early forties, she was probably the outstanding priestess of Bahia after Aninha's death. Everybody had heard of her, and spoke of her respectfully. An international congress of sociologists had held a celebration in her temple the previous year (where they served champagne, Dr. Eustacio told me), and then large replicas of Menininha and some assistant priestesses, like human-size dolls, were made and placed on permanent display in the small museum attached to the Medical School. Lately I was told that a popular magazine in Rio carried an illustrated story of her temple.

This attention was due partly to the force of her personality and partly to the reputation of her temple, known as Gantois. On my arrival in Rio, the distinguished scholar of candomblé, Dr. Arthur Ramos, had talked to me about her with admiration. I read about her temple in his books, and also in the books of his great teacher, Dr. Nina Rodrigues, who had first revealed the candomblés to the world of science. Dr. Nina had concentrated on Gantois, which was then directed by the eminent Mother Pulcheria, aunt of Menininha, and his descriptions so fired the imaginations of Brazilians that they became the nucleus of a whole school of thought. They are unequaled in preciseness and vividness, and are also very sympathetic although presented from the Huxleian viewpoint of his time which denounced the Negro practices as inferior because they were pagan and also no doubt because the Negroes had so recently been slaves. Modern scholars treasure the descriptions, and also the genius which impelled Dr. Nina to appreciate the human worth of candomblé; but they have abandoned the older interpretations of "racial inferiority" in favor of social and psychological considerations.

Pulcheria and later Menininha had secured distinguished Bahians as ogans. Dr. Eustacio was ogan to Menininha's own goddess, Oxum; and I have heard that both Dr. Nina and Dr. Arthur Ramos were ogans. These connections gave prestige to the temple, and were also a reflection of the significance of the temple. The ogans are a sort of board of directors. I learned too that the temples protected ogans when necessary; for example, when Vargas seized the dictatorship, it was necessary for political opponents to go into hiding, and the temples were then very accommodating.

Edison said that Menininha resented him for political reasons connected with the union of candomblés in which he and Martiniano were active, and to which Gantois belonged, and so he thought it advisable to have me introduced to her by someone else. This was easy. Dr. Eustacio da Lima immediately offered to help me. He was "médico-legista" (practitioner of medical jurisprudence) for the state of Bahia, and was therefore also curator of the candomblé museum and a professor at the Medical School. Smiling gayly, he said that the head drummer at Gantois, a black named Manoel, was an old employee at the Medical School, and also an intimate of Menininha's. Manoel would arrange everything; besides, Menininha's town house was just across the square from the Medical School. How lucky! I exclaimed, delighted to find no hurdles in my path. But it was not easy to talk further with Dr. Eustacio despite his courtesy and attentiveness. I think it was because he was so completely the aristocrat that formalities dominated his relationships. Brazilian aristocrats smile and chat and compliment a good deal, but all this adds up to a heavy barrier between individuals. No doubt too he was restrained with me, a stranger from the democratic United States, because he had only recently returned from a voluntary political exile in France.

However, I shall never forget his one effort to entertain me at the Medical School. The Bahia police had lately captured in the highlands a notorious young caboclo bandit named Lampeão, and also his young sweetheart Maria Bonita. Having pursued his bandit group for so many years that the chase had given rise to exciting ballads indicating the sympathy of the people, the federal soldiers decapitated Lampeão and Bonita when they finally captured them. They sent the heads to the office of the médico-legista where they were put up in a preservative brine. These heads, each in a separate jar, Dr. Eustacio showed me enthusiastically that hot afternoon in the cool dark library. Startled, I watched the handsome young professor, so cool-looking in his linens, his hair black against his pale face, holding the jars to the light. "She must have been pretty for a cabocla," he observed, intent on the girl's face, "she was so fair. You can't see Lampeão very well; he doesn't show up because he's already turning black." I know that many Bahians would have envied my privilege.

Waiting for Dr. Eustacio to arrange the meeting with Menininha—and that took several days since Manoel kept odd hours—I talked with others who knew her. One was Dr. Oliveira, who had escorted me to the great market along the bay on a recent Sunday. Wealthy and an aristocrat, he conducted a famous clinic for poor children, and he had persuaded some rich ladies of the city to support a milk fund. Through long and exasperating experience he knew how deeply the people were impressed with teachings of candomblé. They came to the clinic willingly if they were so advised by their priestesses; but, even after they were given careful medical advice and prescriptions, they resorted to herbs and magical formulas of their cult or, more often, used both together. An expectant or nursing mother would come to Dr. Oliveira just as the spirit moved her; but she seldom failed to contribute to the elaborate, costly rites of her cult when she was ordered to do so by temple officials. The doctor knew how many babies were born out of wedlock, how many small brothers and sisters had the same mother but different fathers, how many young ones had to work or beg because there was no man in the household. He knew well the mixture of bloods among the poor—most of the people were poor—and could see no harm in it.

"We are all Brazilians," he would say in his aloof manner. "That is what counts. We have one spirit, and we are becoming more and more one people. The black brings us his wonderful strength and good humor. The Indian brings his melancholy. The enterprising Portuguese brings all these elements together! The one thing that really worries me is the high rate of venereal disease. The rate is terribly high. Possibly 85 per cent of my patients are afflicted with syphilis. Babies get it when they are born—they stand little chance against it. It doesn't seem to hurt the blacks as much as the others. In the upper class we doctors have been able to persuade people to take treatments whether the symptoms are obvious or not. But what can you do with the poor? Even if we offered them treatments free, they are too ignorant to understand and take advantage of them. Well, we are not worried over the race of a man's blood; but we are worried over the disease in it."

Another medical friend with whom I talked directed the insane asylum. Like every intellectual trained at the University of Bahia, he had considerable knowledge of candomblé, and great interest in it. He could not help knowing Menininha—he called her by her formal name of Escholastica. He believed that in her way, among her class of people sprung physically or spiritually from the former African slaves, she was as distinguished as the medical and legal doctors. She was the guardian of a religious philosophy and administrator of its institution. She held sway over hundreds of souls by right of her priestly knowledge and talent and by right of inheritance from the women who had held the post before her. Yes, he knew Escholastica and respected her. What struck him was that so few followers of the fetish temples became insane; at least, almost none were brought to his notice. He decided that the emotional and social outlets of these groups were unusually satisfying. The phenomenon of possession itself, when the god descended in a woman (or in a wayward man) and obliged her to dance, sing, and apparently lose her true identity, he attributed to nothing more abnormal than hypnotism. "Look at the studies of Dr. Nina," he once explained. "He stuck pins into those priestesses when they were dancing, and they never felt the pain. He passed objects before their eyes, and the pupils never focused. He saw them dance for hours and hours without asking to relieve their natural wants, and they showed no apparent strain. These things are not insanity, they are hypnotism. Besides it is only women who are supposed to fall into these states, and insanity is no respecter of sex. Dona Escholastica herself told me that the older a priestess gets and the more she knows of her calling, the more control she should have over her god and the less often she should fall. Now, the course of insanity is just the opposite: people don't get well merely with age and increasing exposure to possession."

I talked also with Dr. Nestor Duarte, a member of the Law Faculty. He was writing a book on the history of the Negro woman in Brazil, and his studies had deeply impressed him with her independence and courage. He knew the mothers well, and naturally also Menininha, whose town house was not far from the university. In his opinion, the Negro woman was an ennobling and modernizing influence in Brazil. She had always been self-reliant economically, in Africa as in slaveholding Brazil, and that combined with her eminence in the candomblé to give a matriarchal tone to family life among the poor. This was a desirable balance, he thought, to the harsh dominance of men in all Latin life. He remarked that candomblé women did not become prostitutes even when poor, that they led a free love life but did not commercialize it. Some even secured a university edu-

75

cation, and a few with means tried to enter professions. They were well developed human beings at a time when feminism was first raising a voice in Brazil. Young Dr. Nestor laughed when I showed him a program I had once been handed in a movie palace in Rio de Janeiro. On the back page was printed an essay entitled, "Is Higher Education for Women Necessary?" It argued that college training did not make a woman a tenderer mother nor enable her to suckle her infant better. On the contrary, it deprived her of charm and reduced her chances of marriage. Yet the highest goal of a woman's life was to marry and have children. Dr. Nestor laughed, thinking of the astonishment these arguments would arouse in Menininha and her sisterhood:

"And Dona Menininha has a husband, Dona Ruth, a lawyer named Alvaro MacDowell, a man as fair in complexion as she is dark. She has two daughters, Cleoza and Carmen, both fair, getting a good education, and both of them priestesses, young as they are. Actually, Dona Menininha supports herself, and I am sure her daughters will do the same even when they are married. That kind of woman has been independent for so long— for untold generations—that I cannot visualize her becoming dependent and shut in even after she climbs into middle-class life. And that's excellent for us in Brazil. Like you in your country, we cannot have healthy men unless we have strong healthy women. Indeed I know Menininha, and I admire her."

Others knew her too. There were some friars of São Francisco Monastery who were making a scientific study of the fetish beliefs of the cult, and Padre Barbosa, vicar of the church of Nossa Senhora da Conceição da Praia and guardian of the records of the old brotherhood of freed Negroes called A Irmandade da Nossa Senhora do Rosario. There were also a German doctor, and an Italian diplomat, and many writers who knew her. She was a personage.

By now I was anxious to meet Manoel, and I inquired again of Dr. Eustacio. "Tomorrow," he assured me, and proceeded to tell me about him.

Manoel, whose much-used nickname was Amor, was now

almost fifty years old. When he was orphaned in boyhood Mother Pulcheria took him into the temple, and he lived there until his first marriage. Ever since anyone could remember, he had been working at various tasks in the physiology department of the Medical School; and by now he knew as much about the subject as the professors. Chance had so arranged his life that his work and his traditional beliefs in candomblé intertwined. One would think this highly fortunate, yet Manoel had acutely mixed feelings about Menininha and her staff, and indeed about candomblé itself. His young second wife, Maria José, nicknamed Zézé, was a priestess made by Menininha, and the couple lived within a stone's throw of the temple. He developed periodic rages with Zézé which were known to the whole cult world, and they always were occasioned by her ritual duties to the temple. He did not want his wife to follow the career of a priestess; yet under the circumstances his battle was vain, for public opinion among the blacks was against him. So he became sullen after a period of shouting and throwing things, and he visited improper houses. Zézé was unhappy and confused, though adamant, and she complained to Dr. Eustacio, and later to me, that when Amor forced her to ignore her religious obligations her goddess invariably punished her. The goddess was the fierce young warrior Iansã, known also as St. Barbara of the lightning. Once, Zézé declared in outrage, Iansã banged her on the head so badly that her eyes were blackened for weeks. On another occasion Iansã twisted her left arm so that it hung useless for months. Amor did not want her to dance in the public ceremonies of the cult, where she dressed gorgeously *à la bahiana* and men were free to stare at her. (Hearing these things, I used to wonder if Amor had become affected by the social views of the upper-class professors among whom he worked.) He did not want her to fall possessed and live out of his reach for days. He did not want her to sleep away from him in the retreats with the other women, because only Heaven knew what might be going on between her and the ogans who visited after their work in town. Zézé was flattered by his jealousy, I believe; and though she was a good woman she would do nothing about it.

77

Amor had three half-grown children by his first wife, who had died some years before, and he tried furiously to keep them away from services. Naturally his whole world was against him, and probably he could never actually have torn himself away from his "mother" and the temple drums. I am sure he really believed in the fetish faith, loved its sociability, and gloried in having university professors—his own employers—turn to him for information about it. After I left Bahia, I heard he had broken up the furniture in his house in a new rage; and, not long after, he died.

The three of us met at the university on the afternoon arranged. "You've already heard of Seu Manoel, Dona Ruth," smiled Dr. Eustacio, "and here he is!"

"You exaggerate, you are too kind, doctor!" exclaimed Manoel politely, talking very fast. "Dr. Eustacio is a prince of men," he added to me, affably and ornately, holding himself very erect and smiling in a forced way. He had a shiny black leathery skin on a powerful rangy frame. He was wearing an old navy-blue suit, a worn black felt hat, and run-down black shoes; and his features merged into the general darkness until he smiled. Then his teeth flashed, glowing like pearls. I thought that one must talk to that man's teeth as one talked to the eyes of other people, because they were the soul of his face, each tooth clean and long and with an individuality of its own.

"We want to take Dona Ruth to see Menininha," Dr. Eustacio suggested.

"I went over this morning and told her," Manoel answered, blinking his small, deep-set eyes rapidly to show this was a serious matter. "She is expecting us. I am at your service."

He walked alongside Dr. Eustacio with his overly erect bearing, guiding us across the plaza of the university into the broad sunny street of the Cruzeiro de São Francisco, and then into a shaded block where Menininha's town house stood. "You saw the dolls in our Nina Rodrigues museum," Dr. Eustacio remarked to me. "The second meeting of the Afro-Brazilian Congress was held here last year to study the candomblé, and we thought we'd show them some real 'daughters of the saint.' So we hired women to sew up dolls, almost life-size, representing Menininha and her women."

"They are wonderful! Just like Menininha!" Manoel assented in his rushing guttural speech. "Dona Ruth, you would swear she was in front of you. What a Congress!"

Then the men saw the priestess and exclaimed. I wondered if any outsider could have suspected her position. She sat in the shaded entrance to her house, a black shawl wrapped about her head and bosom despite the heat, and a tray of sweets on a little stand beside her. Her head was turned away as she stared down the block and exchanged remarks with her daughter Cleoza, who leaned out of a window above.

"Menininha!" called Manoel.

Slowly she turned her large head about, opening her large mild eyes, and she smiled graciously. "Doctor!" she greeted Dr. Eustacio and rose heavily. "How are you, my lady?" she acknowledged the introduction to me, giving me her small plump hand. People said she was proud of her dainty hands and feet, which had not a single blemish because she had not been obliged to do rough work. She was about five feet tall, fat and dark, with kinky hair, and a large tooth conspicuously missing in the front of her mouth. Her clothes were not pretty or neat. But I felt dignity in her, diffident at the moment yet pervasive, accustomed to authority. I noticed her full, heart-shaped face, her small full nose and lips, her cool bronze skin.

"Dona Ruth wants to talk with you, Menininha," Eustacio explained.

"An honor, doctor!" she acknowledged in powerful sweet contralto tones. "To receive a friend of yours is a distinction. And we want to tell you how glad we are that you returned from Paris."

Eustacio waved his fine hand, and flashed a handsome smile upon her. "You see how they flatter me!" he laughed.

I watched them with great interest, one the picture of a ruler of the land, the other the picture of a humble Negro. Yet they treated each other with the courtesy of equals, with the same blandness.

79

"Come along, Manoel!" Eustacio called, and they left.

Menininha led me indoors. She handed her shawl and tray to a young girl and walked into the front room, where Cleoza lolled in the window. "Come in, my lady," the priestess urged listlessly. "Let us sit down and have a little visit."

She lowered herself heavily into a flimsy chair, placing her palms on her thighs. Suddenly she was remote and obscure as a Stone Age Venus. Her shawl gone, sitting in a loose cotton dress, her great breasts flowed over a great stomach which bulged over tremendous thighs supported by powerful legs tapering to small ankles and feet. Her brief sleeves exposed large arms, masses of firm smooth flesh that dimpled hugely at the elbows and ended in seemingly fragile wrists and hands.

"My lady," she said quietly, unlike the usual Brazilian woman, "you wanted to see me?"

"Yes, dona," I replied carefully, "I should like to learn a little about your temple. People speak of it with admiration."

She smiled slowly, proudly. "So, my gringa, it is known even in your country. All Bahia knows us, all Brazil knows us. We are one of the oldest temples in the whole land. At ceremonies the terreiro is so crowded you would think the entire city had turned out. They like to watch us because they know we are genuine, they know that everything under my direction comes straight from the old Africans as taught me by my Mother Pulcheria." From her chair she touched the ground with the first and second fingers of her right hand, reverently, in the spirit of a Catholic making the sign of the cross. "And they like to see us dance." The reflection of a smile passed over her face. "They call us the 'candomblé of fairy feet.'"

I was surprised at this interest in dancing since the Catholic practice did not encourage any form of physical exuberance. I answered inquiringly, "I will consider it a tremendous privilege to see you dance, Dona Menininha."

"You will, one day," she answered unaffectedly. "The ceremonial season is a long time off. It will be delayed at our terreiro because we are completing a year of mourning for the death of one of our principal ogans. The saints do not like to be in a house of death, and we must wait till the time comes for cleansing."

Months later, after I had met many priestesses and ogans (an African word that is truly anachronistic in these matriarchal surroundings, since it means lord or master), after I had seen many ceremonies and experienced something of the emotions to which they gave rise, after I had begun to take their logic for granted, I realized the enormity of my request to Menininha. She was a great leader, her life was passed on a priestly pedestal. One could no more ask her to perform than one could ask a minister to give a casual demonstration of the mysteries of his creed.

I came to know that she was one of the most gifted musicians and singers of her world and, despite her bulk, one of its distinguished dancers. Her own daughters in sainthood, whom she trained for priestly singing and dancing, mentioned her performances with awe. To me also she came to seem a hieratical figure, dancing and declaiming with genius the old polished patterns of her traditions.

On that first afternoon she talked about her ancestry. "This house belonged to my aunt," she said, looking around the room and toward the oval-framed portrait of a woman that hung on the opposite wall. "They called her Pulcheria the Great."

The picture resembled Menininha though Pulcheria was slimmer and stood with her head flung erect. People said she had been a fiery crusader in her time and had wrenched protection for her people from the police. In those days when people still could vote, candomblé groups were alternately wooed and persecuted in the interest of one political machine or another. They always were a source of graft, and Pulcheria had determined to put an end to this abuse. She had the support of her young friend, Eugenia Ana dos Santos, later known as Mãe Aninha. Aninha also was a fighter, and her portraits, even the ones taken shortly before her death, show pride and assertion. That must have been a generation of great and kindly women, I thought, realizing why Martiniano mourned them.

In her disciplined, crystalline voice, Menininha went on,

"In the smaller towns and on the farms the people will not believe that Pulcheria is dead."

I examined the picture again, noting the twisted turban of striped African cloth, the housewifely dress of the Bahian, the gold bracelet, large as an Elizabethan cuff, on each arm, the ropes of ritual beads on her chest, the heavy gold earrings hanging beneath the turban. Obviously she was a wealthy woman, who had never known menial or slave labor.

"I also inherited the temple from her," Menininha said, her eyes on the picture.

I sensed how she had loved that woman, and noticed later that she looked at her two young daughters in the same way. During temple rites she always bowed to the pictures and relics of her aunt, and to her daughters, but she bowed to no others.

"My deceased aunt"—she touched the ground again—"inherited her position from her mother, the great deceased named Julia"—she touched the ground—"and Julia founded the temple after she arrived in Brazil. First she served as a priestess in Engenho Velho—mother and daughter served together. . . . You know how it is in Europe, my lady. We mothers are like the royal houses, we pass our offices to kinsfolk only, usually women." She shook her head and sighed. "The candomblé is a great responsibility. Often I wonder where I can get the strength to go on with it, and whether I have the right to burden my daughters with it."

"Why is that?"

"I have no time for myself! I am the slave of my people, two hundred of them who depend upon me absolutely! Imagine!" She shrugged, but her look was not really troubled.

"There is a great deal I need to learn, my mother," I said, sighing to think of the tremendous imponderables of life in Bahia. "You see, we have no candomblés in North America."

"No?" She was surprised and disapproving. "Don't your people believe in God?"

"Oh, yes, but we show it in other ways. Still, we have much to learn."

"You want to learn from us?" Her tone was cold.

"Yes," I ventured.

"But there are secrets here you may not learn."

"It is not the secrets I want, my mother. I want only to understand your beliefs. I want to learn more about God, and about men because they are my brothers."

Menininha did not answer. There was a silence, broken finally by a stout middle-aged Negro woman dressed in black, who walked panting into the doorway.

"My mother," she saluted the priestess and sank stiffly to her knees, lifting Menininha's negligent right hand to her lips. "A blessing?" she begged perfunctorily.

"Be blessed, my daughter," Menininha granted casually, not even looking at her. "You don't have to stay there kneeling. This is not the temple. You'll get rheumatism on that damp floor. Sit down. What's new?"

The woman found a low stool and placed it alongside Menininha's chair, setting it so as not to look full into the mother's face, as that would have been disrespectful. She sat with her feet planted far apart and her palms thrust down upon her thighs. I smiled to see these women who did not care about being dainty. Their concern was to lay claim to where they sat.

"They talk about this white foreigner," the visitor replied. Her black face was unfriendly. "It seems she wants to learn the dances." She smiled faintly. "No doubt there is something behind it all. No doubt she will spread her knowledge in the show places of her country and charge high fees."

"What nonsense!" Menininha rebuked her gravely. "She is a friend of Dr. Eustacio, who himself brought her to my house. Besides, he says she is a scholar, a doctor of learning. Do not repeat idle rumors. What else do you know?"

"Truly, my mother, I am here on another matter. What shall I do with the things left by my deceased husband?" Ritually she touched the ground before her. "You will dispose of them, my mother? They are all the paraphernalia of the chief butcher for the temple. A great responsibility, and as I know nothing about it, I do not want the things around. I would not know how to take care of them, and the gods would punish me."

"Yes, we have a big job ahead." Menininha was interested now. "We must attend to it. Come along to the back. . . . Will you excuse me for a while, my lady?" she asked, rising slowly. "Rest yourself, the house is yours. I'll be back."

Throughout my stay I remained astonished at the liberties the mothers could take with time. Menininha never did return that day, and I realized subsequently that she was always late, always delaying. It was a privilege of her station, and even taken for granted in a land of aristocracy and slavery. What was time? Time was what you did with it, and she was always occupied. She exacted promptness of her subordinates, but for her personally it was enough to approximate the schedule.

Months later, after I had won her confidence a little, I was told what had taken place in the rear. The two women had gone to the spacious kitchen where private altars were set up representing the permanent ones in the distant jungle temple of Gantois. They sat down at a bare deal table, and Menininha took out sacred cowrie shells which she threw in specific ways in order to read the will of the gods concerning the disposition of this problem. She thereupon found it necessary to instruct the widow in proper deportment. The people of candomblé are on the whole prudish, and the cowries revealed that the widow, despite her ugly face, was resuming adventures she had enjoyed in her premarital past. There were rumors among the people to the same effect, and complaints that she did not mourn correctly because she had been left too well provided for. Menininha was less inclined than usual to be tolerant because she had subjected herself to certain rigors preparatory to this ceremony, which kept her mindful of the obligations to which the widow must conform. So, carefully, she scolded the woman, who said nothing but none the less withdrew herself and her amusements to a distant island resort.

However, as I expected Menininha to return that afternoon, I waited and for a long time watched girls and women pass in and out of the room. I began to think they wandered through merely to look at me though this was not apparent from the masked expression of their faces.

The room seemed to be reserved for visitors. It was long and narrow and full of shadows. Its cheap furniture was lame and dusty, of the stiff style manufactured in quantity for the poorer people of the region. It had two tall windows looking over the street, and Cleoza sprawled against the sill of one, her back slightly turned so that she could not be accused of thrusting her buttocks in my face. She had been there, silent, since the beginning of the interview with her mother. How did one talk with an heiress-priestess aged thirteen, remote and indifferent as she seemed? She resembled Menininha though much lighter in color, and she carried herself in the same way. She was extremely well fed, her beautiful face glowing, her heavy body revealed by a short, snug dress. The people said that her father planned to make a dentist of her, and in his mind this was not incompatible with the priesthood of Gantois. He himself, a lawyer, believed entirely in the candomblé and represented his wife's interests in the police court. He sent his daughters to a private school and dressed them for the purpose in attractive modern clothes. People said that Menininha had been an accomplished seamstress, supporting herself by this means in her youth. Nowadays, however, the junior priestesses made the dresses worn by her daughters. It was one of the tithes they rendered her.

There were other rooms, dark and stale and filled with rickety tables and chairs. Children skipped through them on errands for the daughters working in the kitchen or for their relatives in the neighborhood. Some women usually slept in the kitchen at night when their own homes were distant and they had worked late here in the home of the mother. They threw mats onto the bare mud floor, and these were their beds. Men usually visited after work but never stayed for the night.

I walked to the other window to see what was absorbing Cleoza. "You like it here?" I asked her offhandedly.

"Yes," she replied shyly.

"She's there every afternoon," another girl in the room commented.

It was a choice spot from which to view the Lower City.

People strolled steadily along the narrow sidewalk, glancing up at the windows, seeking the half-familiar faces that watched idly every day. A padre walked past in sweeping black woolen skirts, gathering his folds and looking ahead. (What an extraordinary uniform for the tropics, I thought, with woolen trousers underneath his skirts and a beaver hat on his head! And I had already sweated through my white linen dress!) A beggar hopped up to him, picked his sleeve and whined, half crouching:

"Reverend Father, in the name of the Virgin, the glorious mother of the Christ Child, give me some coins, and may your goodness be rewarded in the lustrous hereafter."

In a hushed stern voice, not looking at him, the padre told the beggar to quit his drinking, to make his confessions, and to attend a church clinic of alms seekers. The beggar was outraged. He looked to young Cleoza for sympathy, then hurried to catch the elbow of a medical student. "Illustrious sir," he commenced timidly, "the rich young gentleman can spare some coins surely. By the wounds of the Christ I need them." The student stopped, embarrassed, and looked at his own starched linens; probably he had not a nickel in his trousers but was living on credit backed by his family. "Go on! go on!" he urged the beggar softly, bringing out a package of cigarettes. I remembered the success beggars found in Rio, where the people always gave a coin fearing that refusal would jeopardize their chance for Paradise.

Then two women came by, genteel creatures whose garments and gait announced wealth and dignity. Cleoza watched them admiringly as they waited at the corner for traffic to halt. The older one wore the fashionable deep mourning required upon the death of a father, husband, brother, or son. Some ladies never escaped from this attire. The younger was in lighter mourning, her corseted plump figure in a black-and-white organdy print. On her head was a modish flat hat of shiny black straw edged with fine white grosgrain ribbon, and against her rouged cheeks swung jet earrings. Her legs, pretty because they were plump, were set off by sheer black stockings and pattered along on slim black high heels.

"What a lovely brunette!" Cleoza sighed to the girl in the room, who pressed up against her to see. "Such a fair skin—such black hair—such style!" She watched the woman cross the wide square past the towered Medical School and enter the ancient Cathedral beyond it. "I wonder what they're going to confess!" Cleoza giggled. "The young one minces so! Like a little circus horse! . . . Suppose she is the one whom Padre X visits!" She grinned suddenly and threw up her hand to cover her face. The other girl rolled her eyes wickedly.

Leaving the Cathedral and walking in their direction were several colored women in the gorgeous gaudy dress of the Bahian. I always found them a wonderful sight. I knew how hard they worked, laundering at some river edge where they rubbed the wash on a handy rock; or peddling their trays; or standing day and night selling in the markets. Going to church was sheer relaxation for them. They gloried in the magnificent interiors of the colonial buildings, in the grand dark quiet of the pews, in brief friendly conversations with the priests, in the parade of fashionable worshipers.

This particular group was chattering gayly, laughing soberly, and punctuating the conversation with slow gestures of hands and arms as though in a dance. The women walked in French mules with wide slow strides, their skirts of bright cotton print ballooning gently, their heads in colored cloth turbans blossoming in the brilliant sun. Cleoza smiled and waved to them, and as they approached she called out, "Give me a blessing, my mothers!" The women answered as they should, "Be blessed, my daughter!"

They paused below the window to chat with her, arms akimbo. "What's the news?" they inquired. "How is my mother?" They asked after everyone in the household, politely ignoring my presence in their full view. The answer always was "Everyone is well, thank the Lord," and the others echoed, "Thank the Lord!" They turned to leave, sped by graceful formalities echoing after them, "Goodbye until we meet tomorrow! . . . Until tomorrow, if God so wills!"

The tropical night fell suddenly, bringing men to visit, and their calls resounded from the entranceway to the women in the back. Everyone ignored me carefully, politely. My strangeness there suddenly struck me, and so I left, murmuring a goodbye to silent watchful Cleoza.

X

THE PHILOSOPHY, the mysticism and emotionality of candomblé always puzzled me. I learned to know it by rote, the way one learns a new language in school, and I became an adept at it; but my reactions were as remote as those of an adding machine to numbers. I grew fond of the people, I admired the quality of their lives—rich as embroidered brocade—but I wanted to know more. I am convinced now that Edison was right when he said the cult followers were actually good Catholics. One had to be reared in that Latin, medieval Catholicism, ignorant of modern beliefs and systems, and indifferent to them, to get at the heart and soul of the people's values.

"I imagine that educating and improving them will really thin out their existences," I remarked once to Edison.

He half agreed with me, but he could not approve of maintaining the unfortunate status quo in general. The people's poverty and backwardness were not trifling matters. "They aren't materialistic," he reflected, "and in that sense too they are not modern. The blacks are kind and affectionate, and even their cult relationships and philosophy are kind. Their cult religion provides an answer for every situation. They seem to need that type of security. It is in fact the only security for them."

"An 'opiate for the masses'?" I half jested.

"Call it that. But the real opiate is their ignorance and illiteracy—for which they are hardly to blame!" he protested impatiently. "Blame the landowners for that, and our whole inefficient economy. In my opinion, candomblé is a creative force. It gives the people courage and confidence, and they concentrate on solving the problems of this life, rather than on peace in the hereafter. I wonder, now, where the blacks would be without candomblé!"

"I notice that the priestesses are very close to the people."

"Very," he agreed. "The fathers and mothers are supposed to know all the answers, and also the few remaining diviners like Martiniano. The daughters know certain answers, depending upon the length of their training and experience, and all the people have a general idea of what's to be done or of who can do it for them, because they all are related to somebody connected with candomblé.

"As in the popular Catholic belief, everything that happens has some mystery combined with it. I suppose nobody is believed to die a natural death, nobody gets married happily just as a matter of course, nobody is successful merely through luck or talent, nobody gets sick for natural reasons—but always there is some saint or god involved who is revenging himself or blessing his protégé, or some black magic is being practiced. The Catholic priests teach the people about the same thing as the mothers do—which is to rely on the saints and on obedience to commands rather than upon their own reason. God is a familiar idea here in this cathedral city. The Catholic priests say that it is important to know His will, but under any circumstances it is obligatory to obey it! The people speak of God 'in the Catholic life,' and of Oxalá 'in the African'; and this means that they believe they are practicing only one religion, although they use two languages in doing it. Their logic goes on from there. God has Jesus and the saints to express His will. Oxalá, who is also Jesus and possibly the whole Trinity, has a number of offspring to express his will, and they are the gods, or orixás (possibly they are offspring only in the sense in which we humans are children of God). Each god reveals some aspect of Oxalá, as the saints do of God. You know that our Catholics do not worship God as much as they do Jesus, Mary, and the saints. And they feel too that Oxalá is remote, old, and pallid. However, the other gods are pretty exuberant: they feud and love like the Greek deities, they descend among their worshipers to play, and they love a certain amount of trouble.

"It's like the Middle Ages. People talk with spiritual beings, and they live partly in this world, partly in the other. Maybe it is truer to say that there is no demarcation between the two worlds. They take god-forces as casually as you Americans take electricity, and both are equally necessary. . . . Can you imagine the comfort of believing and knowing you can reach the ears of your fate?"

"Terrific," I agreed, "though I can barely imagine it. After all, our American generation was reared on a diet of reason and skepticism. Scientific generalizations don't give one much feeling for the nature of faith or of fate. . . . But explain this: Nina Rodrigues tells stories of women falling possessed at any place, any time, even when alone and far from the temple. Does this still happen?"

"Well, the orthodox Yoruba mothers disapprove of it. They try to discipline the priestesses to manifest the gods only when the temple schedule requires it. Otherwise the god and the woman are anarchistic. They want this force under control.

"But candomblé is not always confined within the walls of a temple. Whole cities turn out to celebrate the mysteries at different times of the year. Carnival, for example, was brought by the Catholics, but here in Brazil the Africans took it over, and today it looks like a celebration for the Kings of the Congo instead of the Christian European picnic it set out to be. But we like it—and so do the tourists. Candomblé also took over the janeiras, and during those months before Carnival the Church and the cultists go around blessing everything: automobiles, new buildings, business activities.

"Well, now it's September, and rituals are beginning for the new season. They begin out of doors by the sea and the rivers and the bays. It is now primarily for fishermen and sailors. All the people sail out with their priestesses and priests to special places where they pray to the mother of waters—'mãe d'agua'—for good luck and a good season. There are several such mothers, but the one they love best is Iemanjá, a wife of old Oxalá; sometimes they call her by an Indian name, Janaína. They sing and dance to her in the boats where she may descend, and at the climax they drop gifts into the water, pretty things that a woman would like. They call this the present to the goddess.* If the present sinks to the bottom—and they make sure it will!—the goddess has accepted it and will grant requests. How the drums roar! How the saints ride the horses!"

"I'd like to see that," I said, imagining the gorgeous scene.

"You will," Edison agreed. "But you will have to put up with noise, heat, and lots of children!"

I am sure my eyes glistened in anticipation.

"Colonel Renato won't like it," he teased. "He'll have you on his blacklist. They think the temples are hideouts for radicals."

"I'm an American citizen—" I was outraged.

"But you're living in Brazil, under a dictatorship. It's up to you. I just wanted to warn you. The police are always watching me, anyway."

"If you don't mind my company, I'd like to go."

"It will be an honor. There are a couple of candomblés I should like to see myself, and I want to write some stories about them. My medical friend, Reginaldo, also wants to go. And Aydano too. We'll make a day of it. The workers living in Itapagipe suburb turn out on the third Sunday of this month to sacrifice for the coming year. Let's go there. They sacrifice near a bridge at the spot called Cabaceiras da Ponte, and they stage a fair for a couple of days and nights. Have you ever been to a fair?"

"No."

"Ah-h-h! That's a treat!" He gestured his delight by stamping a circle on the air with the index finger and thumb of his right hand. "Magnificent! They have music and singing and samba competitions. Then they have contests of capoeira. Do you know capoeira?"

"No."

"Of course not. That's another thing the police try to prohibit, and in this case the mothers are with them. Capoeira is a kind of wrestling that the fugitive slaves developed. It's similar to jiu-jitsu and can be very dangerous. I understand that now

* Presente à mãe d'agua.

some academy in Rio teaches it. Up here they've taken the poison out of it by prohibiting the more difficult and violent movements. And they do it to music!"

"Why do the priestesses object?"

"Well, they say it's because the men of capoeira do not believe in God. They drink a lot of rum, they are tough customers, sometimes they are lawbreakers—it's another world. Personally, I think it's because capoeirists are all men, and there's no place for women among them."

"And they have capoeira at the water-goddess celebrations?"

"Yes, at the fair, not at the ceremony itself. Everybody for miles comes to the fair: all the different temple chiefs, even when they hate each other; all the best dancers, men and women; all the best musicians; all the best cooks! You'll really taste African food there! They throw up flimsy pavilions for cooking and serving—and they sell other things too. Each pavilion has been blessed by a Catholic priest, mind you, and has a name, and flies its own bright flag! I tell you, those people don't sleep until the fair is over. They're too excited."

XI

So WE went to Itapagipe that Sunday. Edison hired a boat and a boatman, and we floated in the inlet for hours waiting for a ceremony to begin. Other sailboats also drifted about expectantly. But the hours passed, and nothing happened. Edison had become disturbed.

"I guess this year they couldn't afford to buy the presents," he said. "It's the general economic situation. They must be very poor indeed, and yet they paid for the police licenses for the fair. Business must be worse than I thought. Ordinarily they'll put their last penny into this because they believe it insures good luck for the coming year. And if they haven't even a penny to offer the goddess . . ." He shrugged. "Let's not wait longer, let's go to the fair now. Mother Sabina is giving a big present in the Barra waters next week, and we can see the ceremony then."

We dismissed our boat and climbed ashore. I felt the melancholy of the three young men swing into excitement as we walked up the sloping bank and through some high brush, stepping suddenly into clearings where sheds had been set up. They were flimsy structures of palm leaves and branches, topped with the national flag of Brazil in green and gold, and with pennants of the African gods in brilliant shades. The name of each pavilion was painted in fanciful letters and colors on the lintel above the entrance, personal names like those given to boats, to donkeys, and to sacred drums and capoeira champions. They were names that lifted my mood, absurd but evocative of splendor and legend and the veiled joys of a dream world. One was Flower of Love; another was Beloved of God; a third was Wonders of Araby; others were The New World, The Conqueror, Kings of the East, and Three Lovely Girls. Edison laughed at them, but Aydano turned them over on his tongue for their rhythm and flavor.

The fragrance of cooking food steamed through the heated air. I noticed no efforts to sell, yet the pavilions were crowded with customers. There was a huge output of mingau, which is a sweetened hot drink of tapioca, water, and milk. The people also liked "American" orangeade which I am certain had been bottled in the United States long before because its taste was horribly corrupted by preservative. There also was aruá, a cold and mildly fermented drink made of rice or roasted millet left to season with sugar in clay pots; it was the drink of the cult people. And there was fresh coconut juice drunk out of the shell.

We passed from one pavilion to another in a sun so hot that I felt it suck the water from my flesh. Edison was not sympathetic. "You ought to use rice powder, Miss Stubborn," he said. "It holds the water. After all, Brazilians have learned something about the tropics."

We sampled the foods in different sheds. All were characteristic of Bahia, and were recipes used in temple rites. There were acarajé and abará, both based on feijão mulatinho—a French bean of a tan shade. Acarajé is fried in locally processed palm oil; and abará is boiled, and seasoned with spice and palm oil. The beans are first boiled, then skinned, and finally ground to pulp upon a large gray stone used as a roller. We found one girl busy rolling them. When Aydano spoke to her with a flirtatious leer she giggled, stopped work, and hid her face. This food was not an American's notion of tropical diet; still it was as delicious as it was indigestible.

Perspiration streamed from everyone, and everyone took the heat casually. Brazilians do. I recall being told how the great outdoor elevator connecting the Upper with the Lower City once fell below its landing because it was overloaded. A friend of mine, a Brazilian girl, who was in it said that the passengers simply waited in the fainting heat for assistance to come. They waited about twenty minutes, calling the porter whose name was Aristotle; and then he came with a lever and helped them out. But in the interim they conversed politely, remarked about the heat, and waited without panic. Dr. Oliveira used to say seriously that patience is a virtue of Brazilian women because they are too weak, too undernourished to do anything else. The heat made me feel as though my blood would burst through my skin, and I could now see the usefulness of dark complexions. Some old ladies were obliged to open umbrellas for shade, and girls spread handkerchiefs over their hair braided on top of their heads and tied in neat African patterns.

Finding themselves before the Enchanted Ship, Edison and his friends seized the entire supply of coconuts, giving me a share, and we drained the sourish cold juice and ate the pleasantly tasteless meat. I remembered a cook we had at home who used to warn me every day of the summer that I would die horribly of eating cold apples with ice water. Thinking of her, I took a share of the oranges the others bought, and chewed and drank them with relish. I couldn't get enough of coldness inside of me. Then we bought frozen acaça, a jellied mass of manioc flour that had first been boiled in water and seasoned with salt. Like the other cooked foods, this was served on a dish of heavy banana leaves, fresh and pretty and green.

Standing now in the shade of the Ship with nothing to do, Aydano sought diversion and therefore proposed to Edison with mock formality, "Old Master, tell us some stories!"

Edison smirked at him and scolded: "You know you are not supposed to tell stories in the daytime. Didn't your old mammy say a lizard would get you if you did?"

"Really?" I asked, thinking of similar sayings at home.

"Yes, I guess they didn't want to be disturbed in their work. They say it's a lazy man's way to tell stories in the daytime."

"Well?" hinted Aydano.

"All right, Flower," Edison answered, really pleased to tell his tales. "The responsibility is yours. I'll tell you an Angola tale I heard from Mother Germina, whose 'protector' is the Holy Ghost. It's about the water goddess:

"Once a pregnant lady vowed to Iemanjá, Queen of the Sea, that if a daughter were born, it would be consecrated to her. The great goddess of the depths granted the wish. A little girl was born who grew big and strong, but the mother forgot her vow. The family lived here in Itapagipe, by the sea, but the child was never allowed to enter the water.

"One lovely morning a boat race was held in the bay of Pôrto dos Tainheiros, and the whole family went to it by canoe. The moment the child arrived at the water she became very restless. She screamed, and pulling the dresses of her mother and aunt, she called, 'Mamma, see that pretty lady looking at me! Look, auntie, how the lady is speaking to me!' In a flash, then, she threw herself into the water.

"The mother and aunt cried frantically, and someone sent for Father Cache-Col—the same one who now practices in the south of the state. This Negro, Cache-Col, came as fast as he could, bringing African drums and a golden tray. He told the orchestra to play, and he sang sacred songs, and he showed the tray to the Queen of the Sea. 'Take this, O Iemanjá,' he called, 'and return the girl.' Iemanjá bargained obstinately with him,

95

and tantalized the people by tossing the girl up and then dropping her into the water. The mother was in despair. The big drums roared, never ceasing, beating out songs of the mãe d'agua, the Senhora Iemanjá, from whose womb came all the orixás. Unable to lure the goddess out with the tray, Cache-Col finally threw it to the bottom of the bay, and only after it had sunk into the waves was the child returned. Then Cache-Col saw to it that the child was consecrated as a priestess of Iemanjá."

"Don't the people dislike their gods when they act that way?" I asked.

"Actually, they often feel guilty about them," Aydano answered. "That's when they remember that they have not fulfilled their obligations."

"And on the other hand they are proud of them," Edison added. "Listen, and I'll tell you another of Germina's stories:

"People were gathered in the suburb of Tojuca at the end of the railroad line. Their candomblé was going strong, and a priestess was dancing, possessed of Iemanjá. Suddenly she began to run, and no one could stop her. Madly she raced into the river Catú with her clothes on. She disappeared, and her body did not rise again to the surface. Back on the bank the drums roared sacred songs, calling upon the goddess to return her. After a long time the priestess came out of the water, looking like Iemanjá herself. She was dressed in new garments delightful to behold. She returned to the temple, dancing as never before, and at dawn danced back to the river. She stepped into the water, then stepped out again. And everyone was still with astonishment, for her wonderful clothes were gone and she wore again her old ones. So people say that the Queen of the Sea actually came to earth that night to play with her favorite children in the suburb of Tojuca."

"As Sosigenes Costa said," remarked Aydano dreamily—

> "Handsome daughter of Africa
> Blessed fruit of Africa
> O Bahia of Iemanjá . . .
> Beloved rose—beside the sea . . ."

"And here's another with a moral," Edison continued. "One of Germina's priestesses was worried over the burden of Iemanjá she carried—you know, the ritual obligations she had to fulfill. This was in a period when the police persecuted candomblé. The goddess came to her in a dream, in gorgeous apparel, and told her that the ceremonies could be arranged if she petitioned a certain police captain for a license. The priestess told the dream to her family but did not follow its advice. Just a dream, she thought. Consequently Mother Germina's petition for a license was denied. Only after four days of vainly making applications did the priestess decide to approach the captain named in her dream. And—the captain arranged everything immediately! Furthermore, the present was accepted by the waters. Germina then gave a mild rebuke to her daughter. 'Aren't people unnecessarily obstinate?' she said."

" 'Bahia of Iemanjá,' " hummed Aydano, " 'mystic daughter of Africa . . .' " His eyes smiled.

Suddenly a group of young men appeared near us, singing songs and dancing samba. In almost no time a crowd collected in a small circle, standing two deep to watch one who danced in the middle. The men were dressed casually in white or pastel-colored linen suits, with collarless shirts, and they wore caps or hard straw hats with occasionally a worn felt one. The heat forced most of them to throw off their jackets, which they carried slung over a shoulder or else dropped on the ground. They all lounged in a similar way, with knees relaxed and bent, their backs curved, their heads dropped forward, intently watching the one dancing in the middle. His head fell back on a limp and broken-looking neck; his arms, pressed against his sides, were bent at the elbows and his hands flapped at the wrists. Some of the onlookers accompanied his rhythm by noisily whipping the palm, back, and fingers of one hand against tambourines. Others thrummed as effectively on the crowns of their hard straw hats, laughing heartily. One used an instrument called the cuíca, said to have been brought from Angola, Portuguese West Africa. It was a small hand drum made of a barrel; the farther end was covered by rawhide stretched taut, and attached to the underside of this hide, at its center inside the barrel was a slim hard stick that extended beyond the margin of the uncovered nearer end. The small barrel was held against the side of the body under the left arm, and the stick was pulled forward rhythmically by the right hand, causing the drumhead—now tightening and now relaxing—to produce a monotonous and somehow indecent raw sound. The men laughed a great deal at it, and tuned up a song of slavery days with the refrain, "Let the cuíca roar!" It roared ecstatically.

At the first bellow, another young man jumped into the circle, displacing the first. He danced dramatically, dipping his back enough to break it, flailing his arms in mad patterns, protruding and drawing in his buttocks. "This is samba!" Edison tapped me enthusiastically on the arm. "This is the real thing, not the tripping around you see in the ballroom! This is genius! The blacks forget everything when they use their feet!"

The boy danced furiously for ten minutes, and the tune changed twice. It seemed to me that each onlooker wished to be in the dancer's place. Finally one accompanist motioned the boy to give up the space. He motioned again and again, until the dancer conceded by poking out his belly at the other and so "giving him the embigada," as they say. The other immediately leaped into the narrow ring. They did not fall possessed, but they certainly abandoned themselves to the mood. The eyes and ears of the young men were riveted to the dance and the music.

However, Edison and his friends wanted to move on and see more of the sights. It was now difficult to walk as the lanes between pavilions had filled up with visitors.

After leaving the boy sambists, we met some colored girls walking in a row with their arms around one another's waists and singing a lovely slow samba melody composed for the last Carnival by the now deceased Noël Rosa. Noël grew up an uneducated boy in Rio, a ragamuffin from the slum dwellings in the hills bordering the city, so undernourished and half sick that he passed away at the early age of thirty. Although he was just a moleque, his talent had been great, with a freshness and poignancy beloved by his fellow Cariocans. The capital city so lamented his death that it named a street after him, and this is true immortality for a Brazilian. The girls were singing his serenade, "To the Shepherdesses":

"As the star of dawning rises in the heavens,
And the moon moves dizzied with such splendor,
The shepherdesses, to console the moon,
Walk in the streets singing charming songs of love.

"Sweet shepherdess, morena,
Image of Madalena,
Thou hast no pity for me
Who lives dizzied by thy glance.

"Lovely child,
Thou canst not depart my memory.
My heart will never tire
Of always, always loving thee."

"That makes me homesick for something," I remarked, "though I don't know for what. It makes me feel a yearning."

"That was his way," agreed Edison. "He knew the sadness of our people, and the gentleness." He laughed. "Usually we bear up with things, and we even sing about them. But sometimes we hate, we hate everything. . . . Poor Noël! He was so homely! He had a huge beak for a nose, and no chin to speak of. He said his face was like a rat's, and no girl could ever love it. I don't know if that was true, but he composed wonderful music even if only in compensation."

"Compensation is strictly a matter of opinion," Aydano reflected brightly. "One day I had to meet a friend who was traveling here by boat. So I went downtown early to get a good shave. Later I was informed that my friend would be delayed a whole week. However, I had my shave. Some people might consider that a fair compensation."

Soon we were halted by a copper-skinned, hook-nosed mulatto. "Hello, Dr. Edison!" he called, smiling. "You've come to celebrate Iemanjá with us today? You're going to play and fall with the saint?"

99

The two men greeted each other with the Brazilian embrace.

"Hello, Manoel! Hello, Flower! What's new?" Edison replied, and introduced the man to me. "This is father Manoel, a good man! Hear, Manoel? Where can we find some fun? Not candomblé. But how about capoeira? It is ages since I have smelled sweat and rum. Of course *you* are too pious to go near it. But give us some directions. You must have heard the people talking about it, eh, Flower?" And he clapped the mulatto briskly on his bulky right shoulder.

"They say Beloved of God fights today. I saw a troop carrying berimbaus * off in that direction." Manoel pointed to the left. "In this heat, it's quite a walk," he cautioned, showing how arduous the trip was by rolling his eyes and throwing the fingers of his right hand so that the fourth and fifth ones clicked.

"So what? We are men, and one of us is an American—that means bravery! Besides, we're young, not an old 'saint' like you, eh, Seu Manoel?"

"Right! But don't forget, the gods come tonight at Mother Cotina's. . . . By-bye." And the priest went on his way.

"So he won't watch capoeira?" I asked. "Too much a man of peace?"

"Not at all!" the others protested and chuckled. "But it is true," Edison added, "that capoeirists do not care about condomblé. Maybe they like more roughhouse than they find in the temple, and of course there is little that most men can do among all those possessed women. Feeling is so high between them, you would think they were enemies. Maybe they were, back in Africa. Maybe they are still carrying on an old fight between Yoruba candomblé from the northern west coast and Angola capoeira from the southern."

"But the people are now in Brazil," I reminded him.

"That's right, and have been for two or three hundred years. But Brazil was always close to Africa, especially in trade between her plantation areas and the slave markets of Africa. My

* The berimbau is a musical bow, six feet tall, with a single wire string, that accompanies capoeira.

country bestowed honors upon kings and chiefs of the west-coast tribes! And often the slaves knew more than the Portuguese owners. For instance, they taught some overseers how to smelt iron. In your country, the blacks came to a superior technological civilization, but in my country they were right at home! Many of the Mohammedans knew how to write when their masters did not."

"The Africans brought a good deal here," I commented.

"Absolutely. And with their fetish cults they have kept an intact rich life despite many great changes around them. The Indian mestiço has nothing to compare with it. His life is poor and lonely, his highland country and climate are hard, his religion is strenuous and gloomy and fanatic. There are none of the warm and friendly feelings of candomblé. You can see that from the very appearance of the mestiços when they are forced out of the interior during the terrible droughts. Euclides da Cunha described it in his classic book *Os Sertões*."

Aydano was listening attentively. He and Edison always carried on such instructive conversations; and if fresh material failed them they would fall back upon their memories and quote long verses from their favorite poets. Now he added:

"But, mind you, those African traditions are now Brazilian—and we call them Afro-Brazilian."

I remembered white friends in Nashville and New Orleans, and I had an actual physical awareness at the moment of the opposition between the convictions I had left at home and the convictions I was encountering here. The difference between them was terrible. And, thinking only this, I sighed: "My Southern acquaintances would be horrified. They would think you had lost your 'pride.' Even I, because I am used to them, have to strain myself to follow you."

"Really?" demanded Edison, and the others slowed up to listen. "What can be so difficult?"

"Well, North Americans think in terms of race. A black man is inferior to a white man because of his race."

"What about the black man's culture?"

"That doesn't matter. A black man isn't supposed to have

any of his own, only what he gets from whites; and that he is supposed to hide."

It was very embarrassing to explain these matters, especially in the face of their incredulity. The papers then were carrying the story of the stoning of a German business office in Rio which had hung out a sign, "Aryans only need apply." I remembered this and so, no doubt, did they. Edison broke the silence.

"North Americans!" he exclaimed impatiently. And his friends (who were white, from all appearances) nodded. "What do they care about culture! What can one expect of people who devote themselves to money! Money-mad! For them, even time is money." Then his tone dropped and he said to me tightly: "I beg your pardon, my friend. Obviously you are a great exception. But sometimes anger overcomes one."

We had arrived at the spot where the men were forming for capoeira. Watchers were crowded four deep around a wide circle, and there was not a woman or a priest among them. To one side of the innermost ring stood three tall Negroes, each holding a berimbau with one end resting on the ground. Two more musicians soon came—one with a chocalho, or metal rattle, and the other with a pandeiro, or tambourine. Edison and the others helped me push front, and we were glad of the diversion.

Two capoeirists were squatting there facing the musicians. One was the champion Beloved of God, with the Christian name of Samuel. He was tall, black, middle-aged and muscular, a fisherman by trade. His challenger was The Black Leopard, a younger man, shorter and fatter. They were barefooted, wearing striped cotton jersey shirts, one with white trousers, the other with dark, one with a felt hat, the other with a cap which he later changed to a hard straw hat. Squatting in their hats and bare feet, one had his left arm on his left thigh, the other had his right arm on his right thigh, and they stared straight ahead, resting. It was required of them to keep silent, and the requirement carried over to the audience.

The orchestra opened the events by strumming an invocation, and this monotonous accompaniment too was essential to the occasion. It was a sort of whining nasal-toned framework within which the men executed acrobatic marvels, always to the correct beat, while the musicians chanted mocking verses:

> "I stood at the foot of the cross
> Saying my prayer
> When there arrived Catherine,
> The very image of the Devil.
>
> "Eh, eh, Ah-Ruanda!
> Missy, let's go away!
> To beyond the sea!
>
> "It's a sharp knife, Missy,
> It's for piercing.
> Missy, throw it to this side,
> Missy, throw it to that side.
>
> "Eh, eh, long live my master
> And my mistress, who taught me!
> Master, leave me to the vagrant life!
> Missy, to the capoeira life!
>
> "Missy, may the earth revolve!
> Master, may the world go on!" *

It was a song of challenge and hope and resignation, containing fragments of rebellious thoughts. It did not possess a simple theme well worked out, but it summarized a type of life and of protest. And it opened the fight.

Beloved of God swayed on his haunches while he faced his opponent with a grin and gauged his chances. The fight involved all parts of the body except the hands, a precaution demanded by the police to obviate harm. As the movements followed the musical accompaniment, they flowed into a slow-motion, dream-like sequence that was more a dancing than a wrestling. As the law stipulated that capoeirists must not hurt each other, blows become acrobatic stances whose balancing scored in the final check-up, and were named and classified. Various types of

* This song and those following, to p. 109, translated from the Portuguese of Edison Carneiro, *Negros Bantus*, pp. 149–153, 155, 158, 133, 138–140.

capoeira had evolved, with subtleties in the forms and sequences of the blows and in the styles of playing the berimbau.

Beloved was prodigiously agile in the difficult formal encounters with his adversary, and he smiled constantly while the ritual songs droned on:

> "They told my wife
> That a capoeira man had conquered me.
> The woman swore, and stamped her foot down firm
> That this could not have been."

And the berimbaus changed again:

> "There was I. Oh! There was my brother,
> There was my brother and I.
> My brother rented a house
> But neither he paid, nor I!"

Impertinently, with slow, calculated, beautiful movements, Beloved butted his adversary with his hatted head, catching him lightly in the pit of the stomach, upsetting him so that he fell on his head. Thereupon the orchestra struck up triumphantly:

> "Zum-Zum-Zum,
> Capoeira kills one!
>
> "The cutting knife is bad,
> Prepare your stomach to catch it!"

The challenging echoes silenced, the round over, the two men walked and trotted restfully in a counter-clockwise circle one behind the other, the champion leading with his arms high in the air, and the other grasping his wrists from behind while the orchestra played and sang teasingly:

> "In the days when I had money
> My comrade called me 'kin.'
> After my money was gone
> My comrade scorned me as 'bold.' "

Gradually, having rested, the one in front wheeled to face the one behind, and they parried to the beat of the songs, never still, balancing from one foot to the other, watching for openings.

> "Comrade, attention!
> Capoeira goes at you!"

warned the berimbaus. The two faced each other, Beloved swaying, Leopard backing away, always rhythmically. As Beloved advanced bending from the waist, lowering his head for the telling blow at the other's middle, Leopard curved forward intending to evade him. Actually he created an opening into which Beloved charged with his right leg, his left one stretched parallel with the ground to support him. Leopard's arms swung back loosely, and he fell forward over the butting head in a clean arc. Laughing quietly in appreciation, the two rose, loping in circles to relax while the orchestra applauded:

> "Lo, he is a messenger of the king!
> He is from Ruanda!
> What can one do with a capoeira?
> He is an African sorcerer *
> And knows how to play."

They sparred again, and again Beloved was the one to attack, half squatting as in a Russian dance, swaying, arms curved forward for balance. Instead of following through with his head as before, he worked to one side and suddenly raised up his body. Leopard bent to charge, but Beloved swung his weight to his right leg and cleared his opponent's head with his left, causing him once more to fall sprawling!

Now another insisted upon entering the ring. He had attempted to do so earlier but had been ignored. Impatiently he pushed Leopard aside, pointing indignantly to the corner where scorekeepers were chalking the points on the ground, points Leopard had failed to make. And sulkily Leopard yielded his place.

The hero Beloved wiped his streaming face and back, and bared his head to cool it. Through everything the onlookers

* Mandingo.

remained silent, only shuffling to ease their positions and inner excitement. Soon the bows whined an invocation for the new round:

"Who taught thee this good magic?
It was the mistress' nigger boy.
The nigger costs good money.
Good money needs to be earned.

"Fall, fall, Catharina,
Rise from the sea, come see Dalina.

"Tomorrow is a holy day,
Day of Corpus Christi.
He who has clothes goes to mass.
He who has none
Does—as I do!

"Fall, fall, Catharina . . ."

To me this was a performance incongruous and wonderful; to the others it was wonderful and completely absorbing. To them it was right. But the phrases startled me into conjectures about slavery, rebellion, and mockery, and I was astounded most at the manner of the performance, which robbed capoeira of its original sting. The police had removed the sting, and the blacks had converted the remains into a weird poignant dance. Did the songs carry meaning to the people now? Did they recall the struggles that inspired them, or did they merely dramatize black men, as candomblé dramatized black women? The rows of watchers were still, and their faces were impassive.

Again, the challenger and the champion began to trot with knees bent, arms swinging loose, Beloved amusing himself with intricate little movements of his feet. Suddenly a boy jumped into the center of the ring flourishing a pot of money. He had just made the rounds with his hat requesting contributions for the fighters; and the orchestra, which rules the occasion, had decided that instead of apportioning the money, it should be left to a new pair to try for with their mouths, each fending off the other à la capoeira. The boy announced this decision and placed the pot on the ground while the berimbaus teased:

> "Would you play with a capoeira?
> He is a tricky devil . . ."

And Beloved won! But with the heart of a champion he returned the pot to open the struggle again:

> "Now you can play!"

This time the newcomer won. The crowd broke up, painfully uncomfortable under the blistering two o'clock sun. Edison was delighted with the exhibition, having watched it like a connoisseur, and he boasted later that he had helped to organize a new capoeira club that would hold exhibitions every Sunday.

We turned to leave the fair. But everywhere something arrested our attention, and at one point we were halted entirely by a group of dark women in Bahian dress. They too were gathered in a circle. To one side stood an orchestra of men whose instruments were a hard straw hat, a cuíca, a pandeiro, and a tin dish rubbed and scraped with a fork. They played for a woman who was dancing in the center. It was the same performance as the men's earlier samba contest, but it was less athletic for, as Aydano pointed out in mock solemnity, they wore no trousers. Each woman danced alone, giving up her place to another whom she chose with the embigada thrust of her belly.

I noticed that three women monopolized the dancing, choosing one another fairly regularly. Despite voluminous skirts, their movements were active, stressing patterns made by the thighs and feet and occasionally by the shoulders. As in capoeira, their dance was a series of intricate designs thrown into relief by the monotonous tunes and rhythms of the songs. The upper part of the body dropped limply, head hanging back, chest and stomach relaxed, buttocks thrust out under an exaggerated curve of the back, arms swaying gently while the back of one hand rested on the belly and the other rested at the small of the back. A dancer had the rapt face of a priestess in trance, and only rarely did she sing. The musicians preferred to "pull" the leading lines while the audience responded in chorus.

Each of the three sambists had a unique finish to her dancing. One who was thin and sulky specialized in small steps and an angular design. Another, taller and robust, covered much more space in a florid design, and Edison remarked that hers was the "true" African style. The third, dainty and picturesque, was mannered like a stage dancer.

Sometimes a woman gave the embigada to an impatient young man. Then he leaped into the ring in acrobatic versions of the women's steps, and tapped, flamboyantly and beautifully. Fair day was the day of the sambists!

To tease the women, now and then the musicians ceased suddenly in the middle of a phrase. It caused a shock which even I felt, like that sensed on the temple floor when the orchestra left the possessed suspended in dreadful silence. But here, sober, the dancer was obliged to continue to the end even if unaccompanied. The audience thought this very funny and shook in quiet laughter. Even my three friends, sophisticated scholars and political figures though they were, had to giggle.

"What's it all about?" I asked, piqued at being left out.

"Well, they caught her 'pregnant,'" Reginaldo, the medical student laughed. "Oh, not really!" He laughed harder as he saw my amazed expression. "They just caught her unawares; they've just interrupted her fun, the round of her pleasure. She sort of hangs heavy without the music." He laughed again, amused at the sex imagery. The women were supposed to grow exasperated then, Edison remarked, and therefore they sang this samba to the dancer:

> "Get up there, woman, into the ring,
> For surely a man doesn't know how to step!"

Whereupon the musicians struck up a vigorous song to which the dancer had to shake and twist her hips violently. A berimbau came in with whining notes, and castanets teased in clicks.

Then a song was started inviting the women to compete for
a prize of money, and the words were bold:

> "O woman of the shaking basket!
> Oh, what a basket!
> Oh, double panniers!
> Oh, such a cute basket!
> Oh, a basket for bread!
> Ah, woman of the tiny basket!
> Ah, woman of the so-so basket!"

And when the dancer did well:

> "Ah, woman of the big fruit basket!
> Ah, woman of the fine basket!"

And to persuade others to enter the contest:

> "Who doesn't shake,
>   doesn't make!
> We say, Shake! shake!"

At that the dancer protested:

> "I am shaking!
> But merely to earn,
> And I've earned a mill,
> I've earned a penny."

The onlookers laughed and sang, wiggling sympathetically in
place.

Then a dancer began a new and complicated song. It required her to run back and forth hunting for a key she had lost,
and she searched for it frantically in the skirts of the women and
the purses of the men. At long last she located it in the center
of the dancing ring, whereupon she sambaed enthusiastically in
relief.

> "Have you seen my key?
> Where is my key, nigger?
> I've lost my key,
> The key of my trunk,
> Ai, my father will kill me
> If I don't find the key!

A golden key on a chain of silver!
Ai, dear St. Crispin!
A key of silver!
Where is that key, my Lord of Bomfim *?
I lost it here.
Ai, God in heaven,
What will become of me?

"Oi it's here!
All thanks to God!"

This dancer won the prize of money, and she thrust her belly at a young Negro while the berimbau moaned:

"I want, but I don't want—don't want!
I don't want, but I do—do want!"

We left, determined to find a boat to carry us to the mainland and a cool spot; and we did.

"This is the gold I spoke of, dona," Edison remarked pleasantly as we relaxed on the water. "The people are good, all of them are poets. The things we saw at the fair today go on continually in one fashion or another. They always sing and dance and play, and create colorful designs and never allow each other to feel lonely or poor. Perhaps candomblé doesn't seem so strange to you now."

"Everything seems strange to me," I replied ruefully, "especially as I learn more. But I'm beginning to take these things for granted, and that's a help. After a while I may sense the logic in them. I still have to remind myself that I'm watching reality, and not a marvelous performance."

"It's reality," Aydano assured me. "All these things matter intensely to our people. And we too would find life lacking without them."

"Is it more than entertainment for you?"

"For us it's life, it's the sweep and the poetry of life. When we see these things we know the people are good, and that no dictatorship can last. Only *they* will last."

Landing, we called a taxi which took us to a restaurant in

* Jesus.

my fashionable Rua Chile high in the Upper Town; and out of it a radio roared a samba from the last Carnival. It had won a prize then and was still being sung in all ballrooms and night clubs:

> "What is it that the Bahian has?
> What is it that the Bahian has?

> "A turban of silk she has,
> Earrings of gold she has,
> A necklace of gold she has,
> Scarf from Africa she has,
> And lacework blouse she has.
> A bracelet of gold she has,
> Stiff-starched skirts she has,
> Handsome sandals she has,
> And charm like nobody else!
> How she sways,
> Wonderfully!" *

I nodded to Aydano. "Others agree with you, it seems."

Aydano smiled faintly. "I feel as all Brazilians do. You say that only because you are not one of us. But some day you too will be a Brazilian!"

The radio took up another song, about the traywoman vending her African delicacies:

> "At ten o'clock at night
> In the lonesome street
> A black woman hawks
> Sounding this lament:

>> Ee—Eh abará!
>> Here is abará!

> "In her bowl
> There is fragrant sauce,
> Spices of Africa,
> And acarajé!

>> O acarajé ecô olalai o!
>> Come, see for yourselves, it is piping-hot!

* This song and the one following, translated from the Portuguese of Dorival Caymmi.

111

"All the world loves acarajé!
All the world loves acarajé!
But the trouble it takes to make!
All the world loves abará!
But no one cares to know the trouble it takes!

"At ten o'clock at night
In the lonesome street
The farther off the sound
The sadder its lament.

O acarajé ecô olalai o!"

XII

THE PEOPLE of candomblé had spawned a pamphleteer, whose name was Arcenio Cruz. The speech of these blacks often liquefied the sound of *l* into *r*, so possibly his name was rightly Alcenio. Edison and his friends teased me for speaking occasional words in the style I had learned from the Negroes, especially as I had come up from Rio with a pronounced carioca accent, which is considered swank. Yet I doubt whether the Bahia variations were merely Negro illiteracy since *l* and *r* get exchanged often in both Spanish and Portuguese, and between the two languages. For example, "branco"—Portuguese for "white"—corresponds to "blanco" in Spanish.

Arcenio was a Bohemian, a man who avoided drudgery but was not really lazy. A devout lover of candomblé, he played in his temple's orchestra, singing himself hoarse during the season, and beating the drums day and night without sleep and fortified only by alcohol. He loved life, which was what the gods meant to him, and he feared death—which chased the gods away from the temple—like a screaming nightmare. I have seen him run, eyes glazed, as soon as he heard the beating of the gourds, no matter how distant in the woods, which signified the arrival of Egungun, the Dead.

Still, there were dozens of other ogans as devout, as loyal and assiduous as he. He was unique because he produced a small, four-sheet paper, "The Clutch," in which he reported on the peccadilloes of his friends and acquaintances in a devastating vein which he called "sportive." But no matter how much his stories hurt, his avowed purpose was the pure one of maintaining "moral standards." So he said on August 28, 1938, in issue No. 545 and the thirteenth year of "The Clutch."

I met him one hot Sunday afternoon in November when leaving with Edison for the jungle suburb of São Caetano. At this time parties were being held in honor of Cosme and Damião, the twin saints who protected young children and brought prosperity and joy to their families. We had hired Amor's taxi to go to a celebration given by Mother Didi, and when we stepped into it in the plaza we found Arcenio. Edison exclaimed, surprised:

"Hello, Seu Arcenio! Haven't seen you for months! Have you escaped from the police?"

"Oh, yes, doctor, just a slight misunderstanding on the part of the law. Everything adjusted now." Arcenio spoke very fast, with eager amiableness, and a heavy lisp as though his tongue were caught in his teeth.

"Fine, fine! Now you're free to blackmail the poor folk in the woods again, eh?" Edison chuckled, recalling some of the things he had read. "Come along with us to see the children play, Seu Arcenio, since you are already here, and you can tell us the latest."

"Thank you, doctor. You honor me. I'm just an ignorant tramp and don't know anything; but I'll be happy to accompany you."

Arcenio sat up front with Amor, who was his friend, and watched him drive. It was exciting, for it took special skill and coolness to manage an automobile (this was a Chevrolet 1929 model) anywhere in the city of Bahia because of the extreme inclines, and the cobblestones that were so slippery and so poorly spaced that often the car could not ride over them but had to go on top of the streetcar tracks. Then there followed the likelihood of collision head on with a streetcar coming full speed around the corner. Amor maneuvered easily, merely smiling when the worst seemed about to happen. But it took a coolness beyond normal understanding to drive a car over the dreadful roads of the mato outside of the city, sticky and yielding and full of deep holes. Yet Amor did this smoothly. When we complimented him, our breath half gone from strain, he only smiled shyly.

Arcenio was totally different in temperament. He was noisy and talkative, and so amusing that he roused even Amor to laughter. He had an interesting appearance, being reddish bronze in color with the fine aquiline features and straight jaw often seen in West African sculpture. But his manners were not in the least distinguished. People called him "impertinent," for he forced his nose into everyone's affairs and freely publicized his information and opinions.

"Let's see that sheet of yours, Editor Arcenio," Edison proposed in a jolly mood. To me he explained, with a snicker: "This business keeps him in hush money when it does not land him in the arms of the police. 'The Clutch'—it's aptly named! But it's entertaining, he does a very interesting job."

Arcenio turned around to us in the rear seat (where gentry always sit) and handed us the latest copy. "I'm just an amateur, Master Edison," he said deprecatingly, but he well knew how remarkable it was for a man of his sort to handle literature.

The small paper had two columns on each sheet, and these were broken into short, widely spaced paragraphs easy to read. The first one stated:

On the Street of February Second there is a girl named X who carries on scandalously with several different men. Such conduct does not become a decent woman; and if she is not careful, her esteemed papa will become very angry.

From his seat in the front, Arcenio watched us in the chauffeur's mirror. Edison shook his head while he smiled. "Of course everyone knows whom you're talking about, it's such a little street. You'll ruin the girl's name, man!"

"No, no!" Arcenio was emphatic. "She's doing wrong,

young as she is, playing around with married men. I'm trying to save her, and above all I don't want her old man to go shamed into his grave. He doesn't realize the kind she is, but if she keeps up— Just think how the women will come round after her!"

"I suppose some 'father' is already commissioned to make up a bundle of bad magic to hurt her."

"I shouldn't wonder, but this warning may stop her in time. . . . The whole edition is bought out!" he stated proudly.

"Will you run off another?"

"Maybe."

"If the girl is like some cases I know," Edison told me with a twinkle, "she'll try to buy off the second edition before the ink gets on to it." He looked meaningfully at Arcenio, watching him in the mirror: "And if our dear friend here should be shown to have overreached himself—he may have to go into sudden hiding!"

Arcenio protested, sputtering and lisping.

Edison slapped him on the shoulder, "I'm just teasing, friend, you know it! The best of us have been obliged to go into sudden hiding. . . . Still, you *have* been missing lately?" He pointed questioningly to a paragraph on the first sheet:

For two weeks now THE CLUTCH has not circulated. As a simple precautionary measure, its director-owner sought a judiciary assurance of the free circulation of this newspaper, which is a critical, humorous, sportive, and newsy organ. This was granted by the most worthy Judge, who proclaimed that "there is no reason at all to feel any embarrassment."

"I was just resting," Arcenio answered with a mischievous look. "My liver has been bothering me."

"It couldn't have had anything to do with that charming brunette whose husband is a sailor?"

"I have not the honor and privilege of the lady's acquaintance."

"It couldn't be that you told a tale too hastily?"

"Dr. Edison! I? a man of honor!" And, no doubt to change the subject, he began to sing softly a fanciful song from the last year's Carnival:

"Oh, they announced and they guaranteed
That the world was going to end!
So my folks up there at home
Began to mourn, began to pray.
They promised that the sun would rise
Before the dawn, before the dawn,
So the folks up there in the hills
Left off their samba, left off their samba!

"I believed in this wild talk.
I thought that the world was going to end.
I busied myself with my farewells,
Hastened to make the most of the time.
I shook the hand of someone I had never met!
I kissed the lips of someone I did not know!
I danced samba in a bathing suit!
But this world—it did not end!

"I hailed a chap I'd always hated
And forgave him his ingratitude!
And celebrating the event
I spent a fortune on him!
Now I know that this chap travels
Telling tales that did not happen!
There's going to be disorder!
There's going to be confusion!
Because this world—it did not end!"

We all joined in the refrain, "Because this world, it did not end!"

Suddenly Arcenio signaled Amor to pull the car over to the side of the road, where a child stood. It was a dark little girl, waiting with her head bent shyly, holding a box with images of the day's patron saints. The box was daintily lined with a lace cloth, and the wooden figures of Cosme and Damião, lying upon it, were cloaked like medieval crusaders. A pottery figure of their mother lay watchfully beside them; she was St. Barbara,

116

who is also the African goddess Iansã. On their other side lay sprigs of the dainty plant called melindre (meaning "delicate"), which is a symbol of Our Lady of the Immaculate Conception who is also the African goddess Oxum who helped to rear the Twins.

"My daughter," Arcenio said gently, leaning out of the window, "have people given a lot of charity money to the Twins?"

"Yes, sir," she whispered. "A blessing?"

"Bring your box to me, and you'll get it." The men prepared pennies to drop into her hands. "How many days have you been carrying it around?"

"Three, and you're the third person today, so I'm through. Tomorrow we will play." She looked up excitedly.

"Tomorrow? You're going to eat a lot, eh? Wish some nice things for me, my child?"

"Oh, yes, sir! Goodbye!"

We had passed through the town and were in a densely populated section of the woods. The taxi, moving slowly, secured traction by driving on top of the iron streetcar tracks, between huge cotton trees looming on both sides; and when the car line ended we continued along an ungraded dirt road. Sometimes the road was level, and sometimes there were steep and difficult ascents; dust flew up so heavily, burning our eyes and mouths, that we had to shut the windows. Finally we reached our "street," which was a row of clay houses. When we inquired for Didi, whose right name was Justa, a man pointed to the end of the row and said, "There she lives, in that house built like a castle." We had to inquire several times more before we could actually identify the house. It was better built than the others, of frame in the front and clay in the back, and it was set on a slight elevation as befitted the residence of a Mother.

When we entered the front room children tumbled all over us in a torrent, laughing and calling. Finally they were directed to move in a circle around an old ragged black man who stood

117

in the far corner of the room. The man "pulled" the leading lines of a song:

> "Two! Two!
> My mother gives me to eat."

The children shouted a reply to the saintly Twins:

> "Two! Two!"

He continued:

> "My father gives me to drink."

They shouted, laughing:

	"Two! Two!"
He:	"Come here!"
They:	"Two! Two!"
He:	"I give you to eat!"
They:	"Two! Two!"
He:	"I give you to drink!"
They:	"Two! Two!"
He:	"I have a father Who gives me to eat! I have a mother Who gives me to drink!"
They:	"Two! Two!"
He:	"Whoever gives me to eat Also eats; Whoever gives me to drink Also drinks."
They:	"Two! Two!"

Dona Didi came from the kitchen to greet us, laughing. She had a pleasing, fair skin and a gay smile. She was wrapped in a large soiled apron because she had been cooking for the children's game of eating that was to follow, and her fine straight hair had fallen into her eyes.

"Come in! The house is yours," she called heartily. She pointed to a good-looking mulatto of middle age, dressed neatly in a modish gray suit, who stood in a corner as though he were out of things. "Here is my friend, Dr. Xavier. Keep him company, please! You know, Dr. Edison, he hates our African ways." And she laughed tolerantly as though her friend were a willful child.

Arcenio whispered to us: "Do you know, this man with a lawyer's degree takes care of Dona Didi! He pay for this house and all. He really likes her, though people say she belongs to all mankind."

The crowd of children bobbed around. Women came in to clear the center of the room; chairs and a bed were stood up against the walls. I noticed young women there, one of them pregnant and seeking a happy outcome through the kindness of the child saints; there were adolescent girls who dreamed of having children; and there were twenty-five youngsters ranging from three to ten years of age. Some old women brought in great platters, each piled high with a different delicacy. One platter held caruru (okra sliced and prepared in a special manner, seasoned with palm oil and pepper); another held roasted sliced peanuts; another had boiled chicken; another, vatapá—a tasty preparation of manioc flour seasoned with palm oil and pepper and mixed with boiled shrimps; others, still, held acarajé, large smoking yams, and sticks of sugar cane prepared for sucking.

One platter at a time was laid in the center of the floor on a cloth. Then the old man called, "Advance, children, upon the caruru!" The children dived for it with a howl, gobbling the food in lightning time, eating with mouth, hands, and arms. The more they ate, the more wealth the gods would bring to the household—both wealth and joy, Edison pointed out to me, as Arcenio nodded in smiling approval. No utensils were permitted. When the children picked themselves up from the floor, sighing and giggling with fullness and satisfaction, the vegetable was in their hair, eyes, and noses, and up their arms. Women brought in towels, but the children preferred to clean themselves by rubbing against Didi, the hostess; and thereby she partook of their happiness and plenty. Eating the peanuts was a cleaner performance. The waitresses by now had lost their punctilio, and when they brought in the chicken, they simply threw the pieces onto the floor and called to the children to

119

dive after them. I observed all this with the eyes of my amazed childhood, imagining the experience of having been asked—no, encouraged!—to run wild for the sake of everyone's good. The pace stepped up, boys and girls rubbing themselves off against any adult available, and against the walls, for the sheer pleasure of soiling things. The madder the shambles, the more food eaten, the more ecstatic the romping of the children, the more certain was the happy outcome everyone desired. Still, Didi observed some cautions, begging the children to be careful of her bed and of the clothes of the visitors.

When the food was all eaten, the old man stood up and called as he clapped his hands in march time:

"Have you eaten enough?"

The children shouted a gay response, crouched on the floor:

"Enough!"

He: "Have you drunk enough?"
They: "Enough!"
He: "Have you eaten enough?"
They: "Enough!"
He: "Drunk enough?"
They: "Enough!"

After seven exchanges of this sort, the old man breathed earnestly, "God be thanked!" For the offerings to the Twins had been accepted! Even Edison and Arcenio reflected the general satisfaction in their smiles. And then I too felt good, such was the contagion in the room.

Carefully the old man and an old woman picked up the cloth from the floor, soiled now by food. They called to the others to follow them as they danced around in a circle, counterclockwise, singing solemnly to the skipping samba beat:

"Thanks be to God,
O—O my God,
Praised be God,
O—O my God.

> "Praise be, O my God
> That Cosme and Damião have eaten!"

And they added in some African tongue:

> "Jambururû,
> "Aêrê-ê-ê,
> "O makuindê,
> "For St. Cosme has received."

The cloth was thus danced out of the room. The children and older girls remained, forming a ring and sambaing individually in the counterclockwise moving circle. The old man returned to his corner to direct the singing and dancing. Edison commented to me that the songs were of different sorts: some from the unorthodox caboclo tradition which Didi followed, having brought it from her home state of Pernambuco in the north; and some orthodox Yoruba. The adults were completely absorbed in the children's activities, and stood around laughing in delight.

As the dancing continued, women brought food in tiny doll dishes to an altar of Cosme and Damião in the room. There were also other altars, to twins of lesser prestige, and it seemed to me as though the people could not have enough of multiplying children. There were altars to the girl twins Carmen and Carmelita, to the boy twins Duval and Duvalterço, to the mixed twins Joanna and João. All were served food.

Now the excitement began to produce unusual effects. As she danced, the pregnant girl started to stagger and lose the beats. The others therefore sang to her:

> "O canoe!
> The canoe upset at the bottom of the sea!
> Canoe!
> Don't throw me into glory!"

She ran out and brought in a pole on which she tied a flag of white toweling, probably an emblem of her god Oxalá. The others ignored her, singing and wheeling around. The old man continually brought up new songs:

> "Cosme and Damião,
> Playful child
> Seized his little sword
> Went to play in the river.
>
> "Applaud, O siren of the sea.
> The Twins come, the Two come.
> They are going to play,
> They are coming to play,
> They are coming to wander and to play,
> The Two, the Two."

People watched the pregnant girl happily since her ecstatic actions augured well for her condition, and they said the spirits of the mischievous Twins had entered her head. In fact she sang while the others continued dancing:

> "Cosme and Damião,
> Your house is perfumed with carnations
>   and roses
> And with orange blossoms.
>
> "Cosme and Damião,
> Your fortune has arrived at the Fortress of
>   the Sea.
> St. Barbara sent it."

She danced very fast now, and the others sang to her. She called to them as she danced, and the children answered.

She:	"Look! Look there!"
They:	"Twins, Two."
She:	"Look there, in the country!"
They:	"Twins, Two."

Then the girl gave the embigada to an old woman while the giddy ring of youngsters whirled about them. The old woman, who danced with her eyes closed as though in a trance, passed her turn to a young mother of twenty-four, who already had an eleven-year-old son. The old man sang while the children wheeled madly:

> "White water,*
> Let me be!
> White drink,
> Let me be!"

The ring split into two, boys on the outside and girls on the inside, moving continually. Suddenly one excited little boy yipped out, all unawares, the cry of the great Yoruba god Xangô when he descends into someone:

> "Ka-a-a-biesi-i-i-le!"

The others laughed, to the poor child's bewilderment, and they slowed down to a skip:

> "I bought a tambourine
> For five and a half cents!
> I bought a tambourine for
> Five and a half cents!

> "So—

> "I am going to see Juliana!
> Ju-li-ana!"

And still slower, out of their own happiness, they sang pityingly:

> "Look at the bird who will not stir his head,
>   Look at the raven!
> Look at the bird who does not sing in a cage,
>   Look at the raven!"

They danced in a file through the kitchen and out the back door of the house, circling the grounds singing and dancing, giggling and laughing, casting about the blessings of the Twins.

Dona Didi now invited us to eat. She had freshened herself and changed to a gay Japanese kimono; she had combed her fine hair and powdered her pretty face. Leading us to the kitchen,

* Sugar rum.

she stopped at a little room to show her private altars for the Catholic Twins and for the Yoruba Do'u and Alabá.

"Do you know what they are, my father?" she asked Edison smiling. "Do'u is the child who is born third in triplets, or who is born normally after twins. Alabá is the child who comes after Do'u. And I have other twins here—Crispin and Crispiniano, and Crispina and Crispiniana. So I have plenty of happiness around me!"

I was touched by her genuine feeling. I looked at Cosme and Damião in the center of the throng of child deities, smiling boys standing side by side, shouldering broad daggers.

"Some old folks say they are brothers born of the same mother," Didi remarked. "Others say they are friends who swore eternal loyalty in blood. But it doesn't matter because they love each other like brothers." She looked fondly at a small slim candle burning before them, surrounded by tiny jugs of water, and by tiny bowls, cups, and saucers of food, and by tiny vases filled with flowers. A faint pungency of incense hovered over the corner.

Arcenio interrupted her hesitantly. "I'd like to make a wish, dona."

"Go ahead, my son," she urged him heartily. "The saints accompany it."

"Amen," he responded, moving close to whisper to the upstreaming flame.

"And you, my lady," Didi proposed to me. "Won't you wish? The house is yours."

So I wished silently for good things.

Waiting in the kitchen doorway for us was a black woman in Bahian dress—a Creole they called her—and she turned to direct four others, also in billowing skirts, to place the food on the table. The room was not large enough to hold us all; the floor was unpaved and hilly; the darkness was relieved uncertainly by candles. People outside crowded at the windows to see what was going on. More came in, and children pressed against us, staring with great shining eyes, and asking in small voices for a blessing when prompted by their elders.

"Do you like the lady?" a woman asked her tiny daughter Julieta, whose big eyes were glued on me.

The baby nodded.

"Julieta likes her!" the mother exclaimed laughing, to the bystanders. "Do you like her dress, Eta?"

The baby nodded again.

"She likes the white lady's dress!" the mother announced again. "And I suppose she likes her shoes and silk stockings! Do you think the lady is pretty, my daughter?"

"She's pretty," the little voice piped, "and she's white, white like a sheet. That's why she talks gringa!"

"That's why she talks gringa!" the women agreed, laughing.

"Let's eat and drink," Didi proposed, and I followed the others to a bench at the table which was placed against a wall. "A toast to Cosme and Damião," she called gaily, "in good muscatel that Dr. Xavier brought!"

The people watched us as though it were a marvelous show.

Food was set on the bare wood table in huge platters, the candomblé food of caruru, farofa (toasted manioc flour), feijoada (boiled black beans cooked with dried beef onto which the farofa was poured), boiled chicken, abará, roasted almonds and earthnuts, hard-boiled eggs, fried bananas, millet cooked with coconut milk and sugar, and vatapá. Truly, a groaning table. My appetite could not match that of the others, who ate enormous portions, crouching low over the plates as they wielded their cutlery. To me, this excellent food was not enjoyable, so strange was its cooking and seasoning. It was rich food too, especially on a hot night. But the others ate with gusto, and showed their appreciation by maintaining total silence. At the end came demi-tasses of bitter black coffee, heavily sweetened. Only after we had finished and left the table did the serving women sit down to eat; and they mopped up their plates with their fingers, which they then sucked clean, rinsing their hands finally in a general water dish. Seeing my startled expression, Arcenio grinned; and Edison explained, in the labored English he used for confidential remarks, that this was the way for the temple people to eat.

125

I sat down by the wall, and immediately a little girl of three jumped into my lap. She was a rachitic child, with a blown stomach and fragile protruding bones; her skin seemed to give off rapid chills and fevers. She had lovely eyes, large and shadowed like those of invalids, and fine luxuriant hair. She talked clearly, but at sudden intervals would cry so that her sister, not more than five years of age, would lean over from Edison's neighboring lap to hug and soothe her. They were precocious and charming, and very pathetic.

The mother pulled over a chair and watched. She was a picture of the children tall and grown up, with her blown belly exaggerated by the Bahian dress and posture. To tease the little one, she demanded, "Is the lady a relative of yours?"

"Yes," answered the baby.

"Well!" exclaimed the mother in mock despair, looking round the room and spreading her hands in a hopeless gesture. "All white people are her relatives! I'm the only black one in the family!"

The father approached now, a dark young man, and he asked his older daughter to accompany him home.

"No, sir, I will not!" she retorted. "Because you, sir, drink rum!"

The astonished father started. Edison, shocked for him, came over and coaxed the child to say that she was only teasing because this was the holiday of the Twins.

"But I was not teasing!" she protested, and scampered out of the room.

"This is the day of the children," Arcenio laughed. "And wouldn't it be fine if we could have such a day too?"

It was time to leave, and the people melted out of the house into the woods.

"God go with you!" Didi called cheerily. "I thank you for coming to honor my Twins! God go with you!"

Arcenio led us toward the two-room wooden shack where he had agreed to wait for Amor, the chauffeur. It was nearly nine o'clock. The low-hanging sky was black and clear, and spotted with stars that somehow gave no light. Suddenly the white moon appeared, streaming light over the trees. Girls' voices rose, singing songs of Twins to the accompaniment of a guitar. There was gentle laughter, and once I saw women in flowing skirts cross the path of moonlight.

"On nights like these, they save precious candlelight," Edison remarked.

As we walked on, silent, we heard a howl, and a whining and hiccoughing. Edison thought it was a dog or fox moaning at the moon; I thought it was a woman possessed by some spirit; and Arcenio thought it was a woman who had drunk too much rum. Then we heard the muffled sound of drumming on a large gourd, and the hushed singing of candomblé songs, quiet as lullabies.

"They sing to forget their sadness," Edison commented. "The sadness of our nights! . . . It is even worse in the interior, where houses are two hundred miles apart. The moon shines over the tableland, empty of moving things, and suddenly a horseman appears in the distance."

We reached the shack and went to the rear to look for the key, since the front door was locked. We found a tiny hut sheltering the fetish stone of Exu, the servant of Ogum, god of the roadways. Arcenio got on his knees to point out the lighted candle burning inside, and the popcorn and almonds tossed around on the ground, the remains of a recent sacrifice to that Exu who protected the empty house.

"Compadre," he called softly to the spirit of the stone, crouching to see it, and addressing it as though it were the godfather of his child.

An old blind man stumbled past a tree. "Who's there?" he growled.

"Arcenio, Seu Eliseo."

"All right. I thought some stranger was messing around."

Arcenio straightened up and brushed his trousers. "A man must never forget the saints, dona," he said, half teasing. "If you keep Cosme and Damião in good humor, remembering them

127

with food every now and then, you won't fall off a streetcar, you won't break a leg, your marriage will be happy, you'll have lots of children, and you'll make money."

I laughed. "It's not that I doubt you, Seu Arcenio, but I've never had luck in my life."

"You Americans!" Arcenio waved me off unbelievingly. "But do as I say, and you'll see— Well, friends, come into the house, and I'll tell you a true story about it."

We found the key on the lintel above the doorway after flashing a searchlight that showed up nests and flying things. The interior was neat, but blanketed in dust, as though it had not been used in a long while. The large African drum called "rumpí," used in temple rites, stood in a corner, its head covered respectfully with a towel. On the walls were colorful calendars depicting poetic savage Indians, and lush blonde women in the tights of cancan days.

We gathered around a rough wooden table in the middle of the room, Arcenio fumbling till he found a kerosene lamp. He leaned on the table to light it, his face brightening now and then from the flame; and soon he began to talk with relish, glancing around and smiling.

"This Johnny," he said, "wanted to get married, and he needed money. He had always been poor, and he did not see how he was to arrange matters. One day Cosme and Damião came to his door in a lace-covered box carried by a child who begged charity. He gave the few cents he had, and made his wish to the Twins. Not long after, he got a job as assistant to a table in a gambling house, and the Twins came to him and told him how to lay his bets. He was to play always on the 'animal' 410, and he must never change. The Twins were loyal to him, and he won. Then he married, and his wife was blessed with children. Things went well indeed. He became a banker in the house, and he gained money and fame by always betting on 410. Other people bet with him and also won.

"He had however the obligation to the saints, and so every year he made a great caruru of St. Cosme to feed the children of the neighborhood. As a result his house was full of contos!

"In the meantime his daughters were growing up and going to school, where they learned to feel ashamed of the carurú. 'Father,' they cried, 'this thing is for ignorant blacks only! We're respectable people now!' So their father tried to please them, and he gave the carurú less often, until finally one year he failed to give any at all. Then he announced that he could no longer bet on his lucky 'animal.' The others in the gambling house continued as before, however; they bet against him on his own 410; they won, and he had to pay them off. One night he paid and paid until he was left bankrupt. He went home alone; and people knew he was desperate, so they followed him. Well, they found him—dead. His own family had not known that he had taken poison.

"That was the work of the gentle Twins, my friends. They give generously when you are good to them. And they take away when you ignore them. His daughters had grown too proud, Dona Ruth. Do you know about this in your gringo country?"

XIII

I SELDOM saw the American colony, largely because I was too busy. The immense Negro population was spread all over Bahia, and candomblé activities were unceasing. The effort to understand this life, through the uncertain means of a foreign language, took all my attention. Similar experience with American Indians had taught me that it was advisable to immerse myself wholly in their lives for a time, so that I might get to think and feel like them.

Passing from Negro Bahia, or any part of Portuguese-speaking Bahia, to the American colony meant passing from one extreme to another. For example, I learned that the American ladies, including the wife of the consul and the wife of the Singer sewing machine agent, scorned me for going around with a colored man (his distinctive reputation was secondary.) It went only a little further in Rio, where a Brazilian friend of mine told me in great distress that her American husband had forbidden her to associate with me because I was a "nigger lover." I decided that I could not afford to waste myself in anger. Also, the American colony was afraid of candomblé, spinning wild tales of poisoning, murder, and sex orgies. I who practically lived in the temples, and found well disciplined men and women, could only throw up my hands. I tried to explain that at worst the standards of the blacks were different from those of the Americans; but judiciousness was not what they wanted.

And the Bahians did not like my compatriots. They questioned the behavior of the women, who dressed carelessly and revealingly, drank considerably, and not only flirted in public but talked freely about their affairs of the heart. They condemned the men because they drank even more, and sometimes allowed themselves to fall into scandalous involvements with women. They were harsh in their judgment because they were disappointed, since the Americans who behaved worst in their opinion had at first appealed to them most, with their young charming faces, and their bearing of "Hollywood movie stars." The missionaries were immune from such criticism, and even sympathized with it, but there were only one or two missionary couples.

My regular contact with the American world was through the consul's first secretary, a man named Jorge. He took care of my mail, a tremendously important detail to an American in another land. But our friendship grew through many kind services he rendered me in other ways. Upon my arrival in Bahia, the consul had generously suggested that Senhor Jorge conduct me about the city when he was not pressed by office duties. This Jorge had done willingly, though with the earnest fidgetiness of a maiden aunt.

I think Jorge's inner nature was different because I often detected a sparkle in his eye, and Bahians who knew told me later that he could get drunk at Carnival time as few men did. Possibly at other times also. Jorge himself told me that two fine girls had broken engagements to marry him because of his hilarity at Carnival. Or else, he had broken them because of new perspectives that came to him then. When I met him, he was engaged again—one of those betrothals that hang fire for years, presumably from lack of funds. Jorge was not well recompensed by our government.

He was in his late thirties, a tall slight man with thinning red hair and large brown eyes in a small, fair aquiline face. He was extremely neat and clean, with a fragrance of toilet water on his white linen clothes. His only Brazilian features were his small hands (thin and cold) and his small feet—which he admired, pointing out pityingly that my feet were probably larger than his. The son of an English mother and a Brazilian father of German parentage, he looked like some of the Englishmen seen in eighteenth and nineteenth century paintings wearing a tall cravat.

Although not well educated, Jorge spoke perfect American English, which he had picked up during years of employment in the American consulate. He was not especially proud of it, either because he was too loyal to his own language or because he had no immoderate esteem for Americans. He had the intense local pride of the Latin who has never left his home town. I think he feared the thought of going even to Rio, though he said that was a dream to be fulfilled on his long postponed honeymoon. He was a man who cared to be proper, and he was poor.

Jorge knew that, as I had come to study Negro life, I wanted intensely to see a candomblé. This was before I met Edison, and I asked him to escort me. He refused—the only time he ever refused me anything:

"Never ask me that," he said with quiet intentness, shaking his head a little. "I hate to refuse you, but I'll never go. It's for ignorant people, if you'll forgive me. If you ever see white people there, it is not simply as onlookers, believe me, but because they believe in it."

"Well, what's it like?" I asked, a little exasperated.

"It's superstition, black magic. They are supposed to murder people and to put poison in food, for a price! They hypnotize their victims. You can find some of their paraphernalia at the State Museum of History—the police captured it on raids. I don't know much about it, but I do know it's dangerous.

"The 'Estado da Bahia' carries long articles on the subject. The blacks are always holding secret meetings, killing animals, dancing, and beating drums in the jungles in the dead of night. . . . We'll never get anywhere as a nation until the temples are gone! Those people are all over! Wherever you go, you meet somebody who takes part in candomblé, or who believes in it. Even the police believe in it."

The nearest he would bring me to candomblé was to the pawnshops. These were large impressive places displaying, among other things, magnificent ornaments from the days of slavery. They had belonged to the colored priestesses, some freed and some slave, bought with money they had earned in different ways allowed by the masters. There were bracelets three to four inches in width, worked or cast in gold or silver and ornamented with medallions of metal or of precious stones, bearing the head of some African deity. Some of these were worth a small fortune. Another stunning ornament was made of heavy silver and consisted of miniature fruits, ships, houses, silverware—anything representing value; it was worn suspended from the belt and was a cult charm for wealth and fertility, the pawnbroker believed.

"If you want to know more," Jorge offered, "let us visit Padre Barbosa, the vicar of the Church of Our Lady of Conception of the Beach. He is well informed. Candomblé women visit his church and hold ceremonies, and they perform too in the market place in front of his church. . . . And he is a radical. He meets with the revolutionary students, and speaks to them."

So we made contact with the padre, to whom also I had letters of introduction. I met Jorge at eight o'clock one morning at the consulate in the Lower City, and we walked the few blocks to the church. It stood on the beach, white and cool like a dream in the hot light, apparently remote from the docks and warehouses with their bitter smells of cacao and hides. We walked up the broad marble stairs to the loggia, and then went inside the lofty hallway to see the father bless women and children.

He was a short square man of middle age, reddish in color, with small features; and despite the heat he wore his black serge habit.

"Good morning," I said awkwardly, not knowing how to proceed.

"Come into my office," the vicar proposed energetically. He led us into a high-ceilinged, rhombus-shaped room, seated us around his desk, and then said with warmth and courtesy: "So you have come all the way from the United States! . . . How I would like to see my friends there!"

"Here are letters from them," I answered.

He glanced over the letters with a smile.

"So you are interested in the Negroes! . . . I must show you some old records of this church." He pulled out a drawer of the huge desk and extracted an aged memorandum pad with long pages of bookkeeping size, which he flipped with wetted forefinger and absorbed gaze. "This contains documents dating from the erection of the building sometime after 1736. Here," he said, bringing the pad around to me, "is a record dating from 1750: 'Brotherhood of Our Lady of Conception of the Beach.' Have you heard of it?"

"Is it similar to the Brotherhood of Our Lady of the Rosary of Rio?"

"The same sort of thing," he nodded. "A mutual benefit organization of free blacks, attached to the church. It was for men only. These records are careful statements of membership dues and of sick and death benefits. The brotherhoods are weaker now because the blacks haven't had much of an income since emancipation!"

I tried to tell him how impressed I was with the colorfulness and continuity of Bahia's history. He glowed at my appreciation and affirmed:

"That is so. Brazil has glories. . . . Wouldn't you like to see the church now, before I go on my calls?"

Jorge, who had been listening patiently, offered to show me

133

the nave. The three of us then went into the immensely high, cool chamber where a few desultory worshipers bobbed up and down making obeisances.

"Not so long ago, masters and slaves worshiped together," Padre Barbosa reflected, "and worship was more ecstatic then than now. We were still under the mystical influences of the Middle Ages. People had visions and heard celestial voices. They danced inside the church at Carnival, and they were not always sober when they danced. But they were not supposed to be in the mood of everyday life," he explained in his vigorous manner; "they were supposed to have been lifted out of themselves. And sometimes I think it was best for them to carouse under the motherly eye of the Church, rather than outside."

"I have heard, father, that candomblé used to be performed within the church."

"Yes," he answered me matter-of-factly. "They are devout Catholics, never forget that."

We walked around the nave, following the walls while the vicar pointed out the details carefully. "You have nothing so ancient in your country, eh?" he smiled, pleased over his country's advantage.

"I doubt it. . . . Who is this saint, father?"

It was a Negroid figure in the attire of a Franciscan monk, a hemp band around his temples, a deep cowl on his shoulders, a rope tied about his waist, sandals on his bare feet, tenderly watching the child Jesus sprawled in his arms.

"That is St. Benedict."

"Oh, the Negro saint!"

"He was not a Negro," the padre said emphatically. "He was bronzed and came from North Africa. He was a Moor. He was a sinner, a ruffian, a drunkard, a thief, maybe a murderer. But his soul was saved, and he was sanctified."

"He reminds me of St. Dominic in the United States, and saints like him in the Caribbean islands."

"Very likely. You'll find St. Benedict in all Brazilian churches. . . . Let us arrange a time for visiting other churches in Bahia."

This suggestion appealed to Jorge, although he had no interest in religion and no confidence in priests. He felt that women were improperly fascinated by priests, and tried to prevent his fiancé from going to her confessions. So now, as we left the vicar, he offered to guide me around the eighty churches in the vicinity, those grand gilded edifices of the time when Bahia was queen of the Northeast, viceregal capital of the Empire, opulent in sugar, slaves, and horses, dazzling the eyes of visiting foreigners who recorded the sights in classical paintings and writings. There were churches of different monastic orders within a few blocks of one another, as well as the religious houses of the orders, and they had been built by workmen imported from Portugal, employing materials imported from Europe. I had no great enthusiasm about the churches, being much more interested in the people, but I agreed.

We rode in streetcars up hill and down dale, all over the sprawling city. Always there was music in the air: at five in the morning, troops of people moving to work in singing bands; at ten at night, lone, chanting contralto voices of black venders; in the hot afternoon hours, radios blaring popular songs. There was continuous movement in the streets, especially in an old section called the Descent of the Shoemakers, which was a lower-class shopping district, and in the business section where the brokerage houses and the wharves were located. The high points of the city were crowned by old churches and monasteries, by new skyscrapers, and by the fine homes of wealthy planters and businessmen. The lower parts of the city were occupied by tenement hovels and, at the outskirts, miserable baked-mud huts that housed the poor people—factory workers, laundresses, peddlers, stevedores, prostitutes. When the car reached the edge of the forest, it raced along a shelf of land, swaying with its speed and the sharpness of the curve, and we looked down over a sheer drop that was frightening. There below, among stunted trees and rank grass and everything fallen, stood a village of wickerworked earthen cabins of the poor—entirely at the mercy of heavy rains that washed away the walls of dwellings, loosened the hillside above, and sent clods of mud storming below. Spread on top of the tall grass which yielded elastically, we saw the white wash that the women had just soaped and left in the sun to bleach.

So we visited the enormously rich churches, simple and lovely in their outside whiteness, graced by fine spires and grille-work, rather alarming in their tall dark interiors with the larger-than-life-size figures of tortured saints. I remember best the Church of St. Francis of Assisi, built in 1710, because the interior was done entirely in gold plate, and it was only a stone's throw from Menininha's town house.

It was impossible to visit the Cathedral and the more popular churches without passing through the slum districts, and this was a cause of shame to Jorge. Not on account of the indecent hopeless poverty, but because I as a lady walked there. "My fiancée would never come here," he observed with his air suggesting that the world was a neat checkerboard where everyone had a correct place. "Any Brazilian woman would be ashamed to walk here!" He hastened to add that this was an expression of his admiration, but I rather think that it vented his disapproval of Americans. He himself hated to walk there, since gentlemen never exerted themselves physically. To carry even a light bundle was beneath our social position.

Afterwards we went into difficult quarters by taxi. So it happened that when we returned to Padre Barbosa's church, we had to drive down the Hill of Our Lady of Conception because this was devoted to those desperate ladies "of the world" whose fee is the lowest in the state of Bahia. No woman may walk down this hill (except during Carnival!), and few respectable men care to. The dwellings are old, old ones, really caves cut out of the stony side of the hill. I saw women in the doorways, bodies exposed, hair hanging, saying words which I am told were not for repetition. Later we wandered by mistake into a better quarter where the prostitutes charged much more and lived in charming little houses, segregated by nationality for the convenience of customers. One woman called vehemently to Jorge, "Is that your wife?"

"Of course not!" he replied indignantly.

I should never have disturbed the police if I had continued sightseeing with Jorge; but on the other hand I should have learned nothing about the blacks, who were the poor and the ignorant and therefore were taboo to ladies. But Jorge treated me most graciously, especially in view of the fact that he disapproved of all my purposes; and when he introduced me to his fiancée, a lovely brunette, I knew that he had confidence in my essential respectability.

He even helped me select my hotel room, and this must have hurt him, not only because the connotations were wicked but also because he could afford to live only in a boarding house. We met less often after that.

It is impossible to exist in Bahia without a personal laundress, and so I turned to the American colony for help. Rose, wife of an American businessman, was an efficient housekeeper in her modest way, and I reasoned that she would know a clean laundress. So I visited her one Sunday morning.

I liked her because she was the only hearty American woman I knew there. One felt that she found it good to be alive. She was a typical suburban matron from a Southern state, an aged young woman of forty-seven or so. She was extremely good-looking in a classical way, with the head of Columbia on a tall fine figure. She wore her dark hair swept in curls to the top of her head, and her clear blue eyes were always echoed in her fashionable dress.

"Hello!" she called out in a husky voice when I came, and smiled warmly. "My husband is off to golf with his friend Tom, but they're returning later. Let's sit and chin."

She talked endlessly, everybody in the colony complained; but she was never malicious, though she knew all the gossip. On this morning she told me that her husband was half deaf, which was why she had to shout, and that the two were very much in love. They had not married until their forties though they were cousins, acquainted all their lives, having come from the same state. And of course she had a laundress for me, a beautiful little cabrocha (a Negro mixed with Indian and probably some white blood).

137

Then the bell rang, and Tom's wife walked into the darkened little room where we sat on stiff blackwood chairs of the style Brazilians call John VI. Ann was fifteen years younger than Rose, with glorious red hair, a healthy freckled skin, and neat features; but, unlike most people from Texas, she had no spirit and no interests. She greeted us listlessly, and our conversation was blocked. As I learned later, Ann was consumed by a morbid and self-destructive jealousy of her husband—a restless, disgruntled young businessman from Oklahoma—fancying that his attentions were engaged by the women of their acquaintance.

Finally the two husbands bounced in, exhilarated from golf. Still there was nothing to talk about. Yes, there was some gossip. It was about a young harebrained matron whom they all seemed to like, and they referred admiringly to her aptitude in Portuguese. She should have been present today but, Tom said with enjoyment, was sulking over an insult he had tossed at her in jest.

As we separated, Ann invited me casually: "Come over to the house this evening. We're having a party."

"I'll call for you," her husband offered.

"Or we'll send someone," Ann added. "Wear a long dress."

At eight o'clock Tom called for me in the car of a young Bahian man-about-town named Paulo. Paulo came of a wealthy family prominent in society, and his father had brought the first automobile into Bahia (I saw its picture later). He was pure white, a descendant of recent French stock, and he was crazy about Americans, especially the young matron discussed in the morning. He insisted upon talking English, which was very trying for us because, in addition to faulty grammar, he had a strong accent and lisped and stuttered. He told me that he planned to visit New York for the World's Fair and negotiate some engineering contracts. I imagine he did not realize the negligible importance of the Americans with whom he was running around, because he lived champagne-lit with joy over the entrées he believed they would arrange for him in the United States. Extremely generous, he put himself, his car, and his means at the disposal of his "ianque" friends. He spoke highest praise of his friends when he said, "They look like movie actors." Gossip described Paulo as a great lover, and this was the solid achievement of his twenty-six years.

Paulo put me in the rear seat of his big black car, and he drove careening by a widely circuitous route to Tom's house. This was a large white mansion dating from the time when planters moved in from their fazendas to the city. We entered the vast rooms, sparsely furnished with pieces brought from the United States. Electric lights blazed, and lovely ladies and their gentlemen strolled around. I was told later that this was the gay set of Americans, with their English and Bahian friends, who drank, played cards, and flirted heavily.

I was introduced to the people as they were dancing, and then someone swung me off in a dance. People ogled one another, made a great show of flirting, and jockeyed with heavy witticisms, carried one another off into remote rooms, returned at intervals laughing madly. Yet they seemed tired, and they made me feel awkward. They talked continually about their hangovers, about the bestial boredom of the place, about the candomblés their servants attended, and which they had a faint curiosity to witness also.

"The women, you know," said one gentleman with heavy overtones of meaning, "they dance into a frenzy, then strip themselves naked in the woods and dance some more. Dr. Rudel has seen them at dawn around his place, passed out."

"Ruth came here to study that," Tom interrupted, smiling.

The others looked at me. "Well, how interesting!" the women said. "You must tell us about it. We would like to go with you."

Then an Englishman asked me to dance to the victrola record which he set spinning. He was one of the handsomest men I have ever seen, with a salty humor. He kept a strong sunburn, a clear gray eye, an immaculately brushed head of iron-black hair, a fine figure, becoming clothes. As soon as he returned me to a chair Rose came over to tell me about him. She swore that he and his wife were unhappy together. The wife, she said, used to go out after amours, but then had suddenly settled down to have a baby which had come a few months before. I looked at the wife curiously. She was not beautiful and even had a faintly surly expression; but later, when she invited me for dinner, I found her pleasing, and delighted in her charming London speech. At home they were gay and friendly. At parties they appeared cynical, and hopelessness floated out like mist from their smart patter. The woman wanted another life, but there seemed to be no way out because the husband was well placed here with a huge English concern. He had been promoted steadily, though slowly, from one tiny hole to another larger one. Bahia should not have seemed bad to them but they said that they lived through one four-year period after another while their unused leaves accumulated until they could spend four months in England. They spoke as though they considered themselves uprooted and homeless, and they communicated this mood to the Americans.

I remember a contrary attitude expressed by a young Englishman I met at about that time in Bahia. He was in his late twenties, well educated, intelligent, and of good presence, and he was employed at a picayune salary as clerk in an English bank. "Why do you remain?" I asked. "If your folks are in London, why not go back there?"

From his six feet three inches of bony blond height he smiled down at me, and in his deep gentle speech he said: "The world is crowded. England has little place for young striving men. We must scatter into the undeveloped parts of the world."

"But Bahia!" I protested. "Living here for years at fifteen dollars a month, losing your vitality, forgetting your training . . ."

He bore with me smilingly, and I suppose he had gone through all this before in his own mind. "I was born in Brazil," he went on. "It's a sort of a home, and one must have patience."

The other couple of interest at the party were Brazilians, but they fitted well into the tense spirit of the English-speaking. Rose told me about them also. Actually only the husband was Brazilian-born. He was dramatic in appearance, a tall and handsome native of a northeastern state, and he had inherited some means. Now in early middle age, he had been educated in Methodist missionary schools of Brazil and a Methodist college in Texas. He spoke excellent English, and this helped him develop a profitable business as agent for various American interests.

His wife, Sylvia, was quicksilver. She was not pretty, with her thin small body and prominent brown eyes in a thin brown face, but she was intense and sophisticated. Of Jewish origin, born in Paris, raised in Buenos Aires in wealthy surroundings made possible by her father's flourishing diamond business, she had many accomplishments. She could dance, and play the piano, and sing, and exchange badinage, and these had caused her husband to fall desperately in love with her when she was eighteen. They had married after a whirlwind courtship, and now that she was thirty-four, the mother of a son and daughter, he had grown extremely jealous. This interested the American colony greatly, though they were puzzled by the depth of the husband's emotion.

Sylvia, with her Latin mind, played the game. She told me later, in the cool comfort of her white stone mansion by the sea, that she lived in daily fear of her husband's suspicions; only in his absence did she trill a few notes to herself, and trip a few steps. But I noticed some things at this party and at one or two others. She drank a little wine and sat down at the grand piano in the roomful of people crying for gayety, and she played in such a way that all the men gathered around stirred by feelings of courtship. Only her husband stayed apart. Sylvia told me that after such an evening he would drop the bland smiling face he had for the world, and storm in the privacy of their room. He threatened divorce so often that it even entered her speech and she would say to me, "Oh, I can't go sailing with you to that island [or meet you for tea, or go for a walk, or do anything outside the home] though I would love to! My husband would divorce me!" She managed her home efficiently, and at the same time had heart trouble and migraine which reassured her husband. A robust wife is not charming and probably is not faithful.

When I told Edison these things he was amazed. He had

thought people in the American world had so much to live for, and were so "courageous." Later, an American reporter came through Bahia, and so did a distinguished American painter of ivory miniatures, and both of them decided early, as I did, to turn their backs on the colony and refresh themselves with the full living of the Negroes.

XIV

I CAME to know Zézé, the common-law wife of Manoel Amor, quite well. She always referred to herself as Zézé of Iansã, and not as Mrs. da Silva, to show that she "belonged" to her goddess and not to Manoel. All the priestesses did that, and it reflected their personal independence. To this day I cannot recall the family names of even the greatest of the mothers like Pulcheria, Maximiana, Flaviana, Sabina, and Menininha. Aninha's family name is known—Eugenia Ana dos Santos—because news reporters went after it; but the knowledge really reflects their emphasis rather than hers.

Zézé was a buxom creature in her middle or late twenties. Edison considered her beautiful, and his was the common opinion. Certainly Zézé had been led to expect such compliments because when she occasionally visited me in my hotel and ate with me in the dining room, she would look around and say with a surly look of outraged virtue: "That head waiter is after me. All these white men are. You watch that one come up and talk to me. I could make a lot of money if I wanted to. But I condescended to live with Amor." And in fact the head waiter would come up and with exaggerated bows talk to her in his Germanic Portuguese.

She was a light coffee-color with small Caucasian features and wavy black braids of hair. These, with her good-looking teeth and plump body, made up her beauty. It was of a sort so foreign to my own standards that I could form no judgment of it. But I used to wonder about the mixture of bloods it suggested, especially as her mother and sisters appeared even more

Caucasian in type but referred to themselves as "Indian." It was her "Indian beauty" that led people to remark that she had "condescended" to Amor, who, poor fellow, was black as shoe leather. Actually she had done very well because Amor's regular wage took care not only of her but also of her mother and sisters when necessary. I would say she had driven a hard bargain, and I am sure she knew it.

She valued money, and that was how our association began. Amor had invited Edison and me to his home near Gantois temple, and while there I said that I would like to study candomblé systematically with a priestess, and that I would pay well. Amor looked at Zézé, who with her mannerism of "condescending" offered to take the job. She explained that it would have to be done secretly since it was against the candomblé rules to give information to outsiders, and that I would have to pretend to everyone that it was only friendship between us. So for months I went several times a week to Zézé's little mud house—built for this union by Amor—and talked with her about everything conceivable.

She was extremely conscientious, but bored; however, she was so intelligent that I always learned a great deal, and I have reason to believe that she was accurate. I think the appearance of boredom came from her guilt. She really felt that she should not be revealing temple matters, and she was afraid of Menininha. On the other hand, Amor was glad of this opportunity of securing some revenge on the whole institution of priestesses, especially as it was being done without Menininha's direct knowledge, and for cash.

I now began to understand Amor's jealous resentment of Zézé's career. They would exchange harsh and scolding remarks, she would comment on the women we knew, men would drop in at the house and tease, Edison would sometimes say illuminating things—and after a while these bits made up a story.

The story was strange, and although it took place before my very eyes, unfolding all the time that I was in Bahia, I was blind to it for a long time. From Amor's point of view, it could be said that the cults operated primarily for the purpose of displaying the women at their best and most exciting. They danced in public in the most striking stage setting available in all Brazil, and when they became possessed by a god, they really started to gild the lily. They were arrayed then in dramatic and daring costumes, and danced and embraced and talked as flamboyantly as they chose. People came from hundreds of miles around to watch the wonderful shows produced during the season by such temples as Gantois and Engenho Velho. Nothing in Rio could compare with it.

Consequently the temple women had no lack of male admirers. In fact, as Zézé put it self-righteously, it was a duty of the men to look on and admire. Black or white, poor man or aristocrat, he was expected to applaud. It was taken for granted that men would support the priesthoods in material ways: "O gente!" Zézé would exclaim at my obtuseness. "I declare! Of course, they give! They're glad to give. They know the gods will help them." And it was almost as though she had eyes at the back of her neck, the way she would hunch and wait for some reaction from Amor, who sat or dozed behind her, out-of-doors on a cool cement block.

Edison told me that it was also assumed that the men would make love to the women. Evidently Amor knew a great deal about this aspect of things, since students at the Medical School, where he was employed, often persuaded him to make arrangements for them. They found it more exciting to go to a priestess than to a commercial prostitute in a "castelo," because the priestess was a definite personality, and in her special way a "respectable woman." There was always the chance that she would not accept the lover, a risk that would never be run with a prostitute. And often she would not accept any money, although the go-between did. Edison said that some of the temples made quite a practice of this, not so much the conventional and reputable ones as the newer ones that had male priests. The male priests then used their female associates as decoys, though the women might not be aware of it.

This easy love-making is usual in Bahia, and it is considered brutish, and not virtuous, to refuse it. Even padres are not ex-

pected to give up women, nor does this impair the authority of
their offices. "O gente!" Zézé would cry. "A padre is a *man*,
isn't he? And a man has the obligation to make love to every
women he meets. Even to his own mother. Then it is up to
her to reject him, saying, 'My son, this cannot be—I am your
mother.' " After a while, the idea ceased to appall me.

The most promising of the male sympathizers of a temple
were made ogans and addressed as "father." I have often wondered what the word "father" actually means to a Bahia black.
Most of the time the household is headed by the mother, and in
the cult priesthoods a "father" is only a secondary sort of
"mother." "Ogan" in Yoruba is said actually to mean "lord and
master"; but obviously this was out of place in the woman-
dominated candomblé. A woman's true affection for a man is
shown when she calls him "son," and this seems more in keeping with the logic of the situation. Occasionally Zézé would call
Amor (nearly twice her age) "sonny," and everyone then knew
that things were right.

A man was offered the post of ogan if he had income or
social position. Edison was ogan to Aninha, and now at Engenho
Velho a handsome priestess of Xangô was urging him to transfer
to her. Just as every person has a guardian saint "in the Catholic
life," so he has a god in his head "in the African life"; and an
ogan is asked to assist the priestess who is dedicated to the same
god as the one in his head. Edison's god was "young Xangô,"
and Amor's was an older Xangô—both deities of thunder and
lightning. Quite a household, that of Amor and Zézé, dedicated
to the thunderbolts!

When an ogan assists a priestess, he helps her purchase food
and materials for the altar and feasts of her god. It is a kind of
housekeeping, and it surprises no one when an ogan also requests
the sexual privileges of a temporary husband. This is not supposed to happen, however, during the sacred period of the
ceremonies, for the women are supposed to be cool then and
indifferent to such things; they are then the "wives of the gods."
Evidently Amor had little confidence in the efficacy of the
prohibition. But it always appeared to me that the women were

so absorbed in their "possession" that they were unapproachable at that time. And the imagery of the state called "wife of the god" was carried out quite literally in a "secret" rite for restoring the woman to normal by washing her mouth and sexual organs with cooling water. The god would not like that and would leave for a time the woman he was inhabiting.

A "serious" priestess is supposed to be above interest in sex, and the famous mothers discipline themselves in this respect. But the pressure of the men and their own excitable natures overcome the other women. Yet there are few romances of the sentimental or desperate sort that we know. Maybe it is because most men have little to offer these women, maybe it is because there usually is another man available when the old one has proved a disappointment.

For the men, the temple is a home, an easy and affectionate place with many mothers who give love and take love, who entertain and feed and give advice. In the evening hours and on holidays it is even like a club, where all the men stop on the way from work, and bring along rum and tobacco and some food to eat. Often they bring presents of yard goods "for the god." They play games among themselves, and although men are not supposed to sleep in the orthodox temples they can always go out into the forests growing thickly around. At Gantois, the father of Menininha's daughters, and a few other trusted ogans, had built little one-room houses for themselves where they entertained and slept when they felt like it. In the summertime, I have seen them come and change to cool pajamas and relax in chairs under the trees, and later in the evening walk about with the children. They could do what they liked so long as they did not violate the temple and the temporary vows of chastity of the priestesses. But, in his sharp scolding of Zézé, Amor was always skeptical. This hurt her very much; and, though I believe she was loyal, I should not wonder if it did not put ideas in her head.

Most of the men who visit are too poor to have homes or to afford commercial entertainment. They seldom know their fathers and have often lived on the streets. They are hangers-on, and stability is provided by the black women. And the women have everything: they have the temples, the religion, the priestly offices, the bearing and rearing of children, and opportunities for self-support through domestic work and related fields. If the temples did not welcome the men, they would be left permanently to the streets, where they would become as ruffianly as they have long been in Rio. (In Rio they are called "malandros," wearing odds and ends of clothing so characteristic as to be almost a uniform; and they spend their lives at petty thievery and violence when they are not composing songs.) The women do not voice their fears in this conscious way, but their awareness of it is clear when mention is made of the capoeirists—the street wrestlers whom they hate for their denial of candomblé.

A temple priestess likes to refer to her group as an "association," "a mutual aid society." Martiniano and Menininha often used such language, and Edison also said that the candomblé organization offered the only social insurance of value to the blacks. He said that the men knew this, and that it added to the respect and friendship they felt for the women of the temple. By contrast, contact with prostitutes—the only other women such men could meet—was inadequate, wanting in personal feeling, and it was often tense because the men were poor and the prostitutes were demanding. But if a man, or a woman, were poor, his temple group would try to help him out. They would try to get him a job or introduce him to somebody useful or, if he were in trouble with the police, would hide him without questions. That in fact was how Menininha met the man who became the father of her children. The poor man had crossed with the law, though himself a lawyer, and so he stayed at Gantois until the trouble blew over. He stayed so many months that an attachment to Menininha grew up, and although later he flirted with other women in other temples, his deepest gratitude and loyalty remained to her because she had rescued him. He legitimized their children though Menininha would not allow him to marry her, and he considered Gantois his home, if not always his actual residence.

Menininha did not marry him legally for the same reasons

other mothers and priestesses did not marry. They would have lost too much. Under the law of this Latin Catholic country, a wife submits entirely to the authority of the husband. How incompatible this is with the beliefs and organizations of candomblé! How inconceivable to the dominant female authority! And so powerful is the matriarchal trend, where women submit solely to gods, that men like Amor and Martiniano, and Menininha's consort, Dr. Alvaro, can only fume and scold and quarrel with the priestesses they love.

Most black men, however, cannot afford the cost of a legal marriage or the responsibilities of a family. Fortunately the Catholic Church baptizes children outside wedlock and does not hold birth against a child or against the child's mother any more than the temple does.

Children and men are welcomed by a woman of the temple. They are her family, and she takes care of them as willingly as she takes care of her god. In return, she demands freedom for herself. Most of the women dream of a lover who can offer financial support at least to the extent of relieving her of continuous economic worry; but they do not think of legal marriage. Marriage means another world, something like being a white person. It brings prestige but not necessarily joy in living.

XV

ALTHOUGH the women cherish their independence (making it so glamorous that some men even dress like women in order to enter a priesthood), problems of affection and family remain. They were disturbing at Gantois at this time because Menininha's dear friend and assistant, Hilda, had decided to become pregnant. Zézé told me of developments from day to day, as they occurred. She was enormously interested in them because they crystallized the issues confronting any young career-priestess.

Hilda was her senior "in godhood," and Zézé addressed her as "my mother," because Menininha had made Hilda a priestess twenty-four years before, whereas she had made Zézé only seven years before. Hilda was now about thirty years old, more or less of an age with Zézé so far as that kind of chronology goes, but priestly rank prevented close friendship. However, Zézé knew a good deal about her.

I had seen Hilda at Gantois, noticing her because among the fifty or so plump hearty women of the priesthood, she was the only thin one. She must have been highly strung because she always moved as though she were charging upon something, her eyes appearing intent upon some inner preoccupation, and the silvery quality of her voice marred by her tension. She was fair, quite white in appearance except for her wiry hair, and Zézé thought she had been saving her beauty all these years for a profitable alliance. And now at thirty she had deliberately become pregnant by a man whom Menininha—her mother in godhood and her best friend after her own sisters—scorned.

Zézé said that Hilda had been "crazy for a man" long ago, when she was only sixteen and neglectful of her duties as a priestess. She had met him in fact at the caboclo temple of Mother Germania, and since she was a Yoruba daughter she should not have been visiting there in the first place. In those days, Zézé and her mother used to patronize the same temple. The performances were exciting, although people came as much to arrange love affairs as to see the show. Zézé was a big girl then, and she remembered everything, she said.

It seems that Hilda glimpsed this young man, and wanted him. She had never wanted any other before, nor since, in the same passionate way. He was her color, but he was an aristocrat. His complexion was yellow-ivory, and his crisp hair fell in a beautiful tight wave. He had the soft clear brown eyes that everyone loves, with heavy lashes and sweeping brows. He was tall and thin, his face slight, his hands and feet very small. He was not really handsome, but he was extremely appealing.

She had not yet talked to him, but she inquired among the women and learned that he was a medical student, of fine family, and that he loved candomblé. He spent a lot of time studying the instruments and songs of the rites. They were planning to

149

make him an ogan. He was twenty-two years old, and his name was Diomedes.

She persuaded the mother to introduce them but the young man was aloof, though he behaved agreeably enough. He addressed her politely as "Senhorita" every time they met after that, which was by chance, and finally she decided that he was being careful because he knew her to be a virgin and he wished to avoid possible complications with the police. ("Not that the police would care much about one of her quality!" Zézé interrupted herself.) He became an obsession with her, and she even thought of going to Martiniano for love magic.

One night at the temple, the ceremonial chamber was overcrowded and hot. From her position on the women's side, she saw Diomedes leave for the garden. She followed and, catching him unawares in the dark hot night, said close to his ear (Zézé always knew fine details, and quoted as though from the ultimate authority), "It is hot inside, isn't it?"

Startled, he answered pleasantly: "Good evening, dona. Yes, it is."

They walked a little, commenting on the drummers and the arrivals of the gods, when suddenly rain poured down. They ran to the narrow veranda of the temple, and still the rain splashed on them. "I'm going to open my shawl," she remarked with an air of making up her mind to something, and she did so, spreading it around his shoulders and then pulling it around her own. The shawl was not large enough for the two, so she leaned against him. After a little she moved so that she stood facing him, and soon she leaned against his chest and pulled his arms and the shawl around her. He kept still a moment, possibly surprised, and then he relaxed and began to stroke her breast softly. They did not kiss, but he leaned his head against hers. "It's raining hard —I'm afraid it'll last a long time," he said. Standing this way, and apparently ignoring it, they continued to discuss the evening's rites.

Zézé, who was usually matter-of-fact or indignant, told this tale sympathetically, even enviously. I wondered if it reminded her of an experience of her own.

Continuing with Hilda, she said that the love affair began that very night, and that it made Hilda happy while it lasted. Marriage of course was out of the question, but Hilda asked her lover, "Won't you try to keep me content?"—meaning, "Why don't you keep me as your regular mistress?" But he answered: "No, we must go our different paths. Yours is one, and mine is another. You must live with someone else." Still, he visited her nearly every day, and gave her money when she requested it. Towards the end he stayed with her in her house for nearly two months. It was deep in the woods, and only a worker's hut, but he enjoyed the change from the city and studied for his examinations. Hilda still hoped to tie him to her, loving him dearly, so one night she remarked: "I believe I am pregnant. Who wants a child without a father?"

"Ah, my daughter," he answered coolly, "that is your concern."

The following month she had a miscarriage—because she was weak, Zézé explained pityingly—and they parted. But Hilda followed him, even annoyed him, until she fell ill with appendicitis. Then she was taken to the hospital; but she ran out of it one night in delirium, lying in her nightgown in a public park. Towards dawn someone picked her up, and because she spoke the name of Menininha, who had made her when she was five years old, she was brought to Gantois. And she has remained with Menininha ever since, supporting herself with dressmaking. The appendicitis was only a castigation of her goddess Oxum, whom she had neglected so many years, and it disappeared after she returned to the priesthood.

Menininha was good to her, as she was to all her clients. Maybe she was especially interested in the return of a wayward daughter. She made herself dream about Hilda's future, and tossed sacred cowrie shells, thoughtfully, to see what answers lay in them. Finally she was able to assure Hilda that she would be happier now, in the temple where she belonged, protected against other people's jealousies and ambitions, cared for by her mother and associates, and by her own goddess whom she had so unwisely neglected. She had Hilda find and feed a fetish stone that represented Oxum, her patron, and could remain only in the temple's locked altar room with the other fetish stones. When Hilda's sisters fell ill, Menininha cured them also, to the extent that they could pay her, and so they became novices in this distinguished temple. When they secured enough money, working as dressmakers and laundresses and aided by relatives and friends, they completed their cures, which were also their priestly training. (All clients and novices had to pay in advance, by the gods' mandate.) And so Hilda's entire family was taken into the temple, and made a new friendly world for her.

Now Hilda was pregnant again. Zézé heard her talking about it often with Menininha, and so did the other priestesses because there were no ceilings in the temple and sound traveled over the walls. The man was Rodolfo.

Rodolfo! Even I was startled to hear that. I had never heard a good word spoken for him. Yet he was an ogan at Gantois. Years ago he had been an ogan, then he had transferred to another temple, and now he was back again. His own friend, Dr. Alvaro, Menininha's consort, laughed at him for his flightiness and disloyalty:

"A temple isn't like a woman," he would say to Rodolfo, calling him "wife" so as to belittle his masculinity. "You can't leave it for another and then return. The people won't stand for it."

But it seemed that they did, because of little Mother Hilda.

Rodolfo was dapper and good-looking. Nothing of the Negro was apparent, but only the Indian and the white blood. He had a fine aquiline nose, well cut lines of eyes and face, and a beautifully grained light copper skin. His few silver hairs were in order, and he never seemed to want a shave, like Alvaro. He wore cream-colored silk or linen suits, and white shoes and hat; it was not until the flat hard-straw hat distorted the high dome that Nature had given him, that one realized how stupid and bad his face was. And in his world women wanted him for love because he was tender and considerate, was fair and handsome, and earned a good wage as a foreman of construction. But he was over sixty years old—old indeed by Bahian standards! And in his long life he had given Bahia a large number of dark sons, all by different mothers but still recognizable as his. He had an old wife, people said, but no one ever saw her. I used to wonder if she too loved him and was proud of him.

Zézé's Amor hated him now because he had recently brought an employer of his to Gantois, a tall stout Portuguese who was obviously interested in the women and the social life, and therefore was willing to become an ogan. After a ceremony he had come over to Amor, who was taking care of the drums—Zézé was pleased by this story though she pretended to be outraged—and asked, "Do you know that stout pretty one of Iansã?"

"Yes?"

"I've got to see her, Seu Manoel! I don't care how you arrange it. I don't care what the conditions are. . . . I'm mad about her. . . . I've got to see her."

Amor grunted something. A few days later, when the two men were idling in the ceremonial room, Zézé came in to make obeisances to Menininha and the gods. Amor turned to the Portuguese.

"That's the brunette you mean, isn't it?"

"It is, Seu Manoel, and I'll thank you for introducing us."

"She's my wife—but you can talk to her!" Amor was furious that the other should have entertained thoughts about his woman. And when Zézé passed, Amor called to her, and repeated to the Portuguese: "It *is* this one, isn't it? . . . Zézé, this gentleman wants to talk with you."

"With me? But he doesn't know me. I'm nobody at all—"

"He admires you," Amor said with ominous gayety.

The white man then spoke for himself, "You must have been asleep when you took this fellow," he told her, meaning that she could have bargained for better than a black man. "Your eyes must have been shut—"

"No, they were wide open," answered Zézé, half flattered, and she turned to leave.

153

Just then another white ogan came up, a young clerk in the town whom the women considered handsome for his gardenia skin, well modeled nose, and heavy wavy hair, and Amor found it too much to bear. He followed Zézé to their home and, she said, became so violent that she felt like leaving him. And he linked the episode to Rodolfo.

Menininha was equally impatient with Hilda, it seems. Hilda was sewing dresses for the expected baby, ornamenting them with the lovely drawn work that is called "barafunda" ("confusion") and looks like lace. She was drawing single threads out of cotton cloth to make the barafunda, then sewing them together with embroidery thread to make a flowered design.

"My daughter," Menininha said to her, "you're paler than ever. Go now and lie down. You can sew later. That baby of yours has twenty-two dresses already."

"Maybe I have done too much," Hilda agreed, according to omniscient Zézé, "and I'm ill because the gods are getting envious. Its father doesn't approve at all—that's why he gives me no money for goods. . . . But Rodolfo is really very kind to me," she added hastily, seeing her friend's face harden. "I know you think he is too old for me, but he *is* strong, and he has such fine features. He looks like a white man. . . . I can't take a black one—you know that I have blood of quality myself. What better than he can I get in our world of candomblé? How they scorn us, my mother! I know that Rodolfo is mad after women, but he is a real man for all his sixty-four years—"

"Sixty-seven," Menininha interrupted quietly. "He has an old wife; he has forty-three children that he knows about; he knows every woman of the street—and I don't like the way Alvaro talks about him—"

"True, my mother, but I am still young. I want children. I'm not complaining about my fortune; everyone has his own, and it is hard to please me. And I like Rodolfo. He supports his children—and he makes handsome ones."

"I've given up criticizing him, and for your sake I've welcomed him back to our temple, though I think he is completely unreliable. I don't want to scold uselessly, but I read the divining board, and unhappiness was promised for you, you recall. . . . But I understand your feelings. I was young once too. At least, Alvaro has no other children and no other woman.

"My daughter," Menininha sighed, "we ought to concentrate solely upon serving the gods. But we are both too young for it; even I am. The old Africans always said that a priestess should be so old that she could no longer remember the passions of youth. Well, things are changing, degenerating, there are no old women fitted for our work.

"And soon there may be no young ones fitted either. Shall I expose my daughters to our hard discipline and responsibilities? Alvaro and I quarrel about that now. He says they have too much white blood, from him. Look what happened to Totonia of Engenho Velho, he says. So he wants Cleoza to be a dentist, and he wants Carmen to be a teacher. We have to decide because they are big girls now—one thirteen and the other ten years old. Suppose they get married!" She looked startled at Hilda.

"My mother—" Hilda dropped her work nervously.

"Never mind, Oxum," Menininha called her affectionately by the name of her goddess, "don't worry now. Maybe I'll talk it over with Martiniano. But that is the kind of trouble you will face if you have daughters. Between you and Rodolfo your children will be all whitened."

"If God so wills—" murmured Hilda sadly, wiping her eyes.

"But be certain we'll take fine care of the baby," Menininha assured her affectionately. "I myself will find out what god it belongs to, and what sacrifices we must offer. It may become a priestess when it is still a child!" she suggested cheerily. "We'll find a strong godfather and give it a good name."

"If God wills." Hilda thanked her. "You are very good to me, my mother—" She touched her lips to Menininha's hand and dropped a tear of relief.

"Oxum," Menininha said as she rose and patted her, and left for other duties.

XVI

THERE WERE three chambermaids on my floor at the hotel, three of the sweetest women I have ever known, three of the poorest and most helpless and most gallant. They were extremely curious about me because that is the motherly instinct of Bahia women, and they wondered that I lived alone, without a man, healthy and rich as I was. They were not prying; they just twittered about the room, which they kept immaculate, and inquired lightly and warmly, reassuring as a coverlet on a cool summer night.

One of them was Pureza Gomez. I remember her first because, with all her warmth, she was completely self-effacing, and although she was a mulatto she looked and acted a great deal like the housekeeper my mother had brought over from Germany to raise me. Berta had given me my first picture of womanly kindness and sympathy (she died an Aryan anti-Nazi), and Pureza fitted into it.

Another was Francine, a "French" type with bleached blond hair and dark brown eyes, who looked like a tart because she was so thin and painted but was as good and gentle as a saint. She had a husband who depended on her pitiful earnings, and a young daughter whose bouncing health was her joy, whose very existence was a continuous surprise bringing the brightness of tears to her face.

The third was Augusta, a fair-skinned mulatto with rippling hair and a sweet expansive disposition. She was younger than the others, about thirty years old, thin as Francine, ladylike as Pureza. Since she was still single she had more time to chat, and when she learned that I was interested in candomblé she was pleased.

"I live next to Dona Sabina," she said with a girlish smile that showed missing and broken teeth but spread to her large black eyes, "and I go to her candomblés. They are beautiful, they are always the most beautiful ones given. . . . She has great powers. She gets what she wants. People have seen her turn into a black bat at night and fly over the countryside. They say that some-times she goes as a black cat, and she usually takes a priestess with her—Antonia, I think. . . . She does well by everyone, though."

Then Augusta told Pureza, who told Francine, who told Eulalia working in the laundry. Soon all the hotel employees knew about me, and the three chambermaids would report to me whenever they had a moment to run in. Pureza had never ac-tually gone to a temple because she was raised in an isolated country town, and after she arrived in Bahia she was too busy attending to her husband—common-law husband, of course; but she wished very much to go to one. She had heard bad things about candomblé, but she found them hard to believe because the temple women she knew, like Eulalia in our hotel, were very good women. She listened with interest to Francine, who was white, telling how she always went to a certain mother for advice and information concerning the future, a mother who lived right in the heart of town and whose charges were reason-able. Eulalia once came very shyly to my door at the end of her day's work, wearing the bahiana dress, and said that she would be glad to escort me to the next celebration at Engenho Velho, where her daughter belonged, and to carry my notebooks and camera. She did in fact escort me to several celebrations, dignified and taciturn, acknowledging, as we walked to the streetcar, the greetings of storekeepers and professional men (who, she said, recognized the power of candomblé and therefore were courteous to her and all bahianas) and refusing ever to allow me to pay her carfare.

So it happened that Augusta told us that Sabina was prepar-ing her celebration for the water-goddess. Eulalia, in her firm wordless way, would have nothing to do with it because the Yoruba people considered Sabina as an upstart, a blasphemous, vulgar somebody. Pureza listened with the open-mouthed won-der of a little boy, standing near us and leaning her face on her fist. Francine was delighted, uttering little exclamations of pleas-ure, planning to have someone take her little girl to see. "Those beautiful clothes," she said, "just like in the movies! I love silk clothes. Don't you, Dona Ruth?" Pureza laughed her high te-hee, and they scattered.

I reminded Edison, and we arranged to go. "But what's wrong with the woman?" I asked. "What have they got against her?"

"Well," he said, "she has practically no training, from the orthodox point of view. The novitiate alone is supposed to last seven years after you enter the priesthood. No one seems to know for certain how she sprang up. And she carries on a terrific feud with Mother Constancia, who leads the caboclo tradition that Sabina claims to belong to."

"Caboclo?"

"That's a new type of practice that invokes Indian spirits along with the African gods and Catholic saints. They are the temples that admit men to the priesthood, and generally have a lax discipline. But Constancia has a solid reputation because she was trained in the orthodox Yoruba before she broke away, and she knows exactly what she is doing. The same was true of Mother Sylvana, who was famous for telling the future, and even had clients in Rio. But Sabina has quite a following herself!"

Menininha did not like to hear Sabina's name mentioned.

"*That* one grew up wild! No hand of mother or saint made *her*! 'Sabina of the vine!' She clings to anything for support! And she lets *men* fall! She wants men around her! She wants money too, she doesn't care really about helping people!" Menininha's scorn was withering, yet I am sure that the two women had never met.

Walking once in the Upper Town, on Seventh of September Avenue, Edison pointed her out to me. "There goes a mother, and the old Africans would turn in their graves to see her." He was gazing at a youthful woman in a handsome white tailored suit, wearing a white turban and white leather sandals; her cheeks were rouged, her black hair in a long bob was nicely straightened, and she was chatting in an animated girlish way with the man on whose arm she leaned. Her eager face had an Indian cast.

"Why?" I asked.

Edison smiled. "Well, look at her! They would say, first, that she irons her hair! No true saint descends into a head that has been touched by heat. Then, she has the ways of a white woman. Doesn't she look neat and shiny and modern to you, like something out of a factory? How could anyone tell she was a mother? Look at the straight lines of her figure!" He was amused, and maybe a little outraged. "The African woman is supposed to bulge, she is supposed to look comfortable, like one who carries children and loves men. That's why she's a mother! But Sabina— well, they would think she was too vain, too light-minded."

We noticed her again that evening, this time in the Lower Town near the great markets, and she had changed her costume. Now she wore a bright blue tailored dress with a smart matching toque and blue leather sandals. Edison accosted her.

"Dona Sabina!" he called and gave a little bow. She appeared flustered and answered self-consciously, "Doctor!"

"We have heard about your famous mãe d'agua," he said flatteringly, "and we wonder if we may be privileged to see it." Then he introduced me.

A shrewd look came into her eye. "Yes, your Reverences, I will be honored by your company," she said, smiling very affably. "It begins at eight o'clock Sunday morning at my terreiro, and"—she turned inquiringly to Edison—"I hope we can have a notice in the paper."

"Indeed!" he assured her.

"Fine! You don't think I look much like a mother, do you?" With a hearty laugh she spun coquettishly to show her figure. "I've just been to police headquarters about my candomblé, and the officer said, like a real cavalier: 'Well, I'll have to let you off! You don't look like a mother to me!'" She imitated his voice and manner, and laughed again.

"But of course you are one," Edison said. "Who made you, dona?"

"No one." Her tone was careful. "You know that we caboclo mothers are not touched by any human hand. I was made by the spirit of an Indian who came to me in dreams. He has been dead hundreds of years, and he is my guardian."

It was a touchy subject, and we parted then.

Early the next Sunday morning, a magnificent September

day, Augusta showed us the way to the temple. It was also Sabina's house, and it was behind the back yards of the Barra residential district built along the charming seashore by foreign businessmen. We wound along mud paths, and suddenly, facing the sea, we saw the new white mud-and-stucco compound high on a steep mound.

"That is it," Augusta said, stopping to look admiringly. Two fat naked little boys, her nephews, came running and tumbling, throwing themselves into her arms. "That is Dona Sabina's cow," she went on quietly.

At the foot of the hill, looking for grass in the cleared flat, was the gleaming white cow, beautifully curried, existing only to provide the mother with milk. We climbed the hill on steps cut out of the mud, and saw a yard hung with new washing.

"She's known for that," Edison observed, nodding at the washing "—always clean, even luxurious." He knocked at the shut door.

A black girl unlatched it and, seeing us, shouted to the interior, "They have come!" To us she added, "Wait in here and make yourself at home."

She took us through a narrow hallway into a sitting room in the front. It was cool, with air that had long been shut in by locked windows and drawn shades. The place had the spotlessness of an unused room. The walls had been freshly painted in pale green and rose. The furniture was of the same style as at Felipe Néry's, and I feared to sit on a chair lest it collapse. Noticing this, the girl pointed out a settee to me, then sat herself down in a chair opposite and stared. She was a nice country girl, and she smiled whenever our eyes caught hers.

Two men now came in to remove the furniture which crowded the small room; but they left a large table in the center, which held the presents to the goddess Janaína. Sabina said later that the gifts had been on display in different parts of the house for over a week; gathered in this one room, they made a showing. People were arriving now for the ceremony, and as each one entered he contributed something to the table. Edison urged me to contribute also, and I put down some coins—fished up from the bay later by boys—and scribbled a note, like the others, asking Janaína for success and happiness. Edison liked that and smiled, though he would never do it himself.

Visitors passed around the table and examined the figure of the goddess propped up in a big silvered cardboard boat flying two sails, and with cabin windows cut out of the hold. One sailor doll stood forward at the wheel and another was aft at the rigging. The big body of the goddess loomed over all, with a lyre resting on one arm. She was a pinkish-colored pottery doll of the white race, with a robust form, full breasts, and a fish tail. She had straight brown hair flowing down her back, combed carefully and bound with a paste-diamond tiara; between her high breasts rested a necklace of green brilliants, and she looked voluptuous. Two smaller dolls like her idled around the boat, leaning against the edges, peering over, and acting as her companions. There were little celluloid Janaínas with harps, standing on the table about the boat on wooden supports ornamented with paper flowers. Around the boat was a sea of toilet soaps, bath salts, vanity cases, combs studded with brilliants, rice powder, and lip rouges—the whole range of feminine gifts cherished by Sabina's followers. There were tiny rhomboid greeting cards with gilded inscriptions of "Profound respects to the Princess Janaína," and each card was dated and signed by one or another among the faithful. Later Sabina placed a letter in the big silver boat in which she offered homage to "the richest princess in the world" and asked blessings for her temple, Bom Jesus da Lapa.

Now the priestesses were dressed for their pilgrimage to the sea. They wore silken versions of the lovely bahiana style, stressing the emblematic colors of the day's goddess, which were sky-blue and white. Sabina's costume was more elaborate than the others. It was entirely of white satin of a costly quality, and over her right shoulder she draped a scarf of fine sky-blue moiré. Like the others, she wore a long necklace of white beads emblematic of the great god Oxalá who is identified with Jesus, the patron of Sabina's temple. The men of the temple—male priests called "sons," and the drummers and ogans—wore white suits and small sky-blue sailor hats. Two little girls of six, who screamed their names to be Sidonia and Maria, and a boy of the same age called Dunga, were also dressed for the occasion. The girls wore white, with blossoms in their hair, like little barefoot brides. The little boy wore a green and red velvet suit which Edison thought was really proper for Carnival when the King of the Congo marches through the streets with his retinue. In fact, one of the drummers startled the little boy by suddenly shouting from behind his back, "Hail, the king!" and the other drummers, as though rehearsed, rolled off a long beat with their fingers on the tall drum round which they stood, and echoed vigorously "El Rei!" Dunga's mother, in her white and blue skirts, went protectingly to him, fussing at his garments, adjusting the train, straightening the tiara. I was enchanted on that windy bluff.

Awaiting the signal to move, everyone talked, appraising the day, wondering about the mood of "Dona Janaína," preparing for a very good time, laughing, humming, tapping the drum. The people adjusted good-luck signs around their necks, crosses, and a silvered "seal of Solomon," and always the figa, which is a closed right hand with forefinger extended to ward off the evil eye, and sometimes even ends as a cross. Figas are always worn at the back of the neck, since in front anyone has eyes against danger!

One young man carrying a small African drum now "pulled" a ritual song "begging permission of the sea to commence the ceremony." He stood at the edge of the bluff gazing at the water. Quickening his tempo, he called out in a rough resounding baritone, "Let us march to the waves!" while the high tinkling voices of the priestesses answered in lovely chorus. A white man of the interior country, Sabina's brother-in-law and principal assistant, shot off two salvos of firecrackers. At this, the neighboring slopes grew dark with people crowding to watch, their breakfasts and work left abandoned.

So the procession started down the steep incline, the drummers first, Sabina walking among her "daughters," and ogans at the sides and rear to maintain order; while Edison and I walked behind all, and the children danced back and forth. Everyone in the procession was barefooted except Sabina, who wore white mules with French heels and furry trimmings in sign of her status. She was the only woman who did not carry flowers. Some daughters carried gilded or silvered water-jugs, containing bouquets, on their heads. One daughter stood out because she wore the gold-colored cloth of the goddess Oxum who lives in the top layers of the sea, and she was already possessed, twitching so violently that an ogan had to relieve her of her jug.

The procession wound along the narrow path of red clay that ran through the crude suburb, and finally we reached the broad and busy streets leading directly to the inlet where sailboats waited to carry us across the Bay of the Savior. The sky burned blue overhead, the wind was stiff over the water. "Lovely daughter of Africa . . . O Iemanjá"—phrases of the poem returned to my mind. Several of the priestesses carried the toy ship and presents that were to be thrown to the goddess in the water, others carried the graceful jars, like Greek amphoræ, filled with holy water that was to be pitched to the goddess at the point of sacrifice. They sang caressing hymns to beautiful and wealthy Oxum, to the older voluptuous Iemanjá, and confused them both with Janaína:

> "Oxum, ah, Oxum is a beauty,
> Oxum, Oxum,
> Oxum is a splendor,
> Oxum, oh, Oxum!"

In an ecstasy, the chief drummer Kaún shouted:

> "Janaína!
> Come out of the sea!
> Janaína is a child!
> Come and play on the sand!
> Come out of the sea!"

This is the Middle Ages, I thought, staring at the procession, the bay, the sailboats flying flags of the gods, the crowds guarded by police watching the ceremony and ignoring business and industry.

As though he heard, Edison remarked: "It still takes my breath away, too. But it is the twentieth century in Brazil, in

Bahia. This is the same universe that holds Hitler, Franco, and Mussolini. However, we are in the land of gold, according to our black friends, the country of slaves and candomblé." He laughed without humor. "See how these people believe! It takes the heart out of a man. All this matters most to them and whatever talk they hear of war and labor problems is just so many words, just as remote to them as these doings are to you. Well, maybe they are the only happy people left in the world." There was no contentment in his tone.

Police cleared a way for the priestly procession to reach the beach. Three short and stocky mulatto oarsmen now came wading ashore. Rolling their white cotton trousers above their knees, they carried the sixty-five celebrants through the waist-high water out to the boats. They loaded Sabina and her intimates into the lead boat, then the rest into the others. Watching the bodies cradled in the muscular arms of the oarsmen, I felt self-conscious and awkward; and I burned in an agony when my turn came and one oarsman picked me up. Another picked up Edison, who adjusted his gray felt fedora carefully as the man lifted his slight body high. We were deposited in the lead boat with Sabina, at her command, our dark city clothes conspicuous among the bright garments of the others.

Sails were set full for Mont-Serrat, a cove far down the bay, and they took advantage of the September wind. It was now about ten o'clock, and the sun was hard and brilliant upon the blue water, whitening the horizon and setting the jugs and paste jewelry of Janaína ablaze with broken light. Spirits soared, and Kaún intoned imperiously:

> "Now, yes, now
> It is that we can navigate!
> O fish of the sea,
> O needle of Maria
> Zaniapombo,
> Needle of Iemanjá!" *

* This song and "The Lord preserve us today!" (following), translated from the Portuguese of Edison Carneiro, *Negros Bantus.* "Zaniapombo" (Bantu) = "Creator."

The women rocked and smiled to the mood of the song, and as they passed a cliff at the top of which soared a lovely old white church the daughter named Antonia greeted it with a terrific yell:

"Salute St. Anthony of Barra! Salute St. Anthony of Barra!"

The others joined her happily, since she, like the church, was dedicated to this soldier saint; and they followed with cheers for Our Lord of Good Ending who protects Bahia, being Jesus and also the god Oxalá. Pretty Antonia began to sway as though possessed. Edison whispered to me that he was inclined to underrate these ready trances, imagining that Antonia was merely hysterical over the occasion, and obsessed with the ambition to be ordained a priestess.

The boatload sang gently:

> "The Lord preserve us today!
> Save us, O Lord of Good Ending,
> Save also the moon and the stars,
> Save the sun and its gleam of gold!"

People noticed that Mother Sabina was falling too, so they took up a song for Iemanjá. A relaxed and pleasant expression came over her face, her arms waved, reaching out to embrace the boatload, her body swayed, she twisted and shimmied her shoulders and neck, and she caressed her breasts. She was the goddess. As these actions threatened to tip the boat, her husband held her arms. Then two young daughters felt the contagion, and uttered little cries with agonized expressions on their faces. The drummers beat and tapped. Suddenly, blankly, Sabina started from her trance; she blinked and shook her head, and looked tired and annoyed. There followed a dull period of waiting.

Drummer Kaún became restless, and struck up a song about a drunken sailor:

> "O sailor
> Hold fast the helm!
> Don't let the boat spill! *

* With the double meaning, "Don't let me get dizzy and fall into trance."

I am a sailor
Who comes from Lisbon
Sailing the waves of the sea
I come at half-mast
Bringing a royal dove."

Kaún himself "fell" in the midst of his singing, raising an imaginary bottle to his lips and flopping around as though intoxicated:

"My father is a whisky-sot
My mother is a drunkard."

But the drummers are supposed to remain "sober," even in a tolerant group like Sabina's, and so she whispered to him impatiently and harshly, "Take it easy! Take it easy!" He was too absorbed to notice her, whereupon she shook him severely and blew stiffly into each of his ears. A violent shudder seized the poor fellow, he blinked his large eyes and shook his head with the disoriented look of one aroused suddenly from sound slumber. Immediately he fell into a light sleep.

These fleeting incidents embarrassed me, as though private emotions were being exposed.

The people in the second boat now sang:

"Isn't it, isn't it
My boat that comes?
Loaded, full, with a crowd of sailors?"

A well groomed mulatto girl in blue jumped up singing of Iemanjá, flinging her arms and head happily, an expression of unusual pleasure on her face.

Sabina laughed shortly in surprise, saying that this girl usually danced, when possessed, in a dour spirit. Evidently a new god had seized her! Edison grumbled to me that it was wrong to be the horse of more than one deity! Besides, Yoruba women learn to fall into trance only when their mother commands, in order to reveal the will of a god for a specific purpose. But this was an orgy! The girl's husband, laughing self-consciously and yet with enjoyment, held her lest she tip the boat over. The others shifted position to watch more carefully. Soon the girl's friend, who was dressed in red, also went into a Iemanjá fit, standing up to dance. Her features were set and intent, her eyes torn wide open and at times even crossed, her arms flailing, her head tossing, the image of a tragic fury. They held her to take the pins out of her hair, fearful that they might fly into her eyes. A drum beat with her dance, and she must have come to depend upon it, for the moment it stopped she ceased dancing. She remained in trance, however, her body crouching tensely, her ears so keyed that when a stick dropped accidentally, letting out just one note, she quivered. And when the drum struck up again she danced so furiously that she endangered the boat, and people had to restore her by blowing hard in her ears.

A new song began, about the great deity of pests named Omolu, known in the Catholic world as St. Lazarus and St. Roque. Again women fell into states of possession. So song succeeded song, and trance succeeded trance, and clearly the people were enjoying themselves. Sabina ordered food passed around—balls of manioc served on banana leaves, oranges, candy, and sponge cake. The drums went all the time, and Kaún's wife, overcome by the Twin gods, squealed, and ate roughly and sloppily in their style. For relief, they sang of Nanan, ancient mother of the candomblé gods, and of all the waters of the world; and a couple of young men fell possessed of her, shrieking and dancing. They sang gently, in samba time, about the Virgin Mary who protected the slaves:

> "What day is today?
> It is the day of Our Lady of the Rosary.
> What day is it?
> The day of Our Lady of the Rosary."

Two priestesses danced happily, facing each other. The drum led other songs, tapping excitedly, leaping about the melody and the fundamental rhythm, then quieting into a mournful cadence:

"I come from far away,
From far away, my friend,
From far away.
Ah, I come from far away,
My Lady Oxum."

For now we had arrived at the deep spot prescribed for the offerings, a place free of current. A man stood up swaying, and this was a signal for Sabina to direct the three boats to come close together. Antonia, tears streaming, passed the sacred gifts to Sabina, who carefully dropped them, one by one, into the space bounded by the grouped boats.

"Why are you crying, Antonia, daughter?" people asked in gentle concern.

In deep distress she answered thickly, "No reason—no reason." But she could not halt the tears. I thought that the different exalted moods must have battered her so that the strain of this climax broke her. The atmosphere was indescribably tense.

The heavy gifts plummeted to the bottom of the bay, and a wild shout went up: "Accepted! Iemanjá has accepted! Janaína has accepted! Oxum has accepted!"

The people had received the promise. The coming year would be good to them, for the mãe d'agua had accepted.

Pandemonium broke. Sabina leaped up, dancing furiously and long with Iemanjá, eyes closed. The men labored to keep the boat balanced and afloat. Kaún's wife, Joanna, strove to dive into the bay, longing to join the goddess there, to plummet also to the bottom as a sacrifice. Her husband solemnly pulled her back by the arms. Antonia too tried to leap into the sacred waters; and it was hard to restrain her, for she was strong, passionate and intent. She sobbed tragically, and bent far over the water, pulling her captors after her.

I was caught in the wave of feeling, and fought it. To my relief, Edison chuckled.

"I admire this enormously," he said, "but I can't take it seriously. Sabina has such control over her gods! She can turn them on and off. Now, Menininha is different, and Flaviana and Maximiana—they dole them out. Just look at Sabina. She gives me the impression merely of working hard. In the Yoruba temples a woman in honest trance moves like a sleepwalker, sweeping and sure, and her eye is glazed. I don't believe the women here could stand the needles Dr. Nina used to jab into Mother Pulcheria's priestesses to test their state!"

"But they believe they're doing the right thing, don't they?"

"Surely. But I hate to see the classic tradition corrupted."

"Still, now they know that they will have enough to eat next year, and that their personal affairs will go well?"

"Yes," he agreed.

The boats rocked with the people who fell, and over and over Kaún drummed while the others sang:

> "Our Lady,
> Our Lady Maria was born a flower.
> Yes, I am truly
> Thinking this."

Finally Sabina commanded the people to chant a verse begging permission to leave the holy spot. Immediately they "sobered" up, and began to doze.

Among the three boatloads of nappers, there were none now with whom to talk except the three children who also had been sober and quiet throughout. Now the children had a wonderful time. They mocked at everything that had happened, singing and dancing and laughing, rolling and twitching. Rosa Maria tried a blasphemous word, "Liar!" and then yelled it over and over. It was like saying "unbeliever." The people were "liars," and the ceremony was a "lie." Was she echoing her father, I wondered. For her father, who was Sabina's chief ogan, laughed at her, saying only, "My daughter, don't use that word—it's not nice!" "Liar!" she shouted again.

The boats, unhindered now, returned rapidly; only the children sang. And at the moment of landing, Kaún moaned wearily:

> "I come from far away, my friend
> From far away . . ."

The new good year had begun.

XVII

SABINA'S SHOWY personality intrigued me, being so different from the Yoruba women's, and I decided to see her again informally. If she was truly a rebel, I wanted to know why. And I owed her thanks for Sunday's excursion.

The following Friday then, I walked through the Barra neighborhood, feeling my way to her house. It was so like her, I thought, to live in Bahia's most exclusive section, even if it was at the back doors of the fine houses. I delighted in the wide white avenues—down which nobody sauntered just for a walk! —and looked pleasurably at the spacious homes of white and light-colored stone mixtures constructed in the Spanish and Portuguese colonial styles. Over the years, American and British government officers and businessmen not only had moved in with their families, but had organized an American Club, a British Club, a Yacht Club, and a Jockey Club, to which they admitted selected Germans and Brazilians; and they had thus converted the section into an Anglo-American outpost. Within this space, and within these walls, the same thirty or so families met every day, until the charming area became a gloomy prison to them. But they allowed themselves no release, not even any peepholes. The British Consul, a big handsome man from Canada, used to tell me about them, caustic in his manner but feeling for them deep in his heart. He had immured himself in a beautiful old-style mansion just under the hill of that Church of St. Anthony of Barra—maybe it had been a small monastery attached to the church—and practically no one could penetrate it. I cannot recall now why he invited me, except that he noticed an old pearl solitaire ring on my finger and commented, as though he knew from experience, that such a ring was a ring of sorrow. He proved to be right, and I have the impression that grief was something he had known and fought well, and realized that the others in the Barra could never face.

Beyond the fine avenues, I located the cruder streets and paths leading to the mud-and-wicker huts of the blacks, and I followed them to Sabina's door. Her house was unmistakable, new and large, and elevated above the others—like churches of colonial times!—on the wind-swept mound.

Knocking, I was admitted to the darkened parlor by Odette, Sabina's fifteen-year-old adopted daughter. She left me, and soon Sabina herself came out, smiling broadly and showing a full set of false teeth. The teeth indicated unusual means as well as meticulousness, and so did her spotless modern clothes. Brisk and cheery, she threw herself into a chair and exclaimed in her common speech, "You honor me with this unexpected visit, my lady!" She crossed her legs and her arms, like a college girl.

"You were so kind last Sunday, dona," I answered carefully, not knowing how to change from the formal Yoruba ways to which I had grown accustomed, "that I feel in your debt. So I want to contribute something to the support of this temple." I put some bills on the table.

Sabina was highly pleased, much more so than Menininha or Luzía would have been, because she craved approval. "My lady," she said eagerly, "the guardian of this temple, who is our Lord, Bom Jesus da Lapa, thanks you. . . . Now, my lady, this is our dinner hour. Our food is ordinary, just poor people's food, and we don't even know how to serve it; but I would be proud to have you eat it with me. If you would care to."

I was delighted, of course, and said so. I remembered the formal dining room at the hotel where, because I was a fine lady, I sat all by myself and looked every day at the same men at the other tables—some army officers stationed there indefinitely, the others transient guests on business, but all having the same calculating and exploring appearance; sometimes the wives came down, glum and aloof, but lately attractive women of uncertain character had come up from Rio and São Paulo, brightening the look in the eyes of the men and eventually moving to their tables. The head waiter would come over to me and whisper, "You ought to feel outraged at the presence of those women!" and I would look away so as not to have to respond to the wicked meaning in his eyes, because he was not teasing. And then the food would come, the same food every day:

chicken—surely wild, from its toughness and tastelessness—and eggs and guava. How could I fail to be delighted with Sabina's invitation?

She led me through a corridor to a pavilion in the rear of the house where, she said, they held their ceremonies. I sat down and looked around. It was a large room with huge, hooded window spaces that caught every breeze and retained every shade. The walls were painted a light greenish blue, and on them hung water colors depicting the Indian spirits that "guarded" this temple. They were lined with benches, and tables and chairs were scattered about. It was a comfortable place in Bahia's humid summertime. Odette came to spread a table with a lacy white cloth and ample cutlery, laying the plates upside down to keep them free of insects and falling dust. Food was being prepared alongside the pavilion at an oven under a shed in a kind of corridor cut out of the sloping ground and enclosing the house on that side.

Sabina called me to the table and then, at the top of her lungs, she invited several priestesses working at domestic chores in the inner room. But none, as she explained, had the courage to join me. A young "white" matron from the northeastern state of Sergipe came out to watch us; she was living here temporarily to undergo the priestly novitiate. When she too refused the invitation Sabina twitted her uproariously.

"Woman," she laughed, "the North American lady will think you don't know how to use a knife and fork. She will think you are a monkey, or maybe a bird since you can live without eating. Come on over! Do you think the white lady will bite you, eh? Why don't you show her how proud you are that she came all the way from the United States to learn the songs and dances and medicines you yourself are learning? She just paid me something!" But the woman from Sergipe would not stir. She sat in a corner, bowed, with impassive face.

We ate quietly, Sabina dishing out several kinds of fish and vegetables, and conducting a desultory conversation with her women. As we reached our small cups of bitter coffee—that famous "café pequeno" that cheers the Brazilian heart and soul, cements friendships and nourishes works of genius—Sabina's husband, Benedito, came in. He was the same physical type as she, short and strong. He earned a comfortable living by laying bricks in season; and at other times he walked the streets vending milk and fish. Probably he was the financial mainstay of the temple, and certainly he was proud of his wife's practice. I recalled how deferentially he had addressed her last Sunday when she "fell," calling her "Your Reverence"; and I got the impression strongly that the two were good friends. I had heard that this was Benedito's second marriage, and that he had educated children in Rio.

Sabina hailed him heartily. "Ah, the Old One has come! The Man of the Temple! . . . Odette!" she shouted to the buxom girl.

"Senhora?" Odette answered in a small sulky voice.

"Lay dishes for your father. . . . Do you want to eat, Benedito?"

"Do I want to eat!"

He laughed, and nodded to me while he pulled off his shirt and strode to a washstand in a corner. Having cleaned himself, he walked to the table and kissed the back of his wife's hand, whereupon she returned the salute. I liked the old-fashioned greeting, even though it smacked of feudalism and unhygienic habits; I had seen it even on the sidewalks of Rio.

"Do you want beer, Benedito?" Sabina inquired gayly.

Cheerily her husband answered, "Do I want beer!"

Odette brought him an iced bottle which he emptied into a glass.

"Such heat!" he sighed.

"Do you want meat, Benedito?" Sabina piled his plate with greens, and filled his bowl with soup.

"Do I want meat! . . . And I want feijão!" he snorted in pretended outrage, as though he were being deprived of the staff of life. He wielded his knife and fork busily and daintily, and did not look up.

While Odette served, Sabina explained proudly to me that she was teaching the girl to sew, and that already she had learned to read, write, and figure better than anyone else in the group. Odette worked as though she did not hear a word. She left to sweep the outer corridor, and Sabina went on to say that Odette had already written down many of the candomblé songs. She called to her to show some of these to me, and the young girl returned to do so in her obedient sulky manner. Her writing was crude and awkward, and the spelling was far from standard; but I was struck by the compliant way in which she responded to Sabina's innumerable and trivial calls. She was dressed finely; surely she was destined to inherit the temple. She reminded me of Menininha's daughter Cleoza, so well cared for and pretty, and serious about her duties. Only much later when she was with her friends, older girls and young matrons attached to this priesthood, did she relax and show happiness.

Sabina remarked to me that Odette had a half-brother Antonio who was also being reared at the temple. He came into the pavilion now, dressed simply in trousers, and only after Sabina had urged him in an annoyed tone to put on a shirt, did he return with some ragged makeshift. He was rather undeveloped for his sixteen years, and probably not very bright. He also had a sulky manner, but he could not compare with his sister in appearance. Sabina said quietly that sometimes they suspected his mind was unbalanced, because he had already been possessed by several untamed deities, which caused him to writhe like an epileptic. Her husband was training him to be a bricklayer. He was starting now to mend the straw bottom of a chair when Sabina interrupted him with a request for water. He straightened up slowly and chanted in protest:

"Oh,
I am a waiter, I am
A waiter, a waiter
I am."

Yet he went on the errand, and Sabina hooted, "That boy!"

Women started to wander in, stringing their children after them. Some of the boys collected in a corner of the pavilion and pretended to beat the big drums in a fetish ceremony for the girls; some stood stock-still to stare at me; others imitated the meticulous eating with knives and forks; one boy of seven turned his back and urinated. An elderly seamstress, tall, frail, and white-haired as a New England spinster, arrived to take measurements for priestly costumes, and a Singer sewing machine was brought in for her. The whole easy bedlam revolved around Sabina.

She had a certain presence, a self-assurance and ambition, tempered however by the warm feelings she showed her followers. She loved being the head priestess, the adviser and herb doctor, and she was always accessible. She was interested in everything that people cared to tell her, but she allowed no liberties. Just now she was trying to discipline the children who sprawled over the whole pavilion, like puppies. "Oh, you ill bred creature!" she screamed at one. "Get out of here!" The child went, startled and quiet, but seemingly with such good faith in her that shortly he returned, confident as any house pet. When he recommenced his noise and tumbling, she scolded testily: "The devil! Maria! Such a black heart in one so young!" and cracked him soundly on the buttocks. The child hushed with surprised eyes, but a few minutes later had forgotten and was repeating the offense. "Wayward child!" she shrilled.

Recalling words I had heard in Bahia's back streets, I marveled at the decency of her language.

Sabina sought quiet in order to tell the women about me, while her husband sat in a corner and listened. "In her country of North America they do not know about candomblé. So she has come all that distance to study with me, and after she has learned she will return to her own people and make a lot of money." She preened herself and added challengingly, "Maybe I ought to go to Rio de Janeiro and set up in practice?"

One of the women inquired, timid and surprised: "But she is a lady of quality. How can she belong with us?"

Another asked, "Does she know what our sect is like—that we are Indian, and others are African?"

Sabina then turned to explain to me. "My lady, you should know these things. This temple is protected by Jesus and Oxalá and belongs to Bom Jesus da Lapa. It is a house of the caboclo spirits, the original Brazilian Indians, and does not come from the Yoruba or Congo Africans. Ancient Indians of the primeval forests send their spirits to guide us, spirits that have been dead sometimes for hundreds of years. We worship the Yoruba gods first in our service because we cannot set them aside; but then we worship the spirits because they were the original owners of the land we live in. They were the masters, and therefore they are now our guides, roaming in the air and on the land. They protect us."

She paused and looked around at the listening women. "I'll tell you a story. Once a neighbor of mine was protected by an Indian spirit called Flor de Dia, and he would visit her at dawn. He noticed, however, that she lied and quarreled continually, so in disgust he left her. She became very ill, and for ten years she pleaded with him to return, making costly sacrifices to him. Finally he appeared to her and said that he had been dead these ten years, and was now a hundred years old. You see, her Flor de Dia had been the spirit of a living Indian, but usually one's guide is a spirit that has been dead for centuries."

A black woman now approached Sabina hesitantly from the rear of the house. "Is your ladyship Dona Sabina?"

"The same, my neg'a, at your service."

The woman approached and, dipping, kissed the back of her hand. "I must have some business done," she said, low.

"I don't make any despachos today because it is Friday.* Come tomorrow after two o'clock. . . . Come tomorrow after two o'clock," she repeated as the woman lingered.

Suddenly Sabina began in a vexed manner, "Once I had a fight with Constancia." The expression of her face was grim, and, her eye falling again on the strange client, she repeated impatiently, "Woman, come back tomorrow after two o'clock! . . .

"Yes, it was about two years ago that I had this fight with Constancia. I went to her celebration with my daughter Antonia and my compadre Manoel. I thought it would be very

* Dedicated to Jesus and Oxalá and therefore set aside for good acts and meditation.

176

nice because she is well off since her husband is in the army and draws a salary. Her patron saints are Iansã and Oxalá, who are also mine.

"I was dressed nicely, but just in ordinary clothes. I don't like to go around in bahiana dress. Constancia pretended to be very glad to see me, and she said: 'Ah, my daughter! Here you are, come to honor us in this house of poor people! You who are rich, with fashionable furniture and electric lights!'

"Her caboclo spirit wanted me to kiss her hand, as though I were her inferior—but not I, I wouldn't! I said: 'Look here! We are poor people too! But we are not visiting in the house of poor people, no senhora!' "

I was bewildered by this display of ill humor, and failed to understand why Sabina took Constancia's remarks in such bad part. Yet as Sabina recalled the occasion her mood grew angrier,

"Then her caboclo spirit sang us a song of welcome, like this:

> " 'Here comes wine,
>   Here comes sun,
>   Here comes power.'

And I answered:

> " 'You will be recompensed,
>   You will be recompensed.'

But she was false! She interrupted me while I was still singing in front of the drummers, asking:

> " 'Give me permission,
>   With your permission,
>   With the permission of Zabiapongo,
>   With the permission of the kings of the capangeiros,
>   With the permission of mametu.' *

"But I sang straight through anyhow, and I was going to sing another pretty song to the great mother, the mametugonga, when an ogan cut in on me! Such disgraceful conduct to a

* Zabiapongo, an Angola deity. "Capangeiros," brigand gangs. "Mametu," caboclo word for "mother."

visitor! He dared to do it only because he was Constancia's lover, and he insisted on insulting me in a song of insinuation:

> " 'My mother taught me from a book.
> She was mother of the village of Juremeia.
> Who cares to look will see [this truth]
> Remembering my mother umbanda,
> Protected by St. Barbara of the Thunder.' *

"I was astounded! I was paralyzed there in front of the drums! He was announcing that I was an ignoramus! So I answered him! I sang out loud:

> " 'If you folks don't know me,
> Don't insult me!
> For
> My mother is St. Barbara,
> My father is the Lord of Good Ending!'

"Ha! That was good! Now it was I who was insulting her, and I was winning because they all had to sing and dance to *my* song, which was about their own guardian saints! How the drums beat!

"Then Constancia got up to dance in front of me, and she answered:

> " 'I am she who has pembe;
> I am she who has pemba;
> Only in *my* village
> One finds pemba for curing!' †

"So there she was insulting me again, claiming that only she could cure sickness! She was showing off, and she would have kept on; but the people got tired of the fight and shouted: 'Chetrua! Peace! Call off the fight!' A man whispered to me that no harm was meant, that they would apologize later; but I went on with more insinuation:

* "From a book"=correctly. "Umbanda" (Bantu)=of the cult. St. Barbara of the Thunder=Iansã.
† "Pembe" or "pemba" is West African chalk used in fetish rites.

> " 'My Lady St. Barbara,
> She herself will see me
> As she is my godmother,
> She will come to defend me.'

"And then Constancia fell! I had made her own saint descend in her! She staggered, her eyes stared and rolled, she foamed at the mouth. From all sides people rushed to hold her. I can tell you, her daughters were very embarrassed. Well, I had won. So I remained in front of the drums, and did some more boasting:

> " 'Capangeiro is a fighter,
> Capangeiro has munition,
> Capangeiro wins in battles,
> Just as often as he likes.' "

Sabina smiled now over her victory. She sang the song again, and rose from her seat to dance in place. Chuckling, she continued, "She even tried to steal my daughter Antonia from me, inviting her to dance with her own women!" Her tone was scornful and indignant. "I didn't like that. . . . And all this time, Compadre Manoel was getting frightened. He tried to pull me away, and begged me to return home. 'Father Benedito doesn't know anything about this,' he said, 'and he won't like it.' He kept shaking his head and making faces at me. But I wasn't going to let her take my daughter. I would take hers first! So I sang:

> " 'I call myself capangeiro,
> I don't disguise my character,
> I am the son of Oxalá,
> The grandson of Iemanjá.'

"They were still shouting, 'Chetrua! Truce! Enough!' Then a young man fell for the first time in his life, and he sang to my caboclo spirit:

> " 'There are those who do not recognize me,
> But already have heard tell of me,
> Have heard tell of capangeiro
> Of the village of Oxalá.'

179

"And then I left. I wouldn't even wait for Constancia to waken so I could tell her goodbye. But I gave them all a piece of my mind. I yelled: 'What a house of candomblé! Disgraceful! May you all go to the bowels of the earth! Never again do I visit this devil of a candomblé!' I swore never to visit any other house either, and I never have."

Looking around at her audience, she stated solemnly: "Everybody is jealous of me. They don't like me because I am modern and clean, and they are old-fashioned and filthy. They call me rich! That ogan who sneered, 'Your caboclos can't dance under kerosene lamps, only under electric lights'! And Constancia has a bad reputation. Her throat is full of scars where her lovers slashed her when she betrayed them. The police know. She's not pretty and she's old, but she gets her men by magic."

Edison and Menininha had mentioned Mother Constancia. She was known as a seer, and she was the sister of Sylvana who had first broken away from Yoruba traditions to found the caboclo cults. Sabina had actually begun training in her house, they said, but had quarreled with her and had then tried to plant despachos (sorcery) against her. Evidently Sabina could not forget the feud. Now she snorted:

"These days I have more business than Constancia, I guess. They tell me I ought to set up as a diviner in Rio!"

She relaxed, but only for a moment. Hearing Odette talk to someone in a distant room, she jumped up to investigate. I waited for her, as placidly as I could under the eyes of the women, and after a half-hour she returned. "I will be occupied now," she announced to her people in dismissal, and beckoned me to join her. She took me to the back room of the house and shut the door between it and the pavilion.

At a long table sat a young thin mulatto, neatly though poorly dressed, and with a completely vapid face. "What is your name, my son?" Sabina asked kindly.

"Fernando," he said low.

"He wants me to advise him," she explained to me. "Wouldn't you like to see? You can pay me for it later." Surprised, I agreed, and as Sabina sat down next to her client she remarked, "Seu Fernando, the foreign lady does not understand our language well, so you can speak freely."

On the table was a fine white embroidered cloth—"the cloth of Oxalá, for seeing the future," Sabina remarked. She spread out in front of her eight cowrie shells for divining: "These are the 'de le gun,' and when you throw them on the table, they will help you to see the past of a person." Then she placed a long pretty shell in a pointing position. She spread out a silver chain on which hung the good-luck symbol of brown wood called "figa," the closed right hand with outstretched fore-finger. On her right was a small jug dedicated to Oxalá, filled with sacred water called "maza." She sent her husband for a medium-sized candle, to represent the life of the client; when Benedito put it in her hand, she placed it in a stand on the table, and it burned all through the session. Despite the sticky heat, she had to close the window lest some draft blow out the precious flame. Then she spread out a sacred necklace of twenty-one glass beads; they were milky-white beads dedicated to Oxalá, translucent pearly beads dedicated to Iemanjá, bright blue ones dedicated to Oxóssi, gold ones of Oxum, and more, and all were "closed" on the string by three dark blue beads of Ogum, deity of the roads, quarrels, and warfare. Precious beads, heraldic of the gods that had traveled all the way from Africa.

Fussing with these instruments, Sabina told me that she had prepared for the reading by bathing, and sleeping apart from her husband. This morning she had arrayed herself in a clean yellow frock of Oxum and hung around her neck four long strings of the goddess' yellow beads, "closed" with three large milky ones of Iemanjá. Sabina now asked Benedito to leave; he did so reluctantly, being very curious about the client and me; and in fact he returned later.

Sabina smoothed out the cowries and beads on the cloth before the candle, and requested Fernando, "Put money on the table!"

"How much?"

"Five milreis." He gave her the bill, whereupon she rubbed

181

it along his arms and down his palms on to the cloth, and then placed it under the beads on the table. She chanted, invoking the deities of divination on behalf of the client. She held some shells over the maza water, dipped a couple in it, shook the drops off to her left, and dried the beads with the sacred towel.

"This takes a lot of work," she commented. "It is a specialty. Other temples have an assistant devoting all her time to this—but not I. I have only God." She threw the shells and studied them intently. "Oxóssi is at work here"—she directed her words to the client—"and you will have to make a despacho to get rid of whoever is troubling you."

"What is it?" His voice was anxious.

She shrugged, still looking at the shells. "That I don't know. It might even be a woman. . . . Now, if what I tell you isn't right, stop me."

I was surprised to hear her order a despacho since this was evil magic, supposedly repugnant to the mothers, at least to mothers of the Yoruba persuasion. I recalled having heard Menininha tell, outraged, of a man who had called on her at the town house to request her to prepare a despacho against the lover of a young girl he desired for himself. (This despacho would have been a bundle made up with a black cock and a bloodstained image of the rival, and some subsidiary items.) He had offered her a good sum of money, but she had refused, saying severely: "Sir, you know that I am a mother of our African cult, and therefore a friend of people, not a wicked magician. I maintain relations with the gods, not with the devil. Surely you realize that. I will cure you of sickness, and I will try to advance your happiness in all ways that the gods indicate, but I cannot do the work of the devil."

The man had apologized, she said, saying he meant no harm but loved the girl. However, people later told me that Menininha's second in command, Dona Laura, did practice black magic, contrary though this was to the code of a priestess. But Dona Laura was also said to make it her business to go contrary to the wishes of Menininha, whom she regarded as a priestly rival, and she could not be halted; in fact, she was said to be popular and to have many clients.

Obviously Sabina, whose temple followed caboclo practices, was not worried by the standards that regulated Menininha and most of the other Yoruba mothers. Hearing her refer so openly to magic—though she probably thought that I would not understand such colloquial Portuguese—I recalled too the newspapers in Rio de Janeiro, which several times a week carried stories about the bad magic practiced by Negro men there, fathers of the temples. The Bahia papers did not carry such reports, except rarely, concentrating instead on the religious performances of the mothers. But Bahia men could practice bad magic, and people sometimes gossiped about the despacho bundles they said they saw at the crossroads at midnight. (I never saw one, though I walked through the suburban woods for months.) Martiniano was believed to be the most successful practitioner of them all.

Now I watched Sabina attentively.

She threw shells continuously in different combinations, and I gathered that the pattern into which a throw fell indicated the number of shells to be used at the following throw. Sometimes she used all eight at once, or three or four, or one, and sometimes she gave two or three throws before making a statement. We three stared fixedly at the activity on the table. Each time she moved the big pointer to different sides of a throw, as though such pointing helped her to decipher new meanings.

Steadily she asked Fernando questions. At first he withheld comment, but as she made shrewd guesses, he was finally prompted to pour out a tale of woe. He revealed that he was living with a woman, somewhat older than himself, whom he suddenly had reason to suspect of infidelity. They had been keeping house for a number of years. A man of about twenty lived with them, and Fernando was now struck by the curious fact that the woman had begun to call the man "son," having until then called him "nephew." What could this mean? Surely, "son" meant lover?

Sabina, throwing steadily, eyes on the shells, agreed. "There is a serious disturbance here. But," she went on, "it does not lie in the woman or in the 'son.' It lies simply in your having neglected to make sacrifices to Cosme and Damião. Right?"

"Right," he admitted.

Suddenly Sabina attacked from another front: "The woman wants to leave you but only because she is jealous of you."

Fernando smirked.

Sabina tossed again, and went on: "The woman has no saint to protect her. . . . Now, *you* are living with two women." Pause. "But neither one is bad. You must stay with the older one. The young one is sick because a god is bothering her. You say she claims the young man is setting bad magic against her? Yet she has never seen him? I believe she is mistaken. According to my throws, the spirit troubling her is Oxum, goddess of love. She must come to me to be treated. I'll make it cheap for you because I can see you are poor people."

"But *now*, what will I do about the two women? Shall I leave one or keep both?" Fernando was concerned only with his own state of mind, and practically deaf to Sabina's concerns with his mistress.

Sabina did not answer but continued throwing and tossing. Examining the table carefully, she observed that the older woman had been ill but was so no longer. "Her body is closed to sickness now. But only Cosme will relieve *you* of your troubles."

Fernando muttered that he preferred his sweetheart, even if she was sick, to Maria with whom he was living. Still he could not abandon Maria, he said, having lived with her for six years and knowing her to be a true comrade. But he wanted the new one! As the two women lived far apart, Maria did not know about her rival yet.

Sabina, all absorbed, elaborated: "The young one's trouble is caused by the seven evil spirits, the little demons that serve Ogum. They are all Exus. They harass her, and she won't get well, my son, until she is treated with baths and fumigations. I might as well tell you, she is a medium, she should be in the priesthood. To cure her, Seu Fernando, you must drive Exu away, you must dispatch the evil-doer!"

Fernando appeared neither impressed nor frightened. Perhaps he was tired, or maybe after all his mind was not as vapid as his countenance.

"How much will it cost?" he asked.

Sabina turned to him: "You arrange matters with her. The charge for the sacred bath, the fumigation, and the candle will be about sixty-five milreis."

"I do not make even two hundred milreis a month, dona," he said.

She answered in a low tone: "That's why I'm making it cheap for you. But don't worry." She left for the adjoining altar room containing symbols of African, Indian, and Catholic deities and spirits, and returned with a huge bottle of water. "Throw some of this pembe powder into it," she directed, handing him a small paper packet, "and make a bath for the creature." An absorbed expression on his face, he handed her five milreis. Sabina took him by the arm and, trying to escort him to the door, remarked coaxingly: "You don't live far from here. Come in and make a despacho to settle the creature."

But his thoughts were far away, trapped in the maze of love and duty. "It's a dreadful case, dona, dreadful. The girl even has fever. What will I give her?"

If Sabina was exasperated, if she thought her client was evading her, she gave no sign. Instead she answered calmly: "She needs a bath of special herbs, and a smoking of incense. We will give it to her here. Leave the bath for later on." She handed him another large bottle of water from the altar room. "Mix this water with the powder and give it to her to drink. Look here, really that young man is not at fault! The girl is maligning him, she is imagining things. The trouble with your two women is that they are overambitious, and that is because they are driven by male gods. The gods have to be tamed! The heads of the women have to be prepared for them! All the troubles will be settled when they learn to be priestesses. It's in

185

the shells and the beads. No doctor's remedy will give the young one health—it wouldn't be enough. . . . Does she like to amuse herself? I mean, does she like to sing and dance and have ogans admire her?"

Fernando ignored the question, and asked instead for an amulet to protect his sweetheart.

But Sabina was lost in thought and continued explaining: "It is a matter for her god to decide. The sick one is certainly a medium, that is why she is sick! She does not know how to handle the god within her, and therefore she is unsettled! Don't you understand? She belongs to the god Ogum, who controls quarrels and war."

Fernando seemed unmoved. He muttered that he had lived long with the older woman and yet had never known that she had a son whom she first called her nephew; he did not know if he could trust her; it all looked like a lie.

Sabina returned to the table to throw more shells. Finally she picked the shells up, held them over the little jug while she rolled them among the fingers of her right hand, swung her hand once or twice over the jug, and left for the adjoining altar room. Waiting for her, Fernando exclaimed softly to himself: "Is it possible that he *is* her son! Is it possible?" Sabina brought him three tinted packets of the pembe powder, enough to furnish the girl three curative baths. He took them absently, and exclaimed again, "My good Lord! Nosso Senhor do Bomfim! Can it be!" The man must have been in an agony of mistrust. Suddenly resolving his thoughts, he looked up at Sabina and declared, "I'm going to stay with the two women!"

Little man, thought I, you have a mind of your own! After all the effort that this woman expends to change your thinking! Have you simply used her as a sounding board?

Sabina ignored her client's assertion. Quietly she said: "Bring the sick one here tomorrow. My guide arrives Wednesday and Saturday afternoons."

But still the man could not be swayed. "I cannot, dona. I am working. But *she* might come. She knows you. In fact, she sent me here."

Sabina was overjoyed. "She sent you here! Well, it's the spirit doing this! You're right, you don't have to leave either woman. But you should make your sacrifice to Cosme. You don't have to give him much, just a little food. Do you know how?"

"Maria does. Caruru?"

"Fine! Have her make that. Invite all the children you know, so that they will enjoy themselves and bring you luck. After that, Cosme will advise you about everything."

But these candomblé formulas did not satisfy Fernando; he had not yet arrived at his own solution. "I don't want to leave one woman or the other, not one or the other," he muttered over and over; and finally Sabina led him from the house.

I wondered why Fernando was so difficult to sway. Wasn't he a believer? If not, why had he consulted the mother at all? Was he skeptical of the religion in general? Yet Sabina was confident of winning him, and certainly she had persuaded him to buy medicines that could be only the first step in a protracted relationship. Were the women less skeptical? Or maybe Fernando just had not understood what everything was about?

In Sabina's mind there were no doubts. She returned to the cool pavilion almost skipping, and looking at her husband and me, at her daughter and a priestess tending odd jobs, she burst into a gay and beautiful song,

> "I am an Indian!
> I hail from the woods,
> And of the woods I am king!
> I come from the savage forest,
> But I have a gentle heart."

She capered some samba steps—she really loved to sing and dance—and repeated the song in variations:

> "Oh, from the woods, oh, from the woods,
> Oh, from the woods I have come, I warned you!
> Oh, in the woods I am sultan of the village,
> Oh, from the woods I have come, I warned you!"

187

She halted before me and demanded confidently: "Come here tomorrow to see him—my guide. I'm sure he'll be here. You ought to let him teach you things. He won't ask for much, only about nine hundred milreis for everything!"

She's going to bludgeon me as she did that poor innocent, I thought, taken aback. I must stop her, and yet I can't hurt her feelings; she's positively intoxicated with herself. "I can't afford that now, dona," I answered quietly, "though I appreciate the opportunity. Perhaps you can teach me? You know everything, and you could make it cheaper for me."

"*I!*" she laughed fiercely. She had not expected this reply. "*I* know nothing! I'm just his instrument! It's *he* who knows, and whatever I know, he has taught me. Can't you understand?" Her tone was suddenly angry and despairing, as though she knew she was reaching for something far outside her grasp. "He speaks through me! . . . I tell you, go to any other house and learn what they charge for telling things! Go, if you don't trust me!"

She stopped suddenly, and offered to show me a room where she kept the lovely costumes that were put on the priestesses when their gods descended. We went into her small, well equipped bedroom, where the gowns hung in a huge portable closet. They were beautiful and colorful, as I well knew from the ceremony of the mother of waters, and I was amazed to see how freshly they were laundered, especially since each one consisted of yards and yards of costly material.

"Exquisite," I admitted to her.

"Well, then, come tomorrow," she urged again.

"Ah, dona, I can't. Maybe in another week—"

All at once, as though someone had whipped her, her shoulders shimmied convulsively, her head dropped, her eyes squinted, and her voice mooed deeply. "Huh! Call in the Man of the Temple!" Was she hysterical, I wondered.

Odette heard her mother, looked in with a troubled face, and then went for her father. Benedito arrived shortly, also looking concerned, and saluted the guide by kissing Sabina's hand. The guide, in the new deep voice, asked for ogans Caetano and

Manoel as witnesses. Neither was available. In a low aside, the guide asked Odette to bring a chair, which she then sat in, and she told Benedito to sit with me on the bed opposite her. Hearing people outside, friends and neighbors returning from work, the guide told Odette impatiently to shut the bedroom door and mount a watch. But she then got up to open the door a little, for she wanted to hear and to be heard!

The "Indian" spoke in a murky Portuguese to show that he was a true savage. "What is it that the lady wants?" he asked me. But the enunciation and grammar were so corrupt that the question had to be repeated several times before I could understand. What should I say? I didn't want anything; but I couldn't say that, or the woman would do something desperate.

"Well," I answered carefully, "I did think I would like to learn things from your horse."

The "Indian" laughed a deep "Ho! Ho!" and told the Man of the Temple to listen carefully, and to report to Caetano and Manoel—"for my horse won't remember any of this when I am gone."

"Yes, your Reverence, I am listening," Benedito replied soberly. Nevertheless the "Indian" reiterated the warning at intervals, and to me repeated with maddening frequency: "Do you hear? Are you paying attention?"

The possessed priestess now proclaimed: "My horse cannot teach, my horse knows only what I tell her. She can teach merely songs and dances, but she cannot teach the way of divining by throwing shells on the table, nor can she teach how to cure ills. *I* do these things—not my horse, who is only my instrument. I mount her, and she rides. So you cannot learn from her but only from me. Are you listening? Do you understand, lady? You *must* do as my horse directs, for she is obeying me. Now, when will you return? Other mothers and fathers teach superficial things, but from me my horse has learned fundamentals. So I direct you to study with her—that is, with me, the capangeiro. . . . So you want to learn secrets, lady? You want to do as the daughters do? Sit in retreat, your head bent, seven days alone, without stirring from a dark room, carrying food for the gods on your head, allowing the sacrificial blood to be poured on your head and drip all the way down your body? Do you want to dance with the priestesses, bathe in the foul-smelling sacred water, sing and chant, have my horse pull out your body hairs? *Do you?*"

As I did not answer, feeling the situation was absurd and not of my making, Sabina showed signs of frenzied anger. I decided then to play along and at the next "*Do you?*" I said very low, "Yes, sir."

"Well, that way you will make much zimbi—I mean, money —and will make yourself beloved among the people." Sabina, possessed by "Indian," now interrupted herself by calling over and over in a low voice, "Chetru! Chetru! Chetru!" She resumed in a more even tone: "I order you to pay one conto four hundred in two checks. Do you hear, Man of the Temple? One conto four hundred. Besides, you will provide sacrificial goats, all the foods of the saints, and so on. Everyone in this house will work for you, and at the end you will have to thank them all. It will be your obligation to assist me in all that I do. You can watch anything that goes on in this temple. And remember, the work is strenuous. After three months you will be made a daughter, you will begin a new life in sainthood. . . . At present, you are not ready to 'throw shells on the table'; that knowledge is for those well advanced in the cult. Just to learn that takes three full days. . . . Pay close attention to what I say, for soon it is your time to leave. My horse will direct you how to make your god-costumes; they are costly, and you will need two."

"Indian" halted then to ask Odette in a hoarse aside who was in the house.

"Joanna," she answered.

"Let her come in."

Joanna, black and gaunt, with an anxious face came in and knelt at the mother's feet, kissed the mother's hand, and sat back on her heels respectfully.

"I bless you, my daughter," the "Indian" said, sitting rigid with a commanding set of the shoulders, eyes narrowed, nostrils flattened against the lip. "I bless you," the oracular voice repeated, and Sabina stiffly stretched out her arms to encircle Joanna in a harsh embrace.

The tension slumped, and I felt awkward. What should I do? What could I do? My dilemma was solved when the "Indian" courteously summoned young Antonio to escort me to the streetcar line. Entering the room, the boy stretched out on the floor in an elaborate salute, as required of one protected by the male deity of war, and he kissed Sabina's hand. I rose then to go, relieved, saying I would discuss matters further on another day with the horse.

Antonio was not talkative, but he did answer my questions. As we walked through the darkness that had fallen suddenly, he explained that the capangeiro had arrived off schedule today; and, though he would undoubtedly exhaust Sabina, he was bound to arrive again tomorrow, for he came twice a week and tomorrow was a programmed day. She was also ridden by old Oxalá, and he came two or three times a month, holding audiences with whoever cared to consult him.

Asleep that humid evening in my skyscraper hotel, I had the first nightmare I can recall. I heard the thin painful sound of a desperate shriek, and saw the huge attacking head of a fierce cat whose eyes burned and bore down upon me; and in the split second before my awakening the cat head broke into a sardonic grin. I felt miserable as I got out of bed, trembling and sweating. When my brain cleared, the thought shot out clear, "Sabina, damn her!" The narrow eyes and sniffing nose of the "Indian" framed in fine fuzzy hair, the brutal claws behind the velvet grasp, that deepened voice breaking occasionally into a normal female one, the small stuffy room with everyone in it bent upon making me yield—out of these had come the nightmare. Out of these must come the moods of all those who fall possessed.

"Isn't that conceivable?" I asked Edison the next day, telling him the story.

"I shouldn't wonder. But I am surprised at the pressure she put on you! It's positively unethical! In my long acquaintance with mothers, I've never known one to invoke higher power in order to gain a daughter. Amazing. Mothers do get possessed suddenly to learn how to settle desperate problems like fatal illness, or violations of taboos, or despachos. But to get you! And so much money!" He snorted. "That's why we organized a union of the reputable temples, to outlaw such charlatanism."

When I mentioned the occurrence to Menininha, she considered it beneath her comment. "What is that woman?" she queried rhetorically. "You don't call *her* a mother? She's out only to make a living, not really to help the people, and she has never been trained in any priesthood. She was out after your pocketbook, my lady, and after the prestige of your name. And she lives to fight Constancia, who *is* a great mother, because Constancia baptized her with caboclo. Constancia and Sylvana, those are priestesses! Sylvana never even needed to throw cowries in order to see. Looking out of her doorway, she could tell you anything about anyone passing by. Even the governor consulted her during a general strike. She helped him against the advice of her own gods when he paid her six full contos—and then the gods struck her dead. But the governor was all right because he did what she told him. . . . How can you talk of Sabina as a mother? She cares for neither gods nor people."

I seldom saw Sabina after that.

XVIII

THE TEMPLES often held social dances that had nothing to do with the gods. They were simply occasions for young people to meet, to hear jazz and dance "fox"—and to make love if they chose. At these affairs the bahiana dress was forgotten, and so were the taboos against using hair straightener and rouge. Many were the discussions between Menininha and Cleoza over using rouge, for even at Gantois modern times were knocking. Zézé and Hilda were just a little too old to be influenced by the new trend, and they held it as an additional grievance against Sabina that she used rouge. Bahia life was laden with regulations about women's wear, and during my stay the Archbishop issued new pronunciamentos concerning the length of women's skirts and of the skirts and pants of their bathing suits.

Edison said that the blacks were so crazy about dancing that they would walk miles to an affair if they had no money for carfare—even after a hard day's work. They would dance themselves into a lather until the dawn, and then start the journey back to work. "Only the gods and their black blood keep them from dying of pneumonia," he would say admiringly, for Brazilians love to comment on the physical power of the Negroes. Men and women would be excited by the end of a dance, and lovers might take each other casually, barely hidden in doorways, unaware as though intoxicated, until sometimes a policeman arrested a couple, often first taking the woman for himself. Sometimes out of sheer good feeling, a woman gave herself to the man who paid her carfare home; but she did not necessarily consider that there was any bond between them after that. If he meant to court her, he would have to work at it systematically. Otherwise, the man could not get her even to sit next to him in the streetcar, and as for holding her arm—that was an unheard-of intimacy! The black woman valued her company above rubies.

The noted Mother Flaviana was about to reach her ninetieth birthday, and Edison said one day that her daughters planned a social dance for the occasion. He had often attended these affairs, because he knew the ogan in charge of slaughtering the sacrificial animals; and he had found them entertaining. The ogans and women boasted that Flaviana had made so many priestesses in her near-century of practice that the temple would be rich if they could collect a half-cent for each one.

So, on the Sunday evening of Flaviana's birthday, I accompanied Edison to her "villa" in the woods outside the city near Engenho Velho, riding in Amor's taxi. It was hot and sunny, although so late; Edison sang little songs, as was his habit, and Amor's young daughter listened attentively, sitting up straight in the front seat. The temple was attractive—a solidly built, long, one-story frame structure, dominating several other buildings in the clearing. A pet goat came to greet us, and had to be saved from the car. The bareness of the building struck me. Here as at other temples, there were almost no ornamental flowers, shrubs, or trees; the cut flowers at altars were always purchased at the markets. The towering trees in the near-by woods served exclusively as outdoor altars.

The temple was also the private residence of Flaviana and her own daughters, that is, the daughters of her actual family, and their daughters. It was its private character that had led the ogans, a long time ago, to flank the entrance with two tall shade trees, quite conspicuous in this tropical city denuded of greenery in favor of bare poles strung with telephone and electric-light wires. As an additional reminder of its private character, there was an attractive gabled front over the entrance that was covered with stucco.

Nevertheless the interior of "Flaviana's Villa" was as dank and gloomy as that of any conventional Yoruba temple. The corridor running the length of the house was the required hard-packed mud, and Edison and I walked down it carefully, watchful of wet, slippery spots. We were led to a cell-like chamber at the end, and we stood in the dark until a temple girl switched on a bare electric bulb, saying, "You have visitors, my mother."

Old Flaviana had been stretched on a meager cot, dozing. Now she sat up and in a somewhat confused way received our handshakes—strange greeting to one accustomed to hand kisses— and in return she gave her priestly blessings. Edison told her about me, but I hardly think she listened; she was not even curious enough to look at me.

I thought that in her mind she was not much of this world, her spirit was so remote. On the cot, she held herself rigidly erect, balancing with back-thrust buttocks in the manner of the bahianas, and her old eyes, rimmed red in her black face, looked at things unreal above and beyond us. Her bones and face were dainty, thin, and broad, and her thick hair was snow-white, cropped and curling becomingly in the mannish style favored by the priestesses who bind their heads for carrying loads. She wore a lovely blouse of white drawn work, cut so low and wide that

194

it slipped off a shoulder, and its texture dimly bared her thin breasts.

While her granddaughter brought in chairs for us, she told Edison, in an old cracked voice and in toothless syllables that held the attention, that she had gone to early morning mass to celebrate Oxum, her goddess, who is also Our Lady of Conception. She pointed to the colors of Oxum that she wore, in her gold-threaded necklace and her old-fashioned broad bracelets of heavy red gold set with tomato-coral, in her small gold ear hoops, and in her wide taffeta skirt of rose and gold. Her slim black fingers moved lightly over the finery.

Since this was her birthday, Mother Flaviana had brought out her dolls (the goddess Oxum is a young mother, and the dolls represent the world of little children, without whom she is unhappy). She leaned to the foot of her cot and showed the dolls resting there against divan pillows of gold, pink and pale blue. Fascinated and touched, I saw a girl doll and two boy dolls, and a tiny blond celluloid doll smaller than my thumb, with a nipple in its mouth and wearing a waist-length shirt as Bahia babies do. The big dolls also came from the white race, having blue eyes and reddish hair painted upon their celluloid heads. Flaviana assured us that they had names. The girl doll, though the biggest, was considered the youngest; she had been presented to the mother years before and was mended fresh for this birthday. She wore a crocheted bonnet and a long dress and petticoat, all of blue, and blue crocheted boots. The boy dolls wore charming rompers of white-dotted maroon, with white shirts and black knitted shoes and bonnets. As they looked exactly alike, Flaviana had decided that the smaller one was the younger. She fondled all of them with affection, and she called her granddaughter to bring in the tiny trunks containing their wardrobes.

Now other guests came into the room to congratulate the aged mother and give her presents wrapped in prettily colored paper and gilt cord. Priestesses brought in more chairs, lining them in rows from the cot to the doorway. In the huge ceremonial room near by, musicians were beginning to tune up for the dance. The visitors could barely wait to complete their homage and join the orchestra. Flaviana ceased her chatter, piled the gift packages on the bed, and looked at them quietly. She seemed tired and lost.

Then in a gushing confessional of fright, she mentioned her aches, her weariness, her growing deafness, her age, her great age. (Everyone remembered when she had been beautiful and powerful, when no one would have run away from her.) A young priestess tried to reassure her, saying gently over and over that Flaviana was fatigued from the early mass and from Oxum's arrival afterwards. But the old matriarch did not hear, and dropped back on the cot among the dolls and the new presents.

We followed the others then. Lights were being switched on all over, harsh bare bulbs in keeping with the strident music that the orchestra was beginning to play. "They are all in formal dress," smiled Edison in mild irony, "in summer style, *de rigueur*."

I looked inquiringly at him.

"Just watch them," he insisted. "Every man wearing a white suit and shoes and a blue shirt, every woman wearing a long dress of blue. They are being elegant for the fox. Wonderful of Flaviana to let them go ahead—though she won't appear all evening. She'll stay in there with Oxum."

There were about fifteen men and women present, and the jazz orchestra of four pieces played in a corner. The music was as deafening and vehement as in any college night club; it was all played slowly, and the fox rhythms quite rubbed out, because the men really wanted to play samba. For a time, only girl couples danced, and I suddenly became aware of their unaccustomed tight dresses and "uplift" brassières, the spinal curve of each revealed in all its exaggeration, buttocks protruding heavily as the dancers teetered on new high heels. Though they were priestesses, they had defied tradition by straightening their hair.

"Poor Flaviana," said Edison, "she must have smelled that hair straightening if she did not see it. She has even let them use rouge. Rouge and the hot iron—" He shook his head. "The old

Africans are losing out to the beauticians. No wonder Martiniano is shocked. And Flaviana doesn't say a word."

The girls clung to one side of the room and glanced at the men lounging on the opposite side in apparent indifference to them, talking and laughing as though they were miles away from the dance. Girls and children kept dancing, and the men came onto the floor gradually, each approaching his girl with a serious, set face. At the end of a song, each partner ran as though in terror to the wall where his own sex waited for him.

I found it a heavy affair, blanketed with country gaucherie, but Edison was intrigued.

"Here you see them learning to become sophisticated," he said as he looked about, "leaving Africa for the western world and the twentieth century. They are trying to think as we do. If they had the opportunity, they would be just as conventional as any white person, or as any educated black. They are playing at breaking away from their poverty, even if it means offending the gods. But of course they show their true character anyway: it's the women who aren't afraid to dance, and they keep that bahiana walk of theirs even though the dresses are wrong for it. And look at the woman try to escape from her partner!"

"What?" I was puzzled.

"Yes, she isn't used to being held down by a man! Like Flaviana's granddaughter over there. Before, she was dancing with a girl, and the two of them stood up straight and easily. Now she's with a man, and conscious of it. It doesn't make her happy, she's so young and inexperienced and never had a lover. Just look how serious they are!" Edison was very sympathetic, but he had this habit of putting people under a microscope so that they lost any individual uniqueness and suddenly became instead a congeries of behavior. "Look!" he continued, his eyes glowing as he puffed his cigarette. "The young fellow is pressing their heads together and pushing her towards him—but she is placing a great distance between their legs!" He laughed a little. "She's trying to run away from him!"

"I believe you're interested in her!" I teased him.

"No," he smiled, "but I have danced with her, and it's

197

amusing to watch at this distance. It's hard work leading a woman who feels like that! . . . Now, there's another type that you'll see as the evening warms up. She is older and has had plenty of experience with men. When she dances, you couldn't slip a piece of paper between her body and her partner's; and, sure enough, the man begins to fondle her. The 'dominator,' I call him." Edison snickered, and played at deepening his tenor voice into a virile bass. "He bends her far backwards, and forces his leg into her skirt. The woman loves it, and they become so excited that the children make fun of them. After each number, the dominator claps and claps, calling 'Repeat! Repeat!' Mind you, each number is about ten minutes long!"

Edison was looking over the dance floor as he talked, apparently recognizing his types, although I could not.

"And there's a third type. She's an aloof kind of woman, trying to imitate the upper class. She shows how refined she is by dancing at arm's length from the man!" He looked at me mischievously. "But she winds up just like the other who is being dominated. . . . Now, the man who takes this aloof lady is a character. He's a dandy. He dresses in a starched white suit, so white, so starched; he wears white shoes and even a white hat, and sometimes a white tie. He has squirted toilet water around his face and chest, and even his handkerchief is perfumed: no low human odors will come from him! He'll have the women consider him a man of consequence, with some pennies in his purse. Someone has told him that 'poise makes the man.'

"So he marches up to the aloof woman without a word, but he holds his arms stiffly in the dancing position and makes a little bow. He has seen that somewhere, in the movies or on the stage, and he thinks speech is vulgar under the circumstances. She accepts also without a sound. She may not know anything about him, but he has already found out if she is engaged or single or a virgin, because he plans to get more out of the evening than just a dance. He goes on playing his aristocratic role, not looking at her or talking to her or even touching her: he holds her only by the wrist, so as not to offend by touching her fingers! Nothing intimate between them! She is the same, she holds a handkerchief, the color of her dress, in the hand that she rests on his shoulder. And when the dance is over he doesn't howl or applaud, he escorts her right back to her place and leaves in unbroken silence.

"That is just the beginning." Edison had warmed up to his subject, and got an impish pleasure out of the elaborations. He talked now with imitative gestures and some mockery in his tones. "After a while he approaches her again for a dance, still silent; but somehow soon he stumbles on her foot as an excuse for a remark. When she has answered him a couple of times, he feels he has made a conquest, and he starts rolling his eyes and making faces to the people around, to draw their attention to him. Most men carry on in this way, but they reach this stage sooner with the first two types. . . . Now the dandy whispers compliments in the woman's ear, and she answers out loud that she does not believe him, that she has no luck with men, that no one likes her, that she is *not* a beauty! By now the fellow is making *terrific* faces to the bystanders to show that he is leading her where he wants to take her. The girl cannot see, of course, but she ought to know what is happening because she has seen the same thing with other couples. The men are laughing with her partner. The women are smiling, and they pat her and say 'Neg'a, you've caught a man!' "

We both smiled.

"Maybe you'll catch a couple playing the game of 'eyes,' " Edison suggested hopefully. "It's very popular. A man likes a woman and he signals with his eyes. If she stares back, it means she's interested, in fact has accepted him. They 'talk' for quite a while this way. He'll ask her to dance, addressing her with great formality as 'Senhora'; then he'll get mixed up and say 'Senhorita.' After that, anything can happen, especially if the girl is past twenty years of age."

I was tired of standing and observing, and so I proposed to Edison that we join the others on the dance floor.

"Oh, Dona Ruth!" he answered, somewhat alarmed. "No, we can't. They will talk about us the way I've been doing about them! Then the other men will come over and invite you—and there will be confusion! They will think you are staring at them for a purpose! You must act like a lady!"

He was distressed, and tried to distract me by pointing out a child of six or seven who cried terribly whenever his aunt left him to dance. He thought the little boy had been given too much rum, but the aunt said no, he cried through jealousy. The people seemed to be restrained by our presence, and so we left long before midnight. The buxom young daughter of the butcher ogan insisted upon escorting Edison to our taxi, and took another girl along to whom she clung heavily and remarked sulkily: "Dr. Edison usually dances until one's legs ache! But tonight he did nothing!"

"Ah, my love," Edison teased her in a good humor, "you know well that my heart is yours! You know what an honor it is to have your friendship!"

"Well," she grumbled, "well . . ." And she shook hands limply.

XIX

I THOUGHT about the dance a good deal, because it was so different from any other I had seen, and because it was the first in which men and women joined in the familiar way of our world. It was the conventionality of this dance that drew my attention, and that made it seem out of keeping with all I had come to expect, because the people did not feel at ease with it. The peculiar spirit that was theirs was missing entirely. The women had relinquished command, but the men had not really taken over. There was no idea behind the dance except courtship, no display of virtuosity, no summoning of the gods. But as soon as they could woo, they did, and Edison assured me that after our departure the atmosphere must have brightened enormously.

I discovered that I had become African in my prejudices, as African as Martiniano, as Menininha, as Luzía. I felt that the people had lost themselves when they put on heels for the ballroom and abandoned the patterns that they usually stamped with naked feet on floors of dirt, guided only by drumbeats or the pounding of a gourd or even of a hard straw hat. The songs of the orchestra could not compare with the songs the people chanted in candomblé or at the fair ground, though the traditional songs were hardly more than monotones swaying from one octave to another. But the drums! The men put their hearts into them as they never could into the jazz orchestra. Their rhythms in the background were arresting, vigorous, and clear, edged brilliantly by the lighter sounds of small irons that were tapped now loudly, now gently, and of small baskets filled with shot that were shaken now roughly, now in swooping loops that swished in sound.

And how vivid were the traditional dance forms, from the solemn ones of the Yoruba temple to the mad, gay ones of the street! Temple training stressed polish, and this standard carried over to samba, but not to the fox that I had just seen and was to see again. Fox simply made no sense to the people, but generations had worked and reworked the patterns of the other dances. Each person must have realized that myriads of individuals had danced and beaten to the old rhythms, whereas fox not only was new but did not fit into their scheme of life—probably it had been borrowed from the aristocratic houses in which the women worked.

Edison understood me very well. "And if you could only dance with them," he said, "new sluices of information would be opened."

"How?"

"You would feel things in your very insides. Their dancing is like living: it is their avenue of comprehension and response, it is their mode of thinking, their way of conversing. Do you remember the women of Engenho Velho? Some were in trance, some were out of trance; but all of them were lost in their dancing. You could tell because their movements were sensuous and flowing. That handsome woman, Elizabeth of Xangô, looked as though she were wooing herself, and later, when her god descended, she was in a mood of intense passion—her life had its deepest meaning for her then. Too bad that men are not entitled to this experience unless they are abnormal; they are supposed to be earthy stuff, and the best they can do is to dance in the streets."

I laughed, thinking of the opposite dogma of the Catholic Church concerning its priesthood.

"Yes," Edison repeated seriously, "the people say a man's mind is in the streets, not turned in upon himself where he can be a tool for the gods. He's always 'hot' and excited and worldly. And I think they're right," he smiled.

The people are always right about themselves, I took that for granted. The fascinating thing was to see how their selections worked. Suddenly I remembered a scene in a new caboclo temple we had visited one evening. The rites had begun, and a boy of eighteen was giving a superb theatrical version of samba, leaping high and wide as a ballet star. But the people censured him for bringing the street into the ceremony, though in this dissident temple men were allowed to dance with the women. The boy cried out then that he had merely been playing, not blaspheming any god. But the mother saw vanity and challenge in his wild twists and jumps; she said the gods could not feel at ease unless people were docile and yielding. "Women do not writhe and show themselves," she commented tartly.

"I know by now that women are the chosen sex," I said to Edison. "I take it for granted just as I know in our world that men are the chosen sex. But now I'd like to know what satisfaction a priestess gets out of identifying herself with one particular god? What makes her feel she belongs to Oxum rather than to Xangô or Ogum?"

"Fashion explains some of it," he said. "What makes a monk join one order and not another? He has heard that it represents certain appealing principles, and maybe it is the nearest one to his home, and maybe he has met someone he admires from there. Aninha, for instance, belonged to Xangô, and so lots of her ogans and women belonged to Xangô. Menininha belongs to Oxum, and so do many of her women, while many of the men belong to Oxum's husbands, who at different times were Xangô and

Oxóssi. Besides, Xangô has been a favorite for a long time; he is the virile man, the despotic ruler, the headstrong lover (Martiniano said he was a rapist), and he was even resurrected after death in the form of lightning. Sometimes he's the knight on the white horse; sometimes they think he was like Roosevelt, sometimes like Mussolini.

"The other male gods aren't as fascinating. Ogum governs iron and trouble—quite a sullen type; but iron was a noble metal in barbaric Africa. And trouble? Well, iron went into instruments of warfare. Omolu controls pests, especially smallpox, and some say he is related to Ogum. He is old, palsied, and sly. Oxóssi is a charming young hunter, a prince of the class of Oxum. And old Oxalá is supposed to be as passionless as Jesus. Obviously various influences cause a woman to enter the service of some one god.

"The female gods have great womanly charm. You know about Oxum, who is the dearest daughter of Oxalá, a princess and a perfect sweetheart and wife. Iansã, the stormy Viking, is sometimes said to be the wife of Xangô, and sometimes his sister; and sometimes she enters him so that he becomes bisexual! Often she does mean things to gentle Oxum. Iemanjá, second wife of Oxalá, is the popular water-goddess, and is considered a voluptuous delight. Nana is Oxalá's first wife, and is very old."

"They have distinct personalities, haven't they?"

"Very, and they come out in every imaginable way. The costume of a god tells his or her story. The color tells the age, the length of the skirt tells the sex; shell ornaments are favored by one, beads by another, grass by a third, iron by a fourth, gold by a fifth, a hammer by a sixth, a sword by a seventh, and so on. Each god prefers certain foods, cooked in specific ways; some of them demand fasts, some feasts; each has one day of the week reserved for services or retreats, and each is identified with some saint of the Catholic calendar, so that certain masses have to be said at special times! Each god is represented by a fetish symbol besides, a stone of a certain shape and color, and the stone must be 'fed' and bathed and dressed, so that all this care will cause it to 'grow' and multiply! Sometimes a god 'lives' in a tree, occasionally in a snake, and all these details are known."

"Gracious! How they've worked things out!"

"And that's not all! Each god dances in a standard way, and a priestess must learn this or the god won't feel at home. Yoruba teaches it one way, Angola another, and caboclo differently again. Of course, the woman's temperament can't help coming through. Tia Massí, for instance, is always colorless, but Sabina is as exhibitionistic as a cabaret dancer. Menininha is an artist, cool and skilled and completely in command."

"Still, they're all Catholics?"

"Naturally." He spread his hands and chuckled. "Our Church understands human nature so well! Dona Ruth"—he turned to me—"priestesses get their final ordination within the doors of the Catholic church; every priestess *must* be a Catholic. And certain crucial ceremonies, like death, take place both in the temple and in the cathedral. You should see Bahia during the two months before Carnival! Candomblé and Catholicism are completely intertwined! There is one day called 'the day of the washing of the Church of Our Lord of Good Ending.' Wait till you see it!"

I shook my head over the intricacy of things. "The men," I mourned, "poor fellows . . ."

He laughed. "Some of them don't do so badly," he said reflectively. "Father Bernardino, who has an Angola temple, is even respected by Menininha, and she calls him 'brother' when he visits her. You should see him dance. He rivals the best of the women, although he's a big man. He dances in the woman's way, sensuous and aloof, and he's so competent in his work that the mothers have almost forgotten his original sex. But what a temper he has! That is the remains of his inferiority complex, and he lets it out by shouting, wherever he is."

"Why an inferiority complex?"

"Why, he's a *man*, Dona Ruth, in a world dominated by women! A true priest of the cult should be a woman, and I think Bernardino is honest enough about his cult practice to wish he were truly a woman, instead of just a man acting like a woman. As it is, he has to delegate many crucial functions to a woman of the priesthood, and then it is she who is in command after all, instead of he. It makes fatherhood hollow at times."

I laughed, because I never grew accustomed to this deflation of male authority, especially in a land like Brazil, although female prestige was something I well understood, as did in fact any Catholic Brazilian. "Then who is his god?" I asked curiously.

"Just what you might expect," Edison answered with a certain satisfaction, as though the rules of the cult were working out properly, "it is Iansã, the bisexual goddess. Bernardino is always consistent." He smiled.

I shook my head. "Poor Martiniano!"

"Yes. Did you know he had seated Oxóssi, the hunter? So he can hunt women . . . Well, he's afraid the men-women will dominate Bahia in another generation."

"Misericordia!" I imitated a favorite lament of Menininha's. "My Lady Mary!"

Edison was amused: "A real candomblèzeiro, you've become! But don't worry. The men haven't the character and devotion to hold priesthoods together. They have wild tempers; they fight and call each other names, and beat up their 'daughters'; they are not always honest; and they don't really know the cult traditions. The duties of a 'mother' are tremendous, and the discipline in the old temples is something to marvel at. The women govern through the strength of their moral influence, and seldom need to resort to corporal punishment."

"How does a mother get her training?"

"In the Yoruba temple a priestess gives herself up entirely to a rigid education that lasts seven years! Practically, her soul is given into captivity, because at the end of the seven years her family has to ransom her! She is then reborn, and people talk of her 'age in godhood.' Manoel ransomed Zézé, and so he feels he should own her; but actually there's no competition against the mother."

205

"I see, she always owns," I shrugged. "I wonder if I'd like that."

"A matter of temperament, I suppose," he suggested. "Not all the daughters are tractable. Some grumble; but they do as they are told, the pressure is so great. Anyway, most of them have some junior to boss, because they rank the women in seven-year classes."

I laughed again, surprised at the elaborateness of the system. "Like college," I said.

"More thorough," he twinkled.

"How does one get to be a mother, then?"

"She's supposed to be the oldest in the oldest class. That means that she's had several times the seven-year minimum of training, and has held many responsible posts."

"But Totonia!" I protested.

"I was talking about the model mother. Well, even in Totonia's case, Massí and Luzía are the acting heads, and they've been priestesses since time began. Totonia got it through heredity, because her aunt had such influence among her people; but you see the inheritance became purely nominal. Now, Aninha broke off from Engenho Velho and organized her own priesthood; but she had already been ransomed and approved of. Pulcheria passed her post on to her niece, who then gave it to her daughter, Menininha; but all these women had been thoroughly trained, and Menininha was made when she was practically a baby. Even so, the temple politicians weren't willing to hand the headship over to her without a fight, led by old Dona Laura, who is her assistant now. Laura is her senior according to birthdays, although her junior according to age in godhood; and Laura insisted on being mother. In fact, after Pulcheria's niece's death, there was a sort of interregnum when both Laura and Menininha operated; but Menininha had the advantages of longer training, and of residing in the cult house, because she had always lived there with her great-aunt. So Dona Laura had to eat crow and content herself with being just the little mother."

"Does it work?"

"No," he laughed. "They barely speak to each other, and that is why Hilda rates, because she is Menininha's real confidante and assistant. Dona Laura, indeed, is supposed to be practicing bad magic, which no mother should do; but in that way she draws a following that Menininha isn't interested in, and everybody has to reckon with her because she's dangerous."

"A real political machine?" I asked, incredulous.

"Naturally." He waved his hand, and looked for another cigarette. "Mix African with Latin, and you've got a political organization. Slavery taught by the king of Dahomey, discipline taught by Ignatius Loyola . . ." He exhaled the smoke of his cigarette and left the sentence hanging.

"You keep stressing Yoruba?" I inquired tentatively.

"Because that's the standard training, the classical tradition. The others are less thorough and elaborate, till you reach caboclo and spiritualism, where everything is a jumble."

"Well, it's about time I danced," I said, reverting to the original discussion.

He hooted. "Let me tell you what you're in for! Here's a caboclo dance young Father João da Pedra Preta was showing me: Keep your feet—naked feet—flat, and *never* rise on your toes or lilt. Hold your arms with the insides turned out facing the sky, the elbows pulled in towards your sides, your palms turned up. Suppose you are dancing for Oxóssi, the hunter. Touch your right forefinger to your left thumb and, besides these, let only your left little finger be extended. Shimmy your shoulders. Shake your arms, but keep your shoulders still. Keep your buttocks turned out. Your feet dance in the same tramp-tramp, but the upper parts of your body move in different rhythms, depending upon the drums. Now, flop your body down from the waist, and sweep it languorously from one side to another. Twist your pelvis around."

"I don't think you have confidence in me," I said.

"Americans can probably do anything," he teased, "but I'll believe it when I see you do that dance of Omolu."

XX

MARTINIANO kept his threat, his vow to avoid the temples, and I never saw him at the famous ceremonies. I never saw him anywhere but in his apartment, by appointment, where I was supposed to learn African lore from him. But the more I wished to learn, the less I could extract, because by the rules of his logic, everything became priceless when I wished it. Money, cash, smoothed our relationship gratifyingly, but there were times when I did not offer to pay because I wanted to see how he would act. He would close up like a clam, or become irritable, even though we had already associated for months, and Carlinho and Elena had become easy and talkative with me.

Some people thought he was an intricate character. I think only that he had a natural expansiveness that warred noticeably with the armor of secrecy he buckled around him. For it was an armor. He felt that life, the times, trained death weapons on him. He felt that the temple personnel, if he visited, would greet him with poisoned food. Although he was reputed to be one of the two great African sorcerers in Brazil—the other was Felisbertus of Rio de Janeiro—and respected for it, he would go far out of his way in conversation to bring this up and deny it. "I, a feiticeiro!" he would explode as though he were being charged with grave-robbing. He knew of course that sorcery was illegal under Brazilian law, and also that it had no proper place in the amiable atmosphere of Bahia's candomblé; but he denied it principally, I am sure, because it was of the essence of sorcery to disguise itself. And yet he loved to associate with people, to tell them stories, to flirt with women, and his manner was truly warm and interested. His ties with everyone were of this shuttling character: welcoming and withdrawing; now a pagan, now a Catholic; now a hearty host, now a calculating necromancer.

Edison and I were certain that Martiniano supported himself from the practice of magic, which he had learned in Nigeria, and which he refused to teach people in Bahia. White and black people alike told us they respected him for his talent, and some even believed him to be the devil himself, with his black skin and red eyes, and his devotion to Ifa, the deity of Fate. The police believed he was a professional magician, and watched him. Temple followers thought that he had performed magic for Aninha during his long service at her temple, magic which she needed to have done, but which her priestly vows would not allow her to perform. He was in fact indispensable to her, unlike any other ogan, and her success grew with the association. She was the priestess, he was the sorcerer.

I wanted to see Martiniano at work at his secret trade, and Edison and I put our academic minds to the problem. Question and answer techniques, and even the most ramifying conversations, would not penetrate Martiniano's façade. It became embarrassing, even offensive to continue to prod the old man, and we were risking his friendship. So we decided that in this instance frankness was irrelevant. Instead, we would give him a client.

Edison knew a colored beautician named Rosita who had recently come from Ilhéus on business, and who was disturbed over a love affair. We proposed to finance her consultation with Martiniano provided I might accompany her and observe; and this she readily agreed to do although my own flesh crawled at the indelicacy. Edison made the arrangement with Martiniano—who was delighted in spite of the denials he had steadily made until now—and explained that Rosita wanted me to be present because I was her "comadre" and close friend. "Pronto," Edison said to me, snapping his fingers as though *he* were a magician. "Get going!" And since Martiniano is dead—though in his African belief his soul is about ready to be reincarnated in some baby— I can tell this tale without offense to him.

At about ten o'clock on the appointed morning, Amor drove us to the house. We climbed up the terrible stairway and knocked at the open door.

"You may come in!" Carlinho sang as he ran to us, turning up his pretty face with its shining eyes and flashing smile. And then he skipped off to sit coquettishly on a small trunk in a corner.

"What a *sweet* child!" Rosita called delightedly, and I started to toss him in the air as I did on all my visits.

Martiniano walked in then, smiling and saying as usual: "Good morning, dona! Don't be too good to him, he's a bad boy."

Edison used to explain to me that the old man was simply averting the evil eye by this phrase, lest my admiration injure Carlinho; and the little boy himself was undisturbed by the scolding, because he tugged at my skirt when I let him down and said in a tiny tone, "More—I want more!" Martiniano had to watch me toss him again and turn him upside down in the air, while Rosita laughed and Carlinho gurgled with pleasure. "Two infants," Martiniano remarked half disapprovingly, and turned to Rosita.

"Eliseo Martiniano do Bomfim, at your service," he introduced himself, "and I know already that you are Dona Rosita."

He extended his hand graciously, and she brushed the back of it with her lips. He looked her over admiringly, because she was of the fair type called "Brazilian white" and was dressed smartly in a white suit of mannish cut, a modish straw hat with flowers, and high heels, and used bright cosmetics on her face.

In spite of his African loyalties, the white race and its ways carried great weight with him. He had once said to me—I don't know whether he was depressed or humorous or just dreaming—"If I am born again in Brazil, I want to be white and rich, and I want a white woman instead of the black one I've got." "Would you be a padre?" I asked, thinking of his priestly career in Aninha's temple. "No, no." He waved his hand and laughed. "I don't want any skirts when I'm born again—none of that nonsense. I want to be a man." Edison had not liked that discussion when I reported it to him, because he thought Martiniano was getting too intimate. "He's a lusty devil," he said, "and he still likes to pinch and slap the women, the heavy young ones especially."

These thoughts were in Martiniano's glance at Rosita, and she looked at me a little uneasily. For diversion then, I said, "Seu Martiniano, show us some of your interesting things."

He walked around the room good-humoredly, and stopped before a high altar on which a saint rode at the level of his eyes, surrounded by artificial flowers. "This is St. George of England," he said, "my patron saint." The saint was on a large white fiery horse, dressed in blue-steel armor and a plumed helmet. Martiniano removed the helmet to show his streaming yellow hair.

"That is the god Oxóssi, in the African life, isn't it?" I asked.

"Yes," he nodded. "And on his anniversaries I give him a bowl of fresh flowers, and throw petals on the floor and on my friends who come to honor him. See this?" He pointed to a cloth covering the altar on which had been embroidered a St. George and a phrase in the Yoruba tongue. "I designed it," he said proudly, "and Elena embroidered it."

All around on the walls hung colored prints of Jesus and the Virgin Mary, in different aspects, and prints of St. Anthony and the mulatto St. Benedict holding the Holy Child, and in one corner were snapshots and large portraits of friends and relatives. Carlinho rolled his eyes above his seat against one wall, and Martiniano laughed because there was hanging a monk who carried a folding umbrella.

"The umbrella is supposed to rise when rain is due," he explained, "but this monk is lazy. . . . Well, let us get to work!"

He led us into a little windowless room that was separated from this large one by a glass door hung on the inside with soiled cotton drapes. The room contained a decrepit cot and some chairs; the walls were hung with conventional sacred prints and with two small figures of Saints Cosme and Damião surrounded by flowers. He shut the door, and the room became stuffy and laden with foul odors.

Sitting down on the cot, Martiniano motioned us to two seats facing him; then, raising one little chair with his right hand, he boasted looking at Rosita, "Pretty strong for an old man, eh?" From beside him, he picked up a handsome shallow curved wooden bowl, dark brown in color, aged, and much used. It was spotted with fine sand. On it he put an old shallow basket over which he threw a dirty white cloth. Upon this he dropped the sixteen cowrie shells with which he was planning to divine

Rosita's future. From under the soiled bedsheet, he drew out two handsome old ivory tusks, yellowed and scratched with age, carved in a Sudanese style; metal pins were driven into each tusk, and one had a male face carved on it, with metal pins for eyes.

He dandled the bowl on his lap, showing how it was carved on both sides. "It comes from Egypt," he observed. "See, the inside is divided in half. On each side is a crescent moon with lumps. We call divining the 'moon practice,' and the lumps here are our secrets. Here is another secret, alongside the moon: I mean this design that looks like a harp. Below is the outline of a man with a bow, and below him is a young wolf. Here is a sort of a rosary carved among the designs, made up of little triangles. Every babalaô has an African rosary of cowries called 'opele,' but it is different from this.

"Now, let's get started. Dona Rosita, are you a Catholic?" As she hesitated, he warned her, "If you don't believe in Jesus, we can't do this. I am a Christian!"

"Oh, yes, I believe in Jesus," she assured him, bewildered. "I was just surprised."

"All right. What's troubling you?" As she began to talk, he slipped a five-milreis note under the cloth, and kept flipping a corner so that the money was constantly coming into sight.

"I want this to be a secret, Mr. Martiniano," she begged, swallowing nervously.

"Oh, yes, indeed!" he assured her. "My business is all secret. Even my wife doesn't know. Of course she helps me with recipes and things, but she doesn't know about the cases!"

Rosita leaned forward and spoke intently. She said that she was engaged to marry a man whom she loved better than anyone in the world. Martiniano clucked sympathetically. However, the engagement was secret because her parents opposed the match on two grounds: that her fiancé was many years older than she, and that he was "dark." They wished her to marry a man who was a good deal younger, and white; and she herself thought she would want him if she were not already in love with the first. "What shall I do? I am turning to you because you are old and experienced, and all these people wouldn't visit you if you didn't give sound advice."

The old magician moved restlessly and murmured that one mustn't antagonize one's parents. He took up the sixteen cowrie shells, threw them into the bowl, stirred them with his long fingers, rubbed them in both palms while he muttered invocations to the Yoruba god of divination, Ifa. He yawned as he did this, and perked his head at every new sound in the outer room. He threw the shells again and picked them up. Sometimes he threw all sixteen, sometimes he set a few aside while he threw only those that seemed to have fallen into critical positions, and all the time his hands moved with dancelike gestures. His invocations grew louder while he threw the shells five or six times in succession—and he broke out into a noisy yawn! Then he stated:

"The throws say that you must forget this older man. You must let the matter rest twelve months without thinking of him. You must let this older one go. Or else, shortly after marriage, there will be vexation and anger. You must not cross your parents."

He saw Rosita's expression sadden, and he threw the shells again several times. "They say it is not good to anger your parents," he said softly, looking at her.

"Shall I marry the other?" she asked.

He threw the shells again. "No, rest."

She showed him her engagement ring, a plain gold band dropped on a cord inside her dress. "You see, I really am engaged secretly."

Martiniano grew more animated and threw the shells again, "They say he is the best of all, that old one. But your parents are a hindrance." He looked up and saw Rosita smile. "You must forget all about the other, young one." He tossed the shells. "Now, if you were one of us, I would suggest doing something to change your father's mind. Nothing bad!" he reassured her hurriedly.

She said she was willing to do anything.

"It will cost money," he continued. "You will have to buy a

coral bead like this, a fruit like this, and this spice." He showed a long bead of a tomato color and an odoriferous piece of St. John's bread, and had her bite a piece off the spice to chew for a time. "You will also have to buy a mat and three cowrie shells." Seeing her remove the masticated spice from her mouth, he screamed eagerly: "Give it to me! Don't throw it away! . . . Oh, I won't use it for anything bad. But it's not wise to throw saliva around carelessly—somebody might do bad magic with it. . . . You give me the money for this despacho, and I will get the things. It will come to about sixty-two milreis. Bring the money early next week, and we will begin to work . . . Where do you live? In Ilhéus?—I will give you one of these shells, and keep two for myself. Not for anything bad! I'll keep them until you leave Bahia. Now, you've got to write your name, your father's, and your fiancé's on a piece of paper, and wrap the paper around the shell. Then we start to do things. Oh, it won't hurt your father, it'll just change his mind! We can only begin the work here; you will have to continue it when you reach Ilhéus, and write to me."

"I have another question," Rosita said nervously. "Will I have children?"

Martiniano threw the shells and seemed pleased. Smiling, he said he didn't see why an attractive young woman shouldn't have children. Suddenly his attention was diverted by a sound from outside, and he turned to listen, lifting the drapes to peep through, and opening the door a crack. Unsatisfied, he called his wife for a report, and then with a resigned lift of the eyebrows returned to his work. Throwing the shells two or three times, he chuckled and shook his head. "Oh, I wish I were there to see him—a son. . . . I can see him stand in the doors, in your eyes! Of course you can have a son!"

Rosita, happy, asked how many. Martiniano answered in a flat voice: "The throw says to wait. . . . Don't ask questions."

Rosita said she had still another question, but Martiniano halted her. "First I want your photograph."

She smiled uncertainly and said she had none with her. He explained, "I mean, you are to pay the table."

"What?"

"Aren't you Brazilian, my girl?" he replied impatiently. "The first question I gave you free; but after that you must pay. That is why I put the five milreis on the table, as a hint for you."

Rosita blushed furiously, and gave him the money. "I thought I paid at the end," she said. "This is my next question: Shall I continue with my profession? My fiancé objects."

"He is right," Martiniano nodded. He threw the shells, which confirmed his opinion. He had nothing more to tell her, but he seemed reluctant to bid us goodbye when we rose.

"Dona Ruth," he said in a kindly way, "I have never shown you the things my parents left me, which they brought from Africa. Perhaps you and Dona Rosita would care to see them?"

I looked wonderingly at her, and in a wordless way we agreed that the old man was lonely, and that we would visit with him for a while.

"I never show these to people," he said, as he led us out of the apartment and down a corridor to a locked room. "Only to Dr. Nina and one or two friends. But I know your heart is with them."

This room too was windowless and stuffy, and held a jumbled assortment of candomblé paraphernalia such as I had never seen before. There were wooden and bronze statuettes of gods, with their sacred beads, fans, and swords, all made by Negro artisans of Bahia, now dead; their costumes were tossed about, and also royal scepters of bronze whose heads were carved like human bodies displaying enormous sexual organs. There were fetish stones, containing the very power of the gods, and they were swimming in oil, blood, and alcohol which they had been fed and in which they had been bathed at different times. Dust lay like a blanket, since Martiniano did not allow anyone to handle the god-things, and the room stank with an old mild odor. Picking up a wooden statuette, the old sorcerer said it had belonged to his father, that it represented someone possessed by Iansã. He let me see it in his hand: a breasted figure with skirts, sacred beads around its neck and head, and two wings springing from the head, representing lightning, or—when it became Xangô—representing a hammer. "Iansã protected my father," he said rather absent-mindedly, "so I still make sacrifices to her." He examined a dish of cooked chicken that lay in an alcove, so old a sacrifice that it had molded, and then he bent over a small dish of coagulated blood.

Suddenly he straightened up. "That'll do, that'll do," he said hurriedly, shooing us out and locking the door. "It's just as though that room were full of dynamite—you have to know how to move around in there, or something bad will happen. I wish I didn't have to take care of it, but my parents left it." He smiled and turned to Rosita. "Stay out of these things. You're too fair for that life. . . . Still, I always wanted a woman of this color." And he pointed to the pink palm of his hand.

We were at the head of the stairs then, about to walk down. Martiniano blocked us and said, pretending to chide us, "You mustn't forget to ask my blessing and kiss my hand," and he extended his long-nailed, unclean fingers.

Something about him was new, and confused me. I think it was that he had drawn comfort from our request for help, and that he hated to relinquish his feeling of authority over us. With each step of our descent we left him lonelier, no longer feeling one of us but remembering that he was an old sorcerer at bay.

I never saw him again. Now that he is dead, what can have happened to that roomful of barbaric gods, so precious to the scholars, so fearsome to the cult? And, more important to me, where is little Carlinho, whose singing tones must be ready now to deepen into the voice of a man?

XXI

IT WAS the candomblé women who channelized the life of the folk in Bahia, and so it was a great event when the word spread that Gantois would hold the crucial rites of axêxê to cleanse the temple of the gloomy miasma brought by the death of ogan

Bibiano a year before. The Egungun of death had interrupted life for a year, scaring away the gods of Africa; but after the scheduled rites, followed by masses at the church of the Augustinians, the gods would again descend and dance and enable the priesthood to function to the top of its ability.

I was determined to see the ceremony; but no one was offering to invite me, because it was not considered complimentary or pleasurable to do so. Who wants to come near death? Ogans fled from it when they could, and even the most prominent of the priestesses tried to keep a distance. Unlike other Catholics, these lusty blacks had inherited the conviction that only life as they knew it was good, and they could think of no better future for a soul than to be reincarnated soon in a living baby. That was how Menininha knew that her daughter Cleoza belonged to Nana, for, though Nana had never descended into Cleoza's head, the cowrie shells had revealed on the divining table that the girl's grandmother was reincarnated in her, and the grandmother had belonged to Nana.

Zézé had to dance in the axêxê, being an ordained priestess, but her Amor was walking around very gloomy over the occasion, forbidding his children to go near the temple and scolding his sister-in-law for planning to take her infant daughter Marinalva there, even though the sister-in-law was training for the priesthood. Naturally Zézé would not be so contrary as to invite me; therefore, as with Martiniano, I tried to discover some indirect approach. How could I be reasonable and unobtrusive about it?

One day she called me to lunch with her because, she said, she wanted to introduce to me a visitor from Spain who wished to become an ogan. It was a day of Oxum, and so she would prepare the goddess' special food, a dish of hard-boiled eggs and shrimp baked with manioc. I came early with some cake, and as she was still working at the stove I walked around awhile. I did not like the Spaniard, who clung to her apron strings and talked overaffably and incessantly. He asked a great deal about temple procedures, and it struck me as very peculiar.

The meal could not begin until Manoel Amor returned from

217

work at the Medical School, so I sought companionship in baby Marinalva. She was a tiny thing whose young father had deserted her, and Manoel had generously adopted her, the papers having been drawn up by Dr. Alvaro, Menininha's husband. She did not live with Manoel and Zézé; but her mother or half-sister brought her to the house every day, and she was loved and fondled lavishly. Her appearance had appalled me at first. She was so very ill, with a badly erupted skin and the body and face of a shriveled green mummy. But within six months she had become a different creature. The family combed and washed her straight black hair until it became silken and waving. They washed and powdered her poor broken skin until it healed. They fed her bananas and milk and other good things until her color turned a healthy brown, and she started to walk and squeal and maybe talk. Manoel treated her as though she were rare glass, and addressed her with the tenderness of a boy newly in love. And I wondered if the poor little creature were not indeed becoming the beauty her relatives always thought she had been.

She walked with me around her adopted home; rather, she staggered and ran like a bird, reaching for the fat chickens which tracked heedlessly around, finally heading for the nanny-goat tethered to a distant tree. I led her in another direction, behind the house, so that I should not have to smell the goat, and there we examined the vegetable garden the family cultivated on a slope which was precipitous and deep but very fertile from decaying tree stumps. Fruits grew freely around, and in season one needed only to stretch out and pick a mango or avocado or banana of several varieties.

"Don't, don't!" called Manoel's deep affectionate voice. He came around and caught the baby, who was trying to stuff the dirt and the leaves and the vegetables into her mouth. Smiling, he said: "Come to eat, Dona Ruth. It is an honor to have you." And he led the way with Marinalva high on his shoulder, around to the front, across the sidewalk of cement that ran like a carpet over the red mud, into the neat clean house.

Zézé had set the table in the dining room; although the floor was of packed earth, the furniture was new, and there were shades on the windows. She was busy serving, and Manoel and his children and I just ate and listened while the visiting Spaniard asked Zézé for food recipes and wrote them down, asked about Cosme and Damião, offered to make a contribution of money, and said he wanted to visit Dona Menininha. So the meal hour passed. He would not say a word about his own country, though I tried to put a question, and my wonder grew. I mention his visit because we all learned some weeks later, through the newspaper, that he was eventually recognized in Pernambuco as a Franco agent, though he had been posing as a soldier of Loyalist Spain. I still cannot understand what use he planned to make of the temples.

But Zézé was flattered that day by his attentions, and he gave her a brooch as a token of esteem. Manoel then escorted him to the temple, to show him the grounds and introduce him to the women who happened to be in.

I remained, still wondering how to get around the matter of the axêxê. Zézé rested in a rocker which she placed sideways to me so as to avoid the rudeness of looking me full in the face, and she set Marinalva on her lap. She chewed a bite of banana and then inserted it into the child's tiny mouth, rocking her in the meantime.

Cleoza came down the steps and looked in at the window. "Mother asks," she said to Zézé, "if you can give five or ten eggs for the axêxê tonight."

Zézé's rocking slowed; she shifted Marinalva's position and answered carefully, "I haven't any." Her sister, who was training in Menininha's new class of initiates named "abian," called from an inner room, "Why, of course you have, Zézé! Of course you have!"

I thought I saw a spasm cross Zézé's face. She rose, set Marinalva carefully on the floor, and walked towards the inner room, remarking to Cleoza: "My hens are not laying, but Amor may have bought some. I will see."

219

She returned shortly with five eggs in her hand. Cleoza thanked her and left.

Zézé sat again in the rocker, her face a mask, and picked up the baby. Suddenly she shouted: "Come out here, sister, come out here! . . . *Why* did you have to tell? Why! *She* doesn't contribute anything! She just sits in one place and gives orders, and we have to bleed for it! Where do you think we find our money? How many times has she called on me this week? Just because I live near the temple! Does a ceremony ever come when she does not send to me for last-minute things? Suppose Bibiano is dead: must *I* give eggs? This week alone Amor gave ten milreis, I gave ten milreis, you gave five milreis. That should cover everything if she collected as well from the others! But no! *I* live on the grounds! The *widow* pleasures herself on the Island. . . . Gracious! People! *Gente!*"

Watching with great interest, I saw my opening at last. "I'll help you out, Zézé," I offered, putting some bills on the table. "In exchange, you invite me to the axêxê tonight."

She was surprised and pleased, and the furious rocking stopped. "But it will bore you," she protested in a kindly way. "It is only to speed that old man's soul away from earth. If you feel strong enough to stand it—"

"Yes," I interrupted to assure her.

"Well, you are brave to do it when it is not really necessary. Amor will even lock the children here in the house so they will not get close to the Egun. And there at Gantois my mother has turned everything over to the ogans: they've been slaughtering the sacrificial animals behind closed doors, in the altar rooms, and offering the prayers there so that the women need only to hear them from a distance.

"Come then, if you insist. Dress in white, but wear old clothes because you may have to sleep on the floor. In the morning we go to eight o'clock mass in the church of the Augustinians, to send the soul to God. Come about nine tonight."

XXII

So EVERYTHING was settled simply; I regretted only that Edison could not come. He had not been invited, because his relations with Menininha were still strained. When I arrived, late, the temple seemed deserted, and Manoel appeared to tell me, his black face glum over his rumpled white clothes, that the ogans were still attending to secret matters behind the doors of the principal altar room.

"I'll be glad when all this is finished," he said in his nervous hasty way. "I don't like any of it, not at all—a fearful business. Zézé is in the back with the others. You'd better sit down and make yourself comfortable. They are way off schedule—it may be hours before things begin out here. . . . Menininha has a headache—the ogans have a lot to do in the special rooms. . . . Just take it easy, and I'll be back soon."

Since the night was hot and humid, I stepped out of doors. Gantois was on a height far above Bahia, the old City of the Savior, and the lights of the town were so distant that they appeared like remote fairy pinpricks in the atmosphere. The sky as always was soft and dark, almost a fleshy thing that could be sensed. Gantois stood in a wide clearing in the woods just beyond the trolley line from the Upper Town, but it could not be seen from the main road. The footpath to it was winding and steep, and had been intended to be secret in slavery days when the government opposed gatherings of blacks. Until the enterprising English company had constructed the trolley line, after emancipation, the temple had really been secluded. But now people reached it without difficulty, and steps had been cut in the red clay and carefully buttressed with stone.

Around the clearing, at a little distance from the temple, rose a thick growth of straight and enormously tall trees. It was a virgin wood of great age, in which paths had been cut for the worshipers since certain of the trees were residences of deities, like the fetish stones inside the temple. Little houses were scattered among them where the priestesses and ogans laid offerings to the gods and sometimes kept the sacred garments. Upon occasion, sacred processions of the women danced along the paths to a holy spring at the other end of the wood, with offerings of food and wine, and ultimately the gods descended in them. I looked at these handsome trees and tried to endow them with the living personalities the blacks saw, but my imagination failed me. I had to content myself with knowing that the others sensed a wondrous life where I perceived only wood.

Yet I could not shrug off the difference between my comprehension and theirs. So I turned to look at the temple behind me, and there I was a little more successful. It had been erected by Pulcheria after she had broken away from the mother temple of Engenho Velho and had already become famous. To the eye this was just a rambling clay structure over whose entrance hung a weather-bleached ox horn crossed by two knives, symbols of the hunting god Oxóssi, protector of the temple. Compared with the splendid churches of Catholicism, this did not look like a house of worship; but the glamour of Pulcheria gave it meaning to all who knew. To me it stirred with significance.

I returned to the great room that housed the ceremonies. It was lit very poorly with small electric bulbs, and waiting people squatted and sprawled on the floor. It extended the width of the temple and was half as deep. The floor had originally been covered with a baked red clay, but years of intensive dancing and tramping had broken it in many places. The clay walls had been calcimined in light blue enlivened with rosebuds, but they were now faded and peeling. There was no ceiling, and from the tall roof's rafters hung several electric bulbs and faded crêpe-paper streamers. High above the doorway leading to the interior holy rooms, was an altar of St. George, the Catholic Oxóssi.

Four enormous window spaces had been cut out of the walls, closed now by shutters: one on each side of the temple's entrance, and one on each side wall. Broken benches were piled up against one wall. A fine white dust sifted constantly through the air from the cracked calcimining, laying a gray shroud on everything. The priestesses slept here at night upon woven mats.

As I saw later, a dark corridor connected this ceremonial

chamber with the other parts. The corridor's naked floor ran irregularly uphill, foul from dampness and decayed substances. All doors on the corridor were usually shut because the rooms and the activities were "secret."

Seeing me return, Manoel waved excitedly. He hurried to me, and his husky voice was accusing. "I've been looking for you, dona. Menininha has been waiting for you to give her greetings."

I followed him into the corridor and found Menininha seated in the garish light of an unshaded bulb facing the locked doors of the huge altar room, "room of the gods," which contained sacred paraphernalia. She was on a low stool, her bulk supported on thighs spread far apart, her palms thrust upon them.

"Good evening, Dona Ruth," she said languidly, and proceeded to complain of the splitting headache that had caused her to twist a cloth around her head holding a cool green leaf on each temple.

She looked handsome none the less, and I expressed admiration of her fortitude in carrying on despite the peak heat of the equatorial summer.

"What will they do without me?" she answered. "I am the mother, and these are my responsibilities—though I feel I won't live long. . . . Amor! Show our friend the seat of the old Papa."

So he led me through an open door on the left of the corridor. Always formal with me, he proceeded to lecture like a guide: "Only esteemed visitors are taken in here, Dona Ruth. This room belongs to the father of the gods, Oxalá, who is the same as Jesus in the Catholic life." Suddenly, silently, he extended himself on the floor, touching it only with his palms, toes, and forehead. Rising, he explained: "That is the way we greet him, we who have male gods seated in our heads. . . . It is all white in here because Oxalá is old and has forgotten his passions."

The room was large, with white calcimined walls, no ceiling, and an unpaved floor. Manoel went to a corner behind the door where there stood a large locked closet painted white.

"This is the high altar, the seat of the god," he remarked. "I'll unlock it and show it to you."

223

He did so quite casually, and we examined the interior, which was painted a bright white. It was hung with white lawn and lace draperies and furnished with an ornate silvered cane, a silvered fan and dagger, a beautiful white towel of barafunda, white bowls filled with white rosebuds, and dainty white vases filled with clear sacred water. All these belonged to the god.

"Now I'll lock up," said Manoel. "He will not care for this night of death."

We returned to the big room, which was filling up. The adults were talking and joking, the children were sleeping among them on mats on the floor. We walked over to Zézé's sister who sat with her children on the floor.

"Have you provided for Marinalva?" Manoel asked anxiously.

"Of course!" she laughed, pointing to a bottle of milk, cooked food, warm coverings, a urinal, and a small pot in which she could light a fire. "But I wish it was over! I'm afraid of this!" She rolled large anxious eyes up at her brother-in-law.

"I don't like it either," he growled, and left.

Men were gathering now around the gourds they would use in place of the drums, which were reserved for the gods; and Manoel was the supervisor. The priestesses moved to one side of the room, the left side, near the Oxalá room; lay persons gathered on the other side. It was not far from midnight when the mother sent word to her daughters that she was coming out. Thereupon they arranged themselves according to their seniority in the priesthood, sitting on mats at the foot of her stool. All were dressed in white, in long ample costumes like old-fashioned nightgowns over which they wore dressing jackets. The musicians sat in their usual place on the right side of the room, but without the drums.

Menininha came out quietly and sat on her stool, holding a black shawl on her shoulders. The lesser mother, fair elderly Dona Laura, moved to a stool near her. Menininha had them bring a tall chair for me, and I was seated, as a mark of courtesy, among the daughters who crouched on the floor. Visitors from other temples had come to honor their deceased colleague and were seated near the entrance of the temple facing the mother;

among them was Father Bernardino. Ogans placed dishes and a tall candle in front of the gourd players.

The room was still now. Then Menininha struck a sweet note in her powerful soprano, a song of the axêxê announcing the solemnizing of a death; the words were in Yoruba. She "pulled" a second hymn, calling upon the Eguns, the living deaths. The daughters knelt to her chants, heads bent to the left, and clapped rapidly and lightly in salutation.

The mother then tightened her shawl across her breast and stood up, singing for her goddess Oxum. She sang and danced around the dishes. Unlike the others who danced later, she saluted no one. As she danced, accompanying herself always in a quiet song or chant, her daughters rose one at a time in order of rank, hurriedly and crouching, to give her a coin or two. These she dropped into one of the dishes, making up a collection for the morning's mass for the deceased. Manoel came to me hurriedly to advise me also to make a contribution to each priestess as she rose to chant and dance the farewells. The usual contribution was two hundred reis, but it was courteous to give double that. They arranged for Zézé to signal me the desired sums, and advised me not to stand upright when I offered them but to stoop and to hurry in a self-effacing manner and end with a bow.

Despite her headache, Menininha sang continually, and danced, fumbling with the shawl which had to hide her breasts. She moved lightly and rapidly, and sometimes she was both dramatic and graceful. She sang charmingly, without any tricks or "scattering of live coals," as the people say. One felt she loved to sing and to dance.

As I went to give my dues, I saw that the dishes held food. Zézé had said they were the sacrificial foods of certain high gods who "ate" them. One dish contained roasted peanuts for Omolu, god of pestilence, and also for Ogum, god of highways and cemeteries. These deities did not fear the dead, and so they could visit and were welcomed with their symbolic foods. There was also food for Oxum because she protected the chief priestess: it was a yellow-bean pudding topped with hard-boiled eggs.

There was a dish of okra for the war god Xangô because he protected the deceased; and there was a dish of insipid white manioc for Oxalá, the father of all.

As the sacrificial foods are destined for the gods, not for human consumption, they are allowed to molder or are cooked so tastelessly that it is a labor of devotion to eat them. Similarly, the ornaments used in god-costumes are made of base materials nowadays because, the women explained, they are to be buried with the corpse; but precious ones are passed on to one's daughters although they are always described as the property of a god.

When Menininha had danced through a series of songs, the other priestesses rose singly to dance in order of age in godhood. Zézé estimated later that Menininha, forty-six years old, had served about forty-five years at the altar of Oxum. She was followed by the lesser mother, or iyakekere, Laura, who was about fifty-five years old but had given only thirty-eight years of service to her Oxum. She was quite unattractive as she waddled on legs of unequal length, untidily dressed, and with an indifferent expression on her Caucasian face; but Zézé said she had once been so beautiful as to win a wealthy contractor, a white man now deceased, as a common-law husband. She was followed by the second assistant, or amorô, a fair, good-looking woman named Maria, forty years old, with thirty years of service to her Omolu. The next to rise, with the title of abase, was Eudoxia, a dark gentle woman of forty-nine, with twenty-eight years of service to her Omolu. Finally came Hilda, entitled dagã, thirty years old, with twenty-three years of service to her Oxum.

These were the principal officers, and following them there rose a fine-looking, fair, white-haired daughter with the title of Mother Dada since she supervised the care of the Oxalá room, and besides she had twenty-three years of service to Banha, old retiring mother of Xangô. Then there rose the group of priestesses who had only seven years of service or few more, and these were entitled in Yoruba ebomi, "senior wives of the god." Those with fewer years of dedication were iawô, "junior wives." And finally there were the abian, like Zézé's sister, who

226

had undergone only the preliminary experience of "washing the beads of the god."

I watched the women sitting in status-regulated rows, which none would violate. The "eldest" were in front and had the privilege of sitting higher than the others and of looking squarely at the dancers. The abian dared not look up at all, and when one young girl did, the ceremony was halted for the ebomi America to scold her shrilly.

Status and discipline were preserved by Menininha to the point of discomfort. When I tried to leave the dignity of my tall, narrow chair, wanting to squat on the floor with the abian so as to be near the windows and stretch, Menininha sent me an urgent message to return to the chair and save my face. I looked at the novices sitting ingloriously but comfortably behind the others, directly in the path of the light breezes coming through the now opened windows, and I rejected her command. Confused, she commented to Zézé, the message bearer, "Dona Ruth is like a child!"

As each dancer rose, she touched her forehead to the ground in the direction of the street door, and then in the direction of the dishes; she "begged blessings," half crouching and extending her cupped palms to the mothers, to the gourds, the ogans, and the visitors. Menininha did not salute until her daughters and heirs, Cleoza and Carmen (wakened from heavy sleep under a table) "begged blessings" of her. Then she honored them, touching the ground and her forehead in acknowledgment.

Since no gods descended for this ceremony, everyone danced in a normal state, more or less in the samba style, and each woman's personality emerged in little mannerisms. Cleoza showed unusual gifts. Her movements were graceful, impassioned, and quite lacking in self-consciousness—probably because, like her mother, she had been dancing since the time she could walk. She performed well in varying god-styles, as she showed when she was called to substitute for someone else. Her own goddess was old, cold Nana whose home was the shadowed bottoms of the deepest waters. The priestess America, sister of Hilda, appeared abnormally fat because of dropsy, though she was only in her early twenties, and she danced without any form; but this seemed correct for a votary of Oxalá. Hilda herself, though pretty and romantic in appearance, showed no talent; at best she was conscientious, and the woodenness of her performance may have reflected a tense emotional state. Dona Laura danced like a duck because of her club foot. I was startled by the extreme indifference of her expression, with overtones of scorn and defiance. Zézé remarked later: "Dona Laura is quite isolated. Of course we are all her friends. She is the lesser mother." Her place this evening was at Menininha's feet, but after a while she moved to the opposite side of the chamber to sit with visitors. Hilda then moved into her place. While Zézé counseled me to give larger dues to Hilda, she seemed to forget about Laura; yet Laura had been very courteous to me.

Each temple ordains some children as priests, and there were two such at Gantois. With deep sympathy, I watched them struggle against the boredom, the smothering heat, and the long hours, in their stiff uniforms, prodded to observe the formalities. One was a seven-year-old daughter of the pest-god Omolu; she was obliged to stand up and dance though she was half asleep. As she performed abominably, she was scolded sharply by America, and became so frightened and uncertain that she was told to repeat her dance later. The other child was the same age, a son of Xangô. Being a "man," he could dance only infrequently at the secret rites, and so he was comparatively untrained and stepped rather comically. He also was nervous, and went too fast, rubbing out the syncopation as he skipped to his own march time.

Finally a grown man stood up and danced. He had become the temple's official slaughterer, assuming the post of the deceased. Besides, he was a famed singer, with a repertoire as extensive as my mother's. During this evening he had "pulled" chants in a fine bass-baritone which he varied with a charming falsetto. An orphan, he too had been reared by Pulcheria and consequently knew and loved the ritual. He led the orchestra and chorus when Menininha rested, or when the mood struck him. He seemed to be a humorist, even in this somnolent somber setting; and he resembled an eastern European peasant in his hearty interpretations and his full-mouthed smile. Now he danced samba in the manner of his god Omolu; but to the halting aged steps he gave a comic edge, entirely unlike the dramatic and tortured character of dancers in trance. He sang to accompany his own dance; and between songs, or the lines of a verse, he talked and laughed in such a fashion as to continue the syncopated rhythm.

Manoel walked over to me, glum and depressed. *He* never danced in candomblé, he said, though he also had been reared in Pulcheria's household. He had seen too much of men tempted thereby to desert their sex; his tone was scornful and bitter. He even hated to see the women dance, and he did not care to sing. He said that he had just harshly scolded his drum-assistant Faustino because the old man had gotten himself drunk, and was pounding the gourd erratically and noisily. Indeed, he was dissatisfied with everything. He pulled himself up from the floor remarking that he had to sort out and count the pile of change collected during the dancing.

Nothing interrupted the flow of the ceremony, inexorable and repetitious, through long hot hours. People sought innocent diversions. Manoel came to me repeatedly to ask the time, though there was no need to go by the clock; Zézé sent to advise about dues; Marinalva amused people by dashing, screaming and laughing, across the dancing place and under the feet of the performers; daughters dozed off; children sprawled around, sleeping. Nothing halted the ceremony, nothing lifted the heavy atmosphere.

At one-thirty in the morning there was an interruption. Food was served to some visitors in the white anteroom of Oxalá, while snacks were carried to the others remaining in the dance chamber; the daughters, however, were served only black coffee. At about two o'clock the rites were resumed drearily, continuing until the sun was brilliant at five o'clock. Towards the close Menininha grew philosophical and, touching her heart, which was weak, said aloud in a conversational tone: "I won't live to be old, I feel it. But if I died now, I could say that I have enjoyed something of everything, thanks to Banha, Oxum, and Oxóssi. I always obeyed my mother and my elders." The people murmured assent in Yoruba, saying "Axê," touching their foreheads to the ground at the name of each god.

Matters culminated in a ring dance in which only those could participate who had no mothers. These orphans sang pitiably about their state, for as Zézé explained: "It is a calamity to have no mother! A mother is gold! She carries you in her body, she delivers you with pain!" As they sang, the orphans and the others made gestures of dusting off the spirit of the deceased from around the backs of their heads into the direction of the street. Earlier, the dancers had dusted the footsteps of the people offering coins into the dish holding the food of Oxalá. Somehow this separated the dead from the living, protecting the living, and persuading the guardian angel to withdraw the soul of Bibiano to the feet of Jesus where it could be reincarnated in another person, perhaps that very day. Menininha danced again, honoring Omolu of disease and death, and she prayed while all stood and reverenced with soft rapid clapping, "Oxalá, Banha, we have come to thank you that his [Bibiano's] spirit has gone and freed us of evil; and pray for all of us to God."

It ended, for the time, this great effort to remove death from life; and everyone was cheered to see the bright cool morning. People left to secure some rest before the eight o'clock mass. I accompanied Zézé to her house, and as we walked along, she in bare feet and trailing white gown, with Marinalva slung across her shoulder, she remarked that the ogans were still working. A little while before, possibly at four o'clock, they had swept together the foods in the dishes of the dance chamber. They were the sacred parts and feathers of the creatures that had been slaughtered in sacrifice the previous night; stubs of the candle that had burned while the women danced, and that represented the life of Bibiano's soul; the palm-leaf ornaments, called marió, of Egun; and some of the coins of the collection. All these were death carriers. The ogans put them into a clay dish and tied them into a ritual bundle which they carried out secretly through the back of the house, out of the sight of the women. They were walking now the couple of miles to the Campo Santo, whose patrons are Our Lady of Mercy and Our Lord of Good Ending, walking solemnly and furtively with their awful load to deposit it carefully within the gates. They were preparing to say, "Bibiano's spirit has been led to the place of spirits of the dead, to remain there and not get mixed up with the living." Then they would depart.

I attended the mass with Zézé, and that afternoon I returned to the temple. Under Hilda's direction, the axêxê was concluding in a weary spirit. It was a farewell, and a resumption of life. The temple was freed of death.

Visitors had their footsteps "cleaned" at the dorway, as Hilda handed them water to throw to the right, to the left, and before the door. Mother Dada was dancing alone, and the daughters were kneeling and reverencing with uplifted hands as they sang in Yoruba:

> "Dada, good Mother,
> Ah, tender Mother,
> Dada, precious Mother,
> Who shares all with us,
> Look upon me."

It was a sort of invocation to life.

This was harshly interrupted by Faustino, who, still drunk, began a loud monologue. He talked louder and louder, until Menininha came in and took over the ceremony. Still he talked. She "pulled" a song. He continued talking and fussed with his soiled suit. Suddenly, exasperated, she called in her powerful voice: "I don't like this, folks! If you must talk, do it in the street." It was a shocking reprimand, and Faustino fell silent like the others. She started to sing again. He left, muttering sulkily.

But when he reached the outdoors he rebelled, shouting wildly, yelling that the others would not let him use the gourd, that they defamed him by saying he was drunk and made mistakes. Then he quieted, and soon he was seen urinating. Menininha sang. He returned, grumbling faintly, and went out again. Returning once more, he "pulled" a verse loudly and appropriately, in honor of the goddess then being praised. Menininha startled, hushed herself, then sweetly seconded it. I marveled at her kindliness.

The visitors began to straggle out, and through the windows I saw Menininha's husband arrive. He chatted with neighbors in his shack near by, reading the newspaper, and soon his wife joined him.

She returned only after the last song, and as the official slaughterer, in Yoruba, was giving his blessing to the congregation now freed of the death. He chanted, and the women who encircled him gave the sacred salute, curving over to their left, clapping lightly and rapidly, guided by Menininha, and repeating softly: "Axê, axê." Thus he chanted, in a brisk rhythm, with rising and falling Yoruba inflections:

> "Father, guard me,
> Father, protect me,
> Protect our nation.
> Oxóssi, watch over us.
> Iemanjá and Oxum too,
> Deliver us from evil,
> Deliver us from sorcery."

XXIII

SADNESS AND fear were now officially ended in the Bahia that I knew because after the axêxê at Gantois, the whole city turned out, as though by arrangement, for a glorious holiday called the Washing of the Church of Our Lord of Good Ending. This is the beginning of the fun-making that culminates after a couple of months in the marvelous explosion of Carnival. People began to crowd into Bahia from up and down the coast.

Our Lord of Good Ending, or Nosso Senhor do Bomfim, is the patron saint of Bahia; he is Jesus and Oxalá. The Washing of the church, which is both an African and a Catholic ritual, is scheduled for the beginning of the New Year, and symbolizes fresh beginnings and fresh hopes. In the temples, the "washing of

Oxalá" takes place earlier, even in September, but everybody participates in the Catholic ceremony. It is among the first of the janieras, the series of pre-Carnival gayeties. For want of funds, Bahia had not had a "washing" for several years, but this year the city was intending to do itself proud even though the Pope had just died. The New Year should not be set aside even for death, and there is a folk belief that, whatever you happen to be doing at that midnight point between the old year and the new, you will be doing all through the new. Early in December, Bahians had begun to celebrate, the frequency of the occasions increasing regularly until, by "Washing" time, there were daily festivals. The enthusiasm was very contagious, and soon this blues song joked at the mood:

She: "This is what he wants:
           Good house and good clothes
           And food to be fed to him!
           That is what he wants!
           He wants a life of orgies
           Living on his woman's earnings!

        "This is too much,
           It can't go on.
           Those who don't work
           Have no right to live.
           This lad
           Actually wants me
           To chew his food
           For him to eat!"

He: "She wants me to give up my fun!
           That is impossible!
           But if such a thing should happen
           Our love would die
           And I would have to give up living!

        "It is impossible for me!
           It is easier to stop living!
           Weeping she begs of me.
           Smiling I answer her:
           'Give up my parties! That can never be!' "

Priests of Bomfim Church, which was to be "washed," priests of the Church of Our Lady of Conception of the Beach, from which processions were to start on the march to Bomfim at the other end of the city, and officials of candomblé consulted and decided that the "Washing" would take place on January 12th. The whole city of some 400,000 could "wash," and organize parades for which prizes would be awarded. A prize committee was created, the chairman being Miguel de Santa Ana, president of the Negro stevedores' union. The following day there was to be a restricted "washing" by upper-class families and their servants; and for three days after, there were to be festivals in Bomfim neighborhood.

Edison and I had arranged to meet Manoel and Zézé at my hotel at eight o'clock on the morning of January 12th. It was an exceedingly hot and bright day, wringing the water out of the body and leaving it dizzy and sick. The shade offered relief only from the direct flame of the sun, which spread white over the blue, blue skies, paling the pinks and oranges in the tilings of roofs, but leaving intact the green of occasional trees and the gleaming white walls of the graceful palaces and churches. These buildings stood against the naked sky, framed leanly by rows of tall imported palms, while telephone poles and wires tore through the exquisite picture.

Edison arrived first, and then the couple. But it was not as happy as it should have been, because Manoel and Zézé were on bad terms with each other, and they walked quietly and stiffly, keeping a distance between them and being rigidly polite to us. As we walked through the streets to Father Barbosa's church of the Conception, Manoel showed his mood by trailing far behind and ostentatiously eyeing the masses of women, while he passed calculating comments to Edison. Also, he had dressed in his dark work clothes instead of in his light holiday ones, and made a black streak in the general brilliance. Zézé on the contrary wore a crisp white dress in honor of Oxalá and displayed unmistakably her greater youthfulness and fairer complexion. She had pinned on her dress all the ornaments that I had given her; and she was hatless, in the manner of her class, with her hair braided neatly around her head.

Father Barbosa's church was a cool splendor that day, on the shady side of the broad street that edged the bay. Tall and spacious, its walls were trimmed with white stone, the windows were latticed in white, it was simple, even severe, and elegant. We followed the people who streamed up the broad marble stairway to kiss the hand of the vicar, and we remained on the balcony to watch the bahianas in their glorious outmoded costumes, the aristocratic women in their fashionable hats, and the men all dressed in white.

The proletariat, as the newspapers liked to say, lined below the balcony ready to travel the blistering miles to Bomfim Church. One could have been a newcomer, freshly off the boat or the plane in Bahia, ignorant of the language and the country and yet have known clearly that there was an ecstasy in the air. Man, woman, child, beast, and the things with them were cleaned and dressed elaborately. Many black women had walked all the way in from the country in flimsy sandals which they usually removed and carried on their heads, yet they looked crisp and even classical as they bore on their heads large, gaudily painted jars of water for the "washing." Large horse and pony carts waited in the procession, and also motor trucks, each dressed to represent a castle or a garden in Japan. Men had bedecked the hard-worked donkeys with flowers, and led them proudly, and slowly, so that they would be rested for the competition to follow. Animals and vehicles carried barrels of water for "washing."

Miguel de Santa Ana arrived at about ten o'clock, driving his wife and many daughters in a new LaSalle car. People loved this display of wealth, and whispered that he had been ogan in Aninha's temple; they did not resent him at all but instead were proud of his success. I suppose that, like this day, he symbolized hope. For he too had been a poor black, then a master of stevedores and the head of the union, and now he had a car from the United States and his women wore costly gowns.

Immediately after his car came to rest in the shade of the church loggia, a dark handsome Creole clacked up the steps to us in wooden slippers painted white, balancing on her head a tall silver-painted jar bound round the neck with a fine white towel of Oxalá and loaded with long-stemmed flowers and ferns. She was entirely in white, like a figure of foam: her spreading skirts starched stiff and ending above the ankles, the lace blouse and West African shawl, the turban tied tall above her molded oval face, the heavy strings of beads dropping from her round neck; broad silver bands clasped her firm dark arms. Her clothes were so fresh that they still exuded the odor of the grass on which they had dried in the sun, and yet, as she told us leaning against the shaded wall to cool herself and rest, she had walked the miles from Itapagipe suburb without a bite of breakfast. Father Barbosa came out and teased her, and finally persuaded her to let me take her picture. Zézé stared at her admiringly, and remarked later that she was "a very fine priestess of Omolu" from the distant cacao town of Ilhéus. She used to visit Gantois, and once when she was sleeping there, her Omolu descended violently, driving her for hours among the enormous trees seeking the burial place of some old sacrifice. No one knew why this had happened; but "Omolu must have been punishing her for something," was Zézé's interpretation.

Our attention was distracted by a small mulatto who now stopped at the church. He was dressed in white, and with a very earnest expression was securing his pony by a flowered rope and blanketing it with lacy white towels, perfectly starched; on the back and sides of the animal rested water barrels in white-painted frames, filled with brilliantly colored bouquets of sturdy flowers, and to protect its head, its master had laid a flowered straw hat between its ears.

These instances were repeated over and over, and they touched me with their qualities of devotion and tenderness. Soon we heard the brasses of the firemen's orchestra, and across the avenue from us, spotlighted by the sun, carts and horses lined up in rows. Everything waited now for the final signal to start to Bomfim.

236

Waiting, Zézé caught sight of a mother named Idalice, head of a temple following the Angola tradition, and she exclaimed scornfully, in her uninhibited way: "O people! Gente! Look at her! She's ironed her hair! Gente! A mother touches a hot iron to her head! Gente! A mother so young and flighty!"

Idalice was a friend of Edison's, and he felt moved to speak in her defense. "She is not so young," he protested quietly. "She is more than thirty years old, and she was made by Flaviana a long time ago."

"So she broke away from Flaviana," said Zézé severely, "and changed from Yoruba to Angola. . . . She is of Xangô," she observed, looking again at Idalice.

"How do you know?" I said surprised.

"By her beads, of course!" Zézé laughed shortly. Of course, I rebuked myself silently, since Zézé is of Iansã, she is vitally concerned with the affairs of Xangô, brother and husband to her goddess!

"She is showing off with her beads," Zézé went on, a little sulkily, "wearing them in public. She doesn't need to do that, nor go around offering her hand for people to kiss! My mother Menininha does none of that—that's for the temple."

We saw the procession stir, and so we called a taxi for ourselves, flying gay streamers of colored crepe paper. The pilgrims moved at a snail's pace, too slowly for the taxi, and so we had to halt at intervals. When I stepped out once, to take a picture of the spot, I was astonished to feel the pavement burn through the thick soles of my shoes; yet people had been walking barefooted for hours. A bus came chugging by, its windshield saying in gold letters, "Viva Bomfim!" and bearing a doll dressed *à la bahiana*, with a jug of flowers on its head, surmounted by palm shoots. Open trucks followed, transporting loads of men doing samba, singing, banging tambourines, plucking berimbaus, thumping straw hats, shaking metal bells, shattering the floors with their dancing feet, the fierce sun seeming only to enliven them; and all over the motors were colored streamers, flowers, gilded mottoes, and more men clambering up en route. I stood looking at them, my feet tormented by the heat, and wondered

237

at their endless vitality. Children were everywhere underfoot, ornamented like the donkeys, often barefooted on the broiling pavement, shoes in their hands or on their heads. People massed around, in all kinds of civil and military dress. It was an ocean of humanity, over which the sun burned.

By noon our car reached the long ascent to Bomfim Church, and because of the multitude we had to dismiss it, toiling after this on foot. A center lane had been cleared for the trucks and carts that would parade in competition, and the people—strained and irritated from heat and thirst—peered at them through lines six deep. But everyone strove to behave well, for soon the "washing" would begin.

At the top of the ascent, where the road was cool, a handsome young mulatto was assiduously wiping the sweat from the faces of eight women in priestess garb, each with a gilded or silvered jug on her head and a new stiff broom in her hand. Manoel sneered, and Edison laughed.

That's João da Pedra Preta!" * Edison exclaimed.

"Irons his hair and dances in the temple," Manoel growled in an ugly tone.

I looked at the young father with interest because he was notorious for his love affairs with other men and for his failure to command discipline from the daughters of his caboclo temple. He was supposed to be a wonderful dancer, and I could imagine it from his light, graceful figure. His face was pleasing and pretty, but not weak, and his light brown skin contrasted well against the bright blue polo shirt that he wore opened wide at his throat. He attended carefully to his daughters, all of them much older than he in appearance.

"It is not altogether his fault," Edison answered Manoel. "He is only about twenty-four, and he inherited the post about nine or ten years ago. Naturally he wasn't prepared. He was only seven or eight years old when he wandered into Bahia from the interior, an orphan, homeless, and became the servant of a priest. He lived with gangs of boys like himself, and the only women he knew lived in brothels. Finally old Father X took him

* John of the Black Stone.

238

in and became fond of him, and left him his temple when he died. Really, he's a bright fellow, but what can one expect? He's trying to make his way in the world. . . . Now he's putting his women in competition for the prizes, and they look as pretty as dolls."

Edison understood João's ambitions well, as events proved. Some years later João married: "Yes," Edison wrote, "you read that: married. Married to an old woman, rich and ugly. The marriage was an event in Bahia: reports and interviews in the papers, pictures published in Bahia and Rio, and João wearing spats in the pictures. The best man was an admiral, the captain of ports in Bahia. . . . Day after day, for some time before the marriage, the Rio papers published interviews with him about temple matters."

We did not speak with João, but walked past him to the church. Bomfim had been built long ago by Portuguese artisans, of white stone imported from Lisbon; blue tilings from Holland lined the inside, reminding one of the Dutch conquest, in colonial times, of the state of Pernambuco to the north. The lovely structure, flanked by two towers that rose lightly above a series of simple Latin crosses, stood on a hill and was conspicuous in that flat landscape. A principal cross was sunk between the towers, firm on an elaborate stone-trimmed base set against the severe walls. The window lattices were of carved wood; wide stone stairways led to three entrances at the front and to five doorways at the sides, the broad step at the top being closed by an exquisite gate of iron grillwork. The whole design was simple and refined. The long ascent to the church was framed by sculptured basins and allegorical figures of stone, some supporting and others resting upon fine wrought-iron gates. The church building was surrounded by stretches of green grass that was fenced in by delicate palms. It was a gleaming white dream.

The Catholic priests were beginning to celebrate a mass preliminary to the "washing," and the black faithful streamed in, jamming the building to the doors. But as the four of us were about to collapse from heat and thirst, we went directly to refreshment tables improvised under the palms and ordered cold drinks. The conversation was desultory, with Manoel intent on annoying Zézé by commenting on the pretty women present. Edison said that formerly the church had allowed drinking and courting within its very walls during a "washing." Zézé noticed an elderly white woman dressed in full mourning but barefoot, who held a new broom and waited for the signal to begin scrubbing the church floor. My eye traveled on to a little old black woman dressed so beautifully and distinctively in her bahiana garb that I drew the attention of the others to her. Zézé jumped up and ran to her, squealing, "A blessing, grandmother!" and kissed her hand.

"Ah, my child," the old lady said in measured tones of pleasure, "how are you? How is my daughter Menininha?"

Manoel and Edison then rose to kiss her hand; but when I was introduced she kissed mine. For ninety-two years, Zézé told me loudly, the old Creole had been a votary of Omolu, made by the founder of Gantois.

"Yes," the priestess affirmed serenely. "I've been a part of that terreiro for nearly a century. But I quarreled there, and so I do not go regularly for my obligations."

"But, grandmother, surely there is no necessity for you to go, is there?" Zézé said to show her cordiality. "At your age, you know enough to perform all the obligations for yourself."

The priestess half assented sweetly, and turned to the young man with her to explain the conversation. She was not five feet tall, but she had a graceful and dignified carriage; and despite the heat she appeared cool and starched. She was thin, the shade of autumn leaves. She wore a flowered turban which emphasized her frail face and thin prominent nose; a skirt of harmonizing pattern fell in full folds to the ground; her hip-length blouse, sleeves ending below the elbow, was of elegant tailored barafunda cloth; a shawl of checked cloth was folded across her right shoulder, and she wore simple gold earrings, bracelets, and necklaces. I wondered that in slavery she could have learned her self-possession.

And now, they called out, the "washing" would begin! "The washing! The washing!" people called gleefully. The crowds pressed around the church, and the priests admitted them in orderly groups. Heavy muddy water started to flow down the steps, and Zézé and the others moved away to save their shoes. Manoel sniffed at the whole business: "They'll just soil the church!" he declared sulkily. But I squeezed up the stairs to see. Every man and woman had removed shoes and socks to wade into the flooded interior of the church with jugs and small barrels of water in which cakes of soap floated. They poured and dashed the water everywhere, and scraped the floors vigorously with new stiff brooms, talking and laughing in high humor. I did not disturb them at all with my camera, and my shoes still on my feet. One cheery Negro woman in a snowy priestess outfit of lace and silk, scrubbing away briskly, even called to me to photograph her. I almost wished I could join them.

At sad last, the priests closed the bulky doors of the church. Yet people lingered on the broad top steps outside looking for corners to clean, going over one another's spots, and actually soiling things anew. Young girls in short tight dresses ran around no more gayly than old women with gray heads and bouffant skirts; alike, with knees stiff in the Negro fashion, they bent far over, seeking dirt in the seams of the tiled designs. The priests coaxed for half an hour more before the devotees would leave. How they loved the Lord of Bomfim!

In the elevator returning to the Upper Town, two pleasant-faced women determined to prolong the fun. "My broom is still clean," observed one thoughtfully, holding it for the other to see. "Let's wash some more, at the Church of St. Francis. I'm afraid only of the stones in the square." Others too hated to end, and I felt that the people enjoyed just being together in vast numbers—"bathing in the multitude," as Baudelaire once said. A special world of good meanings was generated from among them. They played and danced and ate and sang and made love around the church for two more days and nights. Ternos and ranchos paraded there, singing and dancing along routes lit brilliantly as the day, celebrating the birth of Christ who was being "washed."

241

On the second night the church set up a huge artificial bonfire. By then the Bomfim square was too packed with people to allow the faintest circulation of air. Electric lamps, strung around the square, on the scaffoldings displaying the ternos and ranchos, and along the façade of the church, boiled the atmosphere like the noonday sun. Occasionally some persons fainted, but others in clusters still sang and danced and trailed the troupes displaying representations of the Bible story, such as fruits, animals, fish, shepherds, and flowers. Some of the troupes had already won large prizes for their costumes and dancing. The town was in a fever, and the marching and singing never ceased. Could Carnival itself do more?

The final festival of Bomfim was held over for Monday, the 16th. The Negroes sponsored it, but everyone participated. It centered on the beach in the Negro quarter of Itapagipe, called Ribeira, but close enough to Bomfim square for one to see the flags flying from poles planted under the palms there. Fishing smacks cruised by, and their sails drew an exquisite pattern against the brilliant blues of water and sky. Indian balsa rafts called "jangadas," manned by two or four boys with paddles, also moved slowly by, graceful and fragile in the distance, like cave-paintings of the Magdalenian period. And as usual, people enjoyed themselves marching and singing, marching and singing, in bands of boys and girls with their arms about one another's waists, dressed in any manner at all. Strangers might link arms and move in rows, singing samba and dancing, joyous though the sun burned the skin off their faces. Sometimes people hired touring cars and passed up and down the streets looking on until they could stand it no longer and also burst out singing and dancing.

Edison and I went there that morning, and the first person we recognized was Aydano, the poet. He was capering down the street leading a procession of youngsters in outlandish costumes. He himself wore an undershirt, trousers, and an enormous fisherman's straw hat, and he sang and danced in a kind of ecstasy while the dust rose eight feet high in the dizzying heat. When we met him for dinner later in the day, he said that his gang had begun early in the morning, before breakfast and would probably go on until the next dawn. He was a changed person after he had bathed and put on clean clothes, very formal and distant, and remained so even after we went to his fiancée's house to see the sights from her balcony.

But in the evening Edison and I went out to see more. Sheds on the beach sold refreshments to hundreds, possibly thousands of people. Colored electric bulbs strung above gave the scene a Moorish quality. The outpouring of energy, the hallelujah of living was overwhelming. Suddenly a friend of Edison's, a university man of old colonial family, began to strum, wonderfully, on a hard straw hat. What *were* they so glad about?

We saw men drinking beer at small tables, not conversing but strumming and singing, about love and fidelity and poverty. How hard it was, they hummed, to have a woman and children when there was no money! A drunken woman came to them and started to sing in a coarse male voice:

> "O, O my God,
> Have pity upon me!
> All the others live so well
> It is only I who live this way!
> I slave, but I have nothing,
> I can't escape this misery!
> O, O my God, such sorrows
> Are not for this world.
>
> "Never having had
> Nor ever knowing
> Happiness
> Or love, tenderness or friendship,
> I live so blue!
> Yet I feel content, for
> I have made efforts
> To live honestly!"

They liked this blues song from Rio, but they were repelled by the prostitute, and they drifted away from her, murmuring: "A woman with a male voice! For heaven's sake, what is this?"

The dancing groups and truckloads and private cars of excited singers blocked the cramped lanes. A car full of famous capoeira men dressed in their gaudy best was forced to a dead stop in front of a bahiana seated on the cool curbstone before her portable stand holding sweets, her legs far apart like some eastern potentate's. There was an actual traffic jam when a group of dancing girls was also forced to halt, and so they tapped in place and giggled.

We got out somehow, and could look up at the clear black sky punctured with cold brilliant stars, and we heard a military band play popular songs in a near-by square. It was like a set from an old Spanish opera. We walked close to the sea in a fresh wind, turning into deserted twisting streets, passing old houses of colonial and slavery times. Edison pointed to a decayed two-story mansion and the slave quarters that had been in use only fifty years before. The house had a dark, vaultlike entrance; but its heavy gates swung idly now, and the once rich owners were dead. Embedded in the tops of the high protecting walls were large pieces of broken bottle glass, soldered in the cement to prevent trespassers from leaping over. This had been made in the days when each new ship in the busy harbor brought dozens and dozens of strange human cargo, when Mohammedan slaves organized religious revolts and the Dutch tried to conquer the Northeast, when the Brazilian army tried for seventy-five years to defeat the fugitive slaves of the Palmares refuges in the interior of Bahia and Pernambuco, when piracy flourished. . . . And all this was not so long ago. Edison, a scion of that dramatic history, sang quietly a song about the Negro slave "Master Domingo" who toyed with the idea of asking his mistress to marry him; Master Domingo laughed, and Edison laughed.

Thus did Bomfim festa end, and even so the city was reluctant. Consequently, on the following day there was a celebration for the chauffeurs who "baptized" and "cleansed" their autos; and girls strolled through the streets with their arms around one another and sang:

> "Ah-h, Bahia!
> Nostalgias are arriving!
> Great sadness overcomes me!"

XXIV

THE SECRET police finally decided to order me out of Bahia, in fact out of the country, just before Carnival, and so I missed that great culminating festa. Edison and I went up to the office of the chief of police to learn what the charges against me might be; but it was impossible to secure any satisfaction. The American consul was afraid to probe. Even my letters of introduction from distinguished personages in Rio did no good. Eventually they told me that I had overlooked some passport technicality.

Plain-clothes men followed me until the moment my boat sailed. I had been told that they wanted to relieve me of my notebooks and pictures; so, with the aid of the British consul and some Bahians, I evaded them and nervously boarded the boat to Rio. It seemed like an extraordinary farce, especially as I had come with recommendations from the federal government. But that, it seemed, was the rub: Bahia, like some other areas, was not in complete accord with the central administration.

I arrived in Rio on the first day of Carnival. The government offices were to be shut for two more days, and by that time the Bahia police wanted me on the high seas, away, anywhere, but not in Brazil. But I was intent upon remaining, and so a Brazilian friend, who was also a lady anthropologist, took me to her summer home in the mountains until Carnival should be over and the government functioning again. We descended on the fourth day, and with other friends went to the chief of the federal police. There my troubles ended. He too was from Bahia, but he thought the order was in error and allowed me to remain for some months longer.

Rio seemed very comfortable after Bahia: nothing to fight for, nothing to hide from. But also nothing to expect. I wanted to know what prizes Zézé had won at Carnival; what was happening to Menininha's new class of initiates; and if Cleoza would really become a priestess. Did Hilda have her baby? And what was going on at Engenho Velho?

I recalled one of my last afternoons there at Engenho Velho

in Bahia's Dark Forest. It was hot, and children were resting among the enormous roots, like gnarled armchairs, of a sacred jack tree that stretched straight into the blue sky, so high that a tall man needed to bend backwards to see the top. The women were preparing for the evening, and the men were still in town. Older boys and girls were helping the kitchen by carrying water up the steep clay steps of the ladeira. Younger ones ran among them mischievously, lacking the ability to fill the gasoline cans with water or the strength to lift them on to their heads and walk up with them. It became as busy around the well at the foot of the ladeira as at a fair, and everyone laughed and teased. Girls of six and seven years promenaded with babies on their arms. The water carriers moved like a chain into the main temple and to the smaller outlying houses. A bahiana sat at the head of the steps next to a house of Exu, and sold sweets.

The women ignored the children, continuing undisturbed at their own routine, although an occasional child might tease and dance with them, and as people happened by, the children were passed from one affectionate hand to another. So they cried and fought unmolested, tumbling among the quieter dogs and goats. I sat and wondered what they thought of themselves. One child of Oxum acted with a superior air, nettling a plain little girl who, though one of the laity, began to shout that she too had a god! The Oxum girl pooh-poohed her, whereupon she yelled and yelled and finally laid her hands fiercely on her own chemise and ripped it apart! Alarmed at this rage, I asked her why she had done this. "Senhora," she answered angrily, "I had to let the wind in to cool me off!" She turned immediately to wrangle with another who teased her roughly: "Say! Who are you! Your father died of a swollen belly!" It became a free-for-all of screaming and pulling and calling. "Hey, you with the cut hair! Hey, you with the falling teeth! Hey, you with the scabby skin!"

They enjoyed themselves immensely, and crowded and fell against me as though I were a tree. Then they turned to examine my light blue linen dress, and talked about my skin that looked pink against their own, and about my hair that was light and "waved in the breeze." They had lovely little faces, with enormous eyes, tiny round features, smooth skins and cottony hair burnt red by the sun; they all wore ragged clothes. One Ogum child leaned, tired, against my leg. "Daughter, aren't you well?" I asked, since the girls were rarely familiar in this way.

"Ah, my mother," she responded sweetly, "I am fine, only I have not eaten."

"When did you eat last?"

"This morning."

"Aren't you hungry?"

"No, because I have pains in my stomach."

"What do you eat?"

"Well, black coffee and dried meat."

"In the evening?"

"In the morning too. I eat twice a day."

Then another little girl came hopping by, followed by a white-haired ebomi scolding her for dancing incorrectly in the temple.

These would be the women of Bahia, I thought, and they all would support the temple, mothering their men and their gods. They would know little else, and would keep those near them from joining the modern world. I missed them in Rio.

Edison came down some time later, having secured a newspaper job; and in his spare time we went to the temple ceremonies there, called macumbas. We had to be certified by the police. The temples were run by men, and seemed cold and tawdry. We missed the warmth and strength of the mothers. Even Sabina, in our memories, towered over these fathers. We haunted music shops to hear recordings of a certain macumba singer, calling himself J. B., who chanted in the warm guttural style of those rascals like Arcenio Cruz who operated in the temples of the traditional mothers. We heard that J. B. had been expelled from the cult, for a time, for having commercialized the songs. Yet he started a fashion, and one ditty, composed by Principe Pretinho in the cult style, became very popular:

247

Who is it who lives in the moon
That brightens the street
Where Cambinda*
Is accustomed to pass?
Who is it, who is it
Who moves about
Lighting for all
Night and day without fail?
It is St. George the warrior,
Who rules on the land,
Who rules on the sea.

There are no solemn conclusions I can draw from my observations in Bahia. In retrospect, the life there seems remote and timeless. I was sent to Bahia to learn how people behave when the Negroes among them are not oppressed. I found that they were oppressed by political and economic tyrannies, although not by racial ones. In that sense, the Negroes were free, and at liberty to cultivate their African heritage. But they were sick, undernourished, illiterate, and uninformed, just like other poor people among them of different racial origins. It was their complete poverty that cut them off from modern thought and obliged them to make up their own secure universe. They lived in the only world that was allowed them, and they made it intimate and friendly through the institution of candomblé, whose vigor and pageantry and promises of security lured others too in Bahia, and were a matter of excitement and pride to the rest of Brazil also.

When I left Rio for the United States, Brazilian friends escorted me to the boat, and one of them said, half teasing but with a certain defiant patriotism, "Now you can tell them that no tigers walk in our streets."

I nodded, and added: "I'll tell them also about the women. I think they help make Brazil great. Will Americans believe that there is a country where women like men, feel secure and at ease with them, and do not fear them?"

* African deity.

Glossary

abará. Fritter of bean flour, chopped shrimp, and pimento fried in palm oil and served rolled in a banana leaf.

abian. Novice; girl whose initiation has not yet begun.

acarajé. Fritter of bean flour, salt, onions, and dried shrimp fried in palm oil.

atabaque. Sacred drum that has the power to summon the orixás.

axêxê. Funerary ritual.

babalão. Male diviner; seer.

babalorixá. Male cult leader; pai de santo.

bahiana (baiana). Women street vendors of Bahia who wear long African-style dresses, shawls, and turbans.

caboclo. (1) Person of Brazilian Indian ancestry; (2) an Indian god worshipped in the candomblés de caboclo.

candomblé. (1) The Afro-Brazilian religious cults of Bahia, with origins in Yoruban religious ritual and belief, created by African slaves and their descendants; (2) the ceremonies honoring the Yoruban orixás; (3) the temple or cult center where the ceremonies are held.

candomblé de caboclo. Religious cult with African, Amerindian, and European influences.

capoeira. A kind of wrestling contest brought to Brazil by Angolan slaves.

Carnaval. Pre-Lenten festival of abandon and liminality, of masquerade and sex role reversal, and of street parades and dance competitions.

comadre. Co-mother, godmother, sponsor, friend.

Cosme and Damião. The sacred twins of the Yoruba; St. Cosmos and St. Damian.

dagã (dagan). The senior filha de santo who makes the offering to Exú.

despacho. (1) An offering made to a spirit to bring about a desired end; (2) an offering made to Exú either to work some evil or to reverse an evil commissioned by someone else; (3) a propitiatory offering to the Exú shrine before a ceremony to keep (send) the Exú spirits away.

ebomi. Female initiate with seven years of service to her orixá.

eguns. (1) Souls of the dead, skeletons, ghosts, ancestors; (2) secret society that summons the souls of the dead.

ekedi. Servant of the orixás who assists the women spirit mediums (the initiates, the filhas de santos) in the candomblé.

embigada (umbigada). Dance move in which the partners dance navel-to-navel, rubbing their abdomens together.

êre. Imp; child-spirit.

Exú. A median spirit; a messenger of higher spirits, good and evil; a trickster; in umbanda, Satan or the Devil.

fazenda. Large estate, ranch, or plantation.

feijão; feijoada. Bean; bean stew.

festa. Holy day; party; festive celebration.

figa. Fetish in the shape of a clenched fist with thumb between fore and middle fingers; often worn for protection from the evil eye.

filha de santo. Lit. "daughter of the saint"; a female initiate in the candomblé; the trained medium who, aided by public dancing and drumming, will be possessed by an orixá.

horse. Spirit medium; the orixás are said to "ride" those whom they possess.

Iansâ (Yansan). Female spirit of wind and storm; St. Barbara; bisexual.

Ifa. Male spirit of divination.

Iemanjá (Yemanja). Yoruban female spirit of the sea, of salt water; the Virgin Mary, Our Lady of Compassion; the Amerindian spirit Janaína.

iya kekerê. The assistant and deputy of the iyalorixa.

iyalorixá. Mãe de santo; female cult leader.

Janaína. Amerindian female spirit of the sea; Yoruban spirit Iemanjá.

macumba. African sect in Rio de Janeiro; black magic; the maleficent variation of candomblé.

mãe d'agua. Female spirit of the Afro-Brazilian cults who inhabits the water; Iemanjá (Yemanjá).

mãe de santo. Lit. "mother of the saint"; high priestess of the candomblé; cult leader; spirit medium.

mãe pequena. Lit. "little mother"; deputy director of the candomblé; the iya kêkêrê.

mato. Woods, bush, forest, jungle.

Nanan (Nana) Yoruban female spirit of rain; spirit of creation; St. Anne.

Obá. (1) Yoruban female spirit of the river Obá; St. Joan of Arc; (2) king; the title given to the ministers of Xangô in the candomblé.

ogan. Male honorary lay protector of the candomblé selected by the orixás; subject to a minor initiation ritual.

olhador. Male seer, diviner.

orixá. The Yoruban term traditionally used to refer to the principal spirits such as Ogum, Iemanjá, etc.

Ogún. Yoruban male spirit of war, iron; St. Anthony (in Bahia).

Omolu. Yoruban male spirit of smallpox and illness in general; St. Roch.

Oxalá. Male spirit of the sky, of procreation; Jesus, Our Lord of Bonfim (Good Ending).

Oxóce. Yoruban male spirit of the hunt; St. George.

Oxún. Yoruban female spirit of the river Oxum, of fresh water; the Virgin Mary, Our Lady of Immaculate Conception.

Padê. Propitiatory offering to Exú that opens candomblé ceremonies.

padre. Father; Catholic priest.

pai de santo. Lit."father of the saint"; high priest of the candomblé; cult leader; spirit medium.

seita. Afro-Brazilian cult center; terreiro.

terreiro. Afro-Brazilian cult center; may refer to the entire center or specifically to the central space where dancing and trance manifestations occur.

umbanda. Cult that emerged in Rio de Janeiro in the 1930s and combines African possession religion with Catholicism, occultism and Allan Kardec spiritualism; it has many regional manifestations.

Xangô. (1) Yoruban male spirit of thunder; St. Jerome; (2) the Afro-Brazilian cults around Recife (Pernambuco and Alagoas).